The Grasp of Consciousness

Collaborators

Alex Blanchet
Jean-Paul Bronckart
Nadine Burdet
André Cattin
Catherine Dami
Michelangelo Flückiger
Isabelle Flückiger-Geneux
Christiane Gilliéron
Androula Henriques-Christophides
Daphne Liambey
Olivier de Marcellus
Alberto Munari
Madelon Robert
Anne-Marie Zutter

The Grasp of Consciousness

Action and Concept in the Young Child

Jean Piaget

Translated by Susan Wedgwood

Harvard University Press   Cambridge, Massachusetts   1976

Library of Congress Cataloging in Publication Data

Piaget, Jean, 1896–
  The grasp of consciousness.

  Translation of La prise de conscience.
  Includes index.
  1. Cognition (Child psychology)   I. Title.
[DNLM: 1. Cognition—In infancy & childhood. WS105
P579b]
BF723.C5P52613   155.4'13   75-43687
ISBN 0-674-36033-8

Preface

When is a subject fully conscious of a situation? How is this consciousness acquired? In other words, what constitutes the dawn of consciousness or, as it is also called in this book, "cognizance"? Now that it is agreed, contrary to the classical behaviorist view, that there is no dichotomy or basic opposition between behavior and consciousness—since cognizance itself constitutes a type of behavior that interacts with all other types—the problem of cognizance is of increasing interest to scientific psychology. For the philosophical psychologist, introspection is fundamental and even has a sort of unlimited power, coextensive with all mental life. The behavioral psychologist has noticed that a considerable portion of behaviors (or their mechanisms) remain unconscious and that cognizance consequently demands the intervention of special activities, depending on other behavior and, in turn, becoming capable of modifying them. It would even seem that cognizance involves more than the incorporation of a new bit of information into an already established field (with all its characteristics) of consciousness. There is a genuine construction, which consists in elaborating not "the" consciousness considered as a whole, but its different levels—that is, its more or less integrated systems. Conceived in such terms, the problem has even come within the scope of psychological research into alertness or "vigilance." Finally, as is well known, it is also encountered by the psychoanalyst in connection with "catharsis."

This book is exclusively concerned with behavior—from material action to operations. The experiments described were conducted in the course of research devised to complete the study of causality at the Center of Genetic Epistemology in Geneva. (However, as cognizance has more psychological than epistemological significance, we are grateful to our friend,

Paul Fraisse, for including this study in his collection, *Psychologie d'aujourd'hui.*) While the concept of cause originates in the actual action, causal structures are profoundly transformed according to the degrees of conscious conceptualization that modify this action. Why then did research into causality lead to the problem of cognizance?

At the sensorimotor level, the few-months-old baby first discovers causal connections solely through his own physical action; only subsequently does he perceive them in the ways objects act on other objects. At the "representation" levels, on the other hand, the child's grasp of causality is initially limited to attributing to the objects activities that are analogous to his own actions; only later will he attribute to objects activities analogous to operations. It might be thought that this is merely a sort of rejuvenation of Maine de Biran's thesis. Indeed, this is how Michotte has interpreted our conception. However, there is a fundamental difference between Maine de Biran's theory and our conception of causality. For the French philosopher, the subject slowly achieves a more or less complete introspection (with an ego consciousness, a feeling of effort as an applied force, and the like) of the causal mechanism of his own action. Subsequently, this is generalized to external objects, through a sort of "induction" of what the subject has thus discovered in himself. We maintain, on the other hand, that the initial psychomorphism of the physical causality and subsequent attribution of operatory mechanisms to the objects themselves constitute basically unconscious inferential processes — processes that lack both this characteristic of immediate intuition postulated by the Biranian theory and, even more important, any relationship with an (initially nonexistent) consciousness of the ego. This was our first reason for seeking to analyze more accurately cognizance of the action itself and how this action is modified through such interiorization.

However, a second, and in fact our main, reason for these new studies is that it was of more general importance to examine the nature and content of the subjects' conceptualizations (including, but not restricted to, the causal explanations) when these do not concern the typical physical situations that we have already studied (transmissions of movements, vectorial compositions, and so on), but the effects of the child's actions alone and of his "practical intelligence": making use of a sling or of an inclined plane, building a sloping path—in other words, easy problems that are solved early in life. In such cases, we first establish what the child is conscious of in his own actions and particularly what he notices of the regulations involved, both in the case of automatic sensorimotor regulations and in that of more active regulations with choice of method from among several possibilities. Then, when the problem under study involves causal relationships, we determine whether this causality of his own action on objects is clearer to the child, or more quickly understood by him, than the causal relationships between one object and another. This whole vast but little-known area is of great importance for psychology and epistemology. From the psychological point of view, cognizance is not merely a sort of interior illumination, it constitutes a far more complex process involving conceptualization. It is these conceptualization processes that have to be analyzed. In other words, although psychologists have tried primarily to determine in which situation a child is cognizant, they have too often neglected the other complementary question of how this happens, a question that demands equal attention. From the epistemological point of view, on the other hand, the interiorization of the actions is at the source of both logicomathematical and causal operatory structures and thus necessitates careful examination.

In this book the situations studied are those in which success in action is achieved early because the necessary coordinations result from simple differentiations arising from more or less automatic regulations of an initially general nature. A subsequent book (*Réussir et comprendre*, Presses Universitaires de France, Paris, 1974) analyzes what happens when success occurs later, as the result of successive stages based on coordinations between distinct schemes and more active regulations involving the introduction of new strategies, while the child is actually in the process of trying to solve a problem.

Contents

The Grasp of Consciousness

1 Walking on All Fours

In the other studies described in this book, the subject carries out actions on certain objects, with his cognizance of these actions depending on his observation of their effects on the objects, as well as of the results and of his own movements. It is therefore useful to begin by analyzing a situation in which the role of the objects is reduced to a minimum, but where the action nevertheless is sufficiently complex for the subject to have trouble grasping it completely, although not so complex that his cognizance is delayed too long. Asking subjects to walk on all fours provides an excellent situation, since most of us could do this before we could walk and because the only material required is a fixed floor, serving simply as a support and not as an instrument or goal. Furthermore, this allows a particularly useful opportunity to check one of our general hypotheses, namely that cognizance depends on active adjustments involving choices of a more or less deliberate nature rather than on automatic sensorimotor regulations. Walking on all fours, of course, because of its familiarity (unless deliberately obstructed), involves only reg-

With the collaboration of Androula Henriques-Christophides.

ulations of this second sensorimotor type and at least one part of the hypothesis would be invalidated if it were accomplished at every age with full cognizance.

The subject is asked to walk (on all fours) about 10 meters, then to explain verbally how he did it. After this, he is asked to use a teddy bear (with jointed limbs) to execute the movements he describes. If necessary, the interviewer gets on the floor and asks the child to tell him which limb to move first, and so forth. Subsequently, the child is asked once more to walk on all fours, this time paying attention to what he is doing, and to give a running commentary. If the explanation is incorrect, he is asked to perform in the way he has just described to see whether it is right. Finally, if he feels another task is necessary, the interviewer suggests that the child walk on all fours quickly across the room and stop immediately when so instructed—at which point he is asked to describe how he started his last movement.

Level IA

At this level, four-year-olds (and sometimes slow developers up to the age of seven) describe their actions as follows (Z or its reverse Σ pattern): one hand, then the other one, then one foot, then the other one (or the feet first). This differs both from the N or its reverse Ͷ pattern (right or left hand, then the foot of the same side, then the other hand and the second foot) and from the X pattern (left or right hand, then opposite foot, then other hand and remaining foot).

Examples

SYL (4,4) walks a few meters (pattern X). How are you doing it? *I'm moving my hands, arms, feet, and legs, and my head.* But what first? *I'm moving everything at the same time.* (then with the bear) *First that one* (left foot), *that one* (right foot), *that one* (left hand), *and that one* (right hand). Now walk on all fours again yourself and really look at what you're doing. (Gives same description.) Someone else told me that it was like that (description of

X). Is that right? *No, first that one and that one . . .* (Z). Show me how I've got to do it (on the floor). *This hand, then that one, then this foot, then that one* (Z).

PAU (4,7) walks according to pattern X. How do you do it? *You put both legs and then both hands.* Show me on the bear. (Right foot, then left, right hand, then left.) Is that how you go on all fours? *Both feet and then your left hand and right hand.* How? *Both feet at the same time, then one hand, then the other one.* Show me what I've got to do (on the floor). (One foot after the other, then one hand after the other.) Get on the floor and do it the way you've just told me. (He puts both hands forward at the same time and gets stuck.) Is that how you told me? *Yes.* Do it again and tell me what you've done. (Again Z.)

NAD (4,9) has the same reactions as the other two: both hands, then both feet, each time one after the other, and so on. When she is asked to walk on all fours in this way, she tries, then hesitates and reverts to the X pattern. What did you move first? (She still gives the same description.)

MIC (4,6): After the same reactions as the others (*first my hands, first one and then the other. After that my legs, one and then the other*), except, surprisingly enough, for making the bear walk in the X pattern, MIC gets down on the floor again and walks, trying to give a running commentary: *I take this hand, then that one, then one foot and one foot* (his actions constantly bely his words). When the interviewer suggests the X pattern, he says, *No, it's animals that do it like that* (and he shows it again with the bear). Do it again yourself. (He does it according to X and again describes it as Z.)

The Z solution clearly indicates these subjects' complete lack of awareness of how they actually walk on all fours, since none of them actually do it this way. (Although most subjects walk according to pattern X, pattern N is sometimes encountered.) Why then does pattern Z immediately come to their minds? This is surely because, if the subjects are asked to give an order of succession about which they themselves have no clue (*I'm moving everything at the same time*, says SYL), they are likely to describe the simplest order, that is, first hands, then feet (or the other way around), but always *both* hands before *both* feet (or vice versa) starting each movement with the same-side foot or hand (otherwise the pattern would be] or [and not Z). Of the 34 four- to eight-year-olds with this type of reaction, 30 Z opposed to only 4] were encountered, which is a fairly clear indication that these children are describing the simplest construction and are not attempting to determine the actual order of their movements.

MIC's manipulation of the teddy bear is, however, worthy of comment, since unlike the other subjects, he makes the bear move according to pattern X. We might have considered this pure chance, since immediately afterward he tells the interviewer to walk on all fours according to pattern Z, which is also the pattern that emerges from his (incorrect) running commentary on his own renewed slow motion walk; but there is his immediate response, at the end of the questioning, to the suggestion of the X pattern. Unlike SYL, he does not say it is wrong, but *it's animals that do it like that*. In other words, he seems to conserve as a memory image the way dogs, cats, or horses move, but this does not help him at all to become actively aware of his own movements; it seems easier to observe others than himself. To sum up, at this level the Z pattern seems to be chosen only because it is the simplest. As will be seen later, subjects at more advanced levels often start off describing the Z pattern, but progress to N or even X.

Level IB

The five- and six-year-old subjects give an N-type description: hand, then foot (or the other way round) of the same side, then the two successively of the other side. This solution, not encountered with four-year-olds, is found with about one-third of the seven- to ten-year-olds and even with adults (who, however, walked according to pattern X).[1]

Examples

COL (5,6) starts off by describing the Z pattern, which he also uses when telling the interviewer how to walk on all fours. On the other hand, when he himself is asked to crawl again, this time slowly, and take note of what he is doing, he says, *Right hand, then right foot, left hand, and left foot* pattern N, even though he walked according to pattern X. Walk on all fours again, slowly. *First that one* (right foot), *then right hand, then left foot and left hand* (inverted N pattern). Now do it and tell me what you're doing as you go along. (He walks according to X, while describing the inverted N pattern, then adapts his walking to match the latter.) Once more. (This time he walks the whole time according to X.) *My right foot, my right hand, my left foot, and my left hand.*

ART (6,2) walks according to pattern X. *I lift my legs and my hands.* How? (She starts off again according to X.) *That one* (right foot) *and that one* (left foot). And afterward? *Right hand and left hand* (thus pattern Z). Same thing for the bear and for the instructions to the interviewer. However, when she is asked to walk slowly, noting carefully what she is doing, she says, despite her X pattern, *Right foot, right hand, left foot, left hand* (thus inverted N). When she does it quickly, she reverts to describing the Z pattern. And now walk on all fours again

1. Before giving her paper at the 1970 Symposium on Genetic Epistemology, Professor Henriques tried out the experiment with several of the participants (she made them walk on all fours on the floor, as well as answer questions!). Logicians and mathematicians favored the N solution, while physicists and psychologists opted for the X pattern.

slowly and tell me at the same time what you are doing. *Right hand, left hand, left foot, right hand, left hand, left foot, right hand, right foot . . .* and so forth. In fact, having started off according to X, she then adapts her movements to match what she is saying and walks according to N.

LAI (6,11) walks according to pattern X, then, without saying a word, points to his right foot, right hand, left foot, and left hand (inverted N). He starts off by making the teddy bear move according to pattern Z, then changes this to N. However, he tells the interviewer to walk according to X, then, back on all fours himself, he walks slowly, with his commentary initially correctly describing pattern X, then reverting to N without noticing that his words no longer match his movements. Finally, the bear is again made to move according to N.

This N pattern, not encountered with four-year-olds but clearly predominant with fives and sixes, is also favored by a third of the seven- to ten-year-old subjects and, as mentioned above, by some adults. Unlike the Z pattern, it is a perfectly feasible way of walking on all fours, although the X pattern is far more common. What is important here is that most subjects describe their movements as if they formed an N pattern, whereas in reality they move in an X pattern (COL, ART, and LAI), and so are not fully conscious of their own movements. Sometimes it does happen (but this is in no way equivalent) that such a subject may try to match his movements to his commentary and move according to N (for example, ART, who at the end of the session stops walking according to X and begins moving according to N).

In this example there is, therefore, no cognizance conceptualized from a previous action, but there is influence of the conceptualization on the subsequent action. This difference is most significant. It indicates that when a child describes his movements only after he has stopped walking on all fours, his actions are directed by simple automatic sensorimotor regulations, which are not sufficient to make him actively conscious of his every movement. Still, when asked for a running commentary, he may even start to hesitate before putting a foot or hand forward, forced to choose between several possibilities: such a choice is a basic characteristic of an active regulation, which as a rule leads to full consciousness of the actions in question. In this particular case, it is true, there is no actively regulated action followed by a conceptualized and adequate cognizance, but instead, first a conceptualization that does not match the action, then an active adjustment resulting in the action matching the conceptualization and thereby becoming conscious. However, even if the active adjustment here stems from an incorrect conceptualization of the subject's action, these examples do demonstrate the need for a distinction—the value of which will become increasingly clear—between the two types of regulations, that is, between those that are automatic and those that are active.

Stage II

Half the subjects at level IIA (seven to eight years) systematically give what may now be simply termed the X solution, which previously was given only by LAI and even then not at all systematically. Two-thirds of the level IIB subjects (nine- and ten-year-olds) give this X solution.

Examples (Level IIA)

MAR (7,6) starts off walking on all fours according to X, but her description is of the Z pattern: *To walk like a little cat, I put my right hand, then my left hand, then my right foot and afterward the other one . . . always like that.* Try again. Did you notice what you were doing? *My right hand* (pause) *after it's the left hand, right foot, left foot* (still Z pattern). Very good. Try once more and see what you are doing. (She walks again, this time slowly.) *Right hand and after* (hesitation) *I put my left foot and then left hand and afterward my right foot* (thus now X pattern). Show me with this teddy bear. (X solution.) And now have another try yourself. (She again describes the X pattern.)

JEN (8,11) first of all describes her movements according to pattern Z, then those of the teddy bear according to N, then again her own movements according to Z, and then according to N. However, when she is suddenly told to stop: *Now, go on. Right hand and left knee, then left hand and right knee* (pattern X). Now do it very quickly. *My right hand and left knee, then left hand and right knee.* Do you remember what you said before? (She repeats the Z description.) Was it right? *No, it was wrong.* Show me on the bear. (X solution.) Do you do the same? *Yes, I think so.*

Examples (Level IIB)

RAU (9,8): Can you walk on all fours? (pattern X). How do you do it? *I put my knees and hands on the floor. I go forward with my right hand and with my left knee as well, then I put my left hand forward, I put my right knee* (so, immediately, an X solution). Show me on the teddy bear. (X solution.) Now, I'm going to walk on all fours; you tell me what to do. *Put your right hand forward, left leg forward, left hand forward, right knee forward.*

JAC (10,6) crawls according to pattern X: Tell me what you did. *I knelt down, put both hands on the floor. I put my right hand forward, then left knee; my left hand, then right knee.* (Straightaway, an X solution.) And on the teddy bear? (Again, the X solution.)

JUL (10,3), by contrast, starts off by describing the Z pattern, then makes the bear move according to N. Is that how you said just now? *Not quite, I said that hands and feet had to be together.* Try doing it again. (N description followed by N pattern ac-

tions.) Now, do it very quickly. (Moves according to
X.) How did you do it? *Left leg with right hand and
left hand with right foot* (in other words, X pattern).

There is thus at this second level a clear grasp, or cognizance, of the individual movements involved in walking on
all fours. How does this come about if, as has been hypothesized, the automatic regulations that direct sensorimotor actions cannot alone make this possible, when walking on all
fours at ten years of age (or indeed at any age, see note 1) is
clearly no less automatic than at four or five? To what extent
are active adjustments directly or indirectly responsible for
the accurate descriptions furnished by the level IIA and, above
all, the level IIB subjects?

Two types of reaction seem worthy of comment in this
respect. Firstly, the questioning may interrupt, or at the very
least diminish, the automaticity of the subject's movements,
thereby causing him to "stop and think"; this introduces an
element of choice and forces the subject to make a conscious
decision regarding his next action. Three methods of arousing
this reaction were evolved:

(a) The subject could be asked to walk on all fours slowly
and to try and observe exactly what he is doing (this request
proved unnecessary for children like MAR who did so spontaneously); here, of course, the slowing down from the natural
speed diminished the automaticity. A variation of this
method consisted in asking the child to walk on all fours
quickly, as in the case of JUL.

(b) Subjects could be requested to move according to the
pattern they themselves had previously described, which
slows them down and so lessens the automaticity.

(c) The most effective (see JEN) proved to be when subjects
were asked to stop crawling and then to recommence; this
again resulted in a break in the automaticity.

All these methods in fact proved largely ineffectual at levels
IA and IB (two-sevenths of the subjects progressed only from
Z to N) and effective at stage II (at level IIA five-sixths of the

subjects progressed at least from Z to N, and for levels IIA and IIB together eight-ninths of the children progressed in this way, with some of them finally giving the X solution).

The second type of reaction is exemplified by level IIB subjects like RAU and JAC, who spontaneously give the X solution and therefore do not fall into the preceding categories (progress to the X solution after at least a partial break in the automaticity of their movements). Here, in all probability, the subject thinks about how he moves right from the beginning and in so doing substitutes a certain number of choices for his automatic movements (as we all do when, for instance, in the middle of running downstairs we suddenly, for some reason, try to take active control of our steps and so probably slow ourselves down unnecessarily).

However justified these remarks may seem, there remains the problem of understanding why the various factors that cause a diminution in the automaticity and make the subject begin to think about his actions do not result in progress until level IIA, which sees the beginning of operatory reversibility. In fact, there is a close natural link between this reversibility and what is involved (a sort of retroaction) when a subject becomes conscious of an action that normally takes place autonomously and quasi-automatically, and he must have achieved a certain level of conceptualization before this can counterbalance the automaticity. Indeed, when a stage I subject is asked to walk on all fours according to the pattern he himself has given, he generally moves as before (except for COL and ART in IB), with perhaps a little hesitancy, while from age seven on, all subjects modify their movements. This appears to herald the beginning of the retroaction that is inherent in the subject's attempt to determine what he is actually doing. Does this lead to a grasp of the principle of reversibility, or is it the other way around? Clearly, it is in the modifications of the action that the explanation of the formation of reversible operations must be sought, and we have often stressed the role of anticipation and retroaction in this development. In this respect the essentially automatic character of the actions studied here constitute a rather special case. However, it is precisely because it is special that it can be accounted for only in the general context of the actions at these levels. From such a viewpoint, the only valid reason for the declining resistance of the automatic responses around the ages of seven to eight lies in the general tendencies that during this period direct the child toward retroaction and anticipation and that are manifested more clearly in his overall behavior than in the particular situation analyzed in this chapter. Here, as in all analogous cases, for an effective conceptualization of the earlier distortions, which at levels IA and IB prevented the subject from making an accurate observation of his own action, the subject must have recourse to the inferential coordinations that enable him to make sense of observations that contradict his expectations. Naturally, the more distorted his observations are, the greater the delay in his acquisition of these coordinations.

2 The Path of an Object Launched by a Sling

The sling used in this experiment is of the simplest type: a wooden ball 5 cm in diameter, tied to the end of a string that the subject releases after swinging it around a few times, aiming it at a target. Even very young children manage to do this and, according to Diodore de Sicile, the inhabitants of the Balearic Islands were particularly good at it because the mothers used to hang their tots' bread on the end of a pole and make them go hungry until they had hit it using their sling (Encyclopedia, Diderot and D'Alembert, 1751, p. 337). However, sensorimotor success does not always lead to accurate conceptualization (in this case, of how one aims and the object's flight path) and it is interesting to find out why.

Throughout this chapter, for the sake of clarity, the reader is asked to picture a clockface as representing the circle described by the sling's rotation (see Figure 1). Positions of targets and subjects, and points on the circle where the sling is released (referred to as "release points"), are all designated with reference to the imaginary clockface.

With the collaboration of Michelangelo Flückiger.

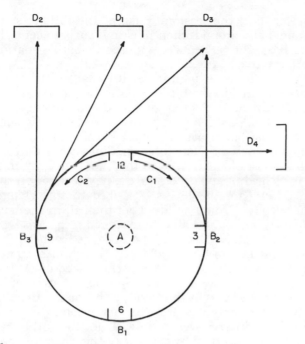

Figure 1

    A: location of the hand when rotating the sling.

    B: possible positions of the subject.

    C: direction of rotation of the ball (C_1 = to the right, C_2 = to the left).

    D: target (rectangular box).

    1 to 12: positions on the circumference where the ball is released when the subject lets go of the string.

    NOTE: It is only in the situations described in the supplementary experiment that the box can have its opening at the top.

The session starts, in most instances, with the interviewer holding one end of the string and demonstrating the circular movements described by the ball at the other end (in a horizontal plane on the floor and without pointing to any targets) and asking the subject in which direction the ball would go if it were released. The actual release points are not specified, but the interviewer sometimes swings the ball in a clockwise direction (subsequently referred to as "to the right of 12 o'clock") and sometimes counter-clockwise ("to the left") to see if the child predicts opposite directions. After this, the subject has a try himself and only after this is a rectangular cardboard box used as a target into which the child has to try to send the ball, simply by releasing it. In other cases, the interviewer starts the session by asking the child to swing the sling around and around, then release it so as to send the ball into the box. The subjects' responses in both situations are most informative.

For the part of the experiment with a target, the box is initially placed outside the circle of rotation, at the 12 o'clock position, with the subject crouching down outside the circle at the 6 o'clock position: the position of the box is such that the string must be released at about 9 o'clock for a right rotation and 3 o'clock for a left rotation. Since almost all the subjects age four or older succeed in this motor task, there are no major steps leading to success in the physical action that can furnish criteria for the levels described in this chapter—although, of course, some children get the ball in the box more quickly than others, and all differences in responses were naturally most carefully analyzed. Because, as has been said, our main interest lies in how and when the child becomes conscious of his actions, the basic question asked of each subject concerns where he released the ball; he can answer verbally or simply mark the spot on the floor (with, for instance, a small cross), or make a drawing, or repeat his action in slow motion, or instruct the interviewer on how to get the ball in the box. In addition, the interviewer can alter either the position of the target (to the left or right of 12 o'clock) or that of the subject, or he can ask the latter where the ball would go if it were released at specific points. As shown by the examples, until stage III of the eleven- and twelve-year-olds, there remain marked differences between what the children do and what they say they do!

Finally, as we shall describe later in this chapter, the interviewer takes a whole group of subjects outside the classroom onto the school grounds, where he asks them to stand up and swing the sling in space. Initially, he does not specify the plane of rotation: vertical, oblique, or horizontal (over the head of or in front of the child)—although, where necessary, he does make suggestions. Here, a drawing is indispensable for judging the child's representation of his actions.

Level IA

Examples

LAU (4,7) is shown what to do by ALA (4,10). ALA is successful and LAU explains: *He turned and it went in the box.* How did he do it? *Because he didn't . . . he made it turn a lot.* A second attempt by ALA is unsuccessful because, according to LAU, *he turned a lot.* What should he do? *Turn less.* LAU then tries three times, starting off by swinging the sling around and then stopping her rotation movement at about 6 o'clock and simply throwing the ball. Are you doing the same as he did? *Yes.* After three more analogous attempts, ALA explains to her, *You've only got to turn it.* LAU does this, releases the ball at the side, and gets it into the box. After this, she sometimes releases the ball at about 4 o'clock (left rotation) and sometimes throws it. These throws are from the 6 o'clock and not the 12 o'clock position, as if the ball should come from where the subject is and go diametrically across the clockface to the box opposite.

TOM (4,5), initially without a target, copies the rotations correctly. What would happen if you let it go? *It would go zoom (round and round), then zoom (the ball would go off).* Where? *Over there* (roughly opposite). *If you make it turn very hard, it turns right up to there* (back of the room). He does not realize that the ball's trajectory is determined by both the release point and the direction of rotation. With the interviewer acting as the target and standing opposite him, TOM releases the ball first at 12 o'clock (right rotation), then at 6 o'clock (clearly thinking the ball will travel straight across from 6 to 12 and so reach the target, but instead it goes off to the left), and then finally at 9 o'clock, which is correct. How did it go? *From the other side* (left as opposed to right rotation) *it goes too far; like that* (right rotation) *it goes there* (to the target). When it comes to telling the interviewer what to do, he says: *You've got to let it go quickly, then it goes over there* (direction not specified), without any reference to the release point. And to go there (to one side)? *You've got to stand there* (opposite). And there? *Stand there* (again opposite). After some correct releases, the interviewer says, Now show me how it went. *Like that.* (Like LAU, he simulates a few rotations, then a release point opposite the target, near the subject with the ball crossing the circle of rotation from 6 o'clock to 12 o'clock.) How would you make it go over there (to one side)? *It's too far.*

HER (4,10) has a target (box) from the outset: he rotates to the right and misses, then to the left and releases involuntarily at 3 o'clock, almost getting the ball into the box. Does it matter which way you turn the sling, does the ball always go off in the same direction, regardless? *Yes.* Where does it go? *To the same place.* After several misses he gets the ball in the box (from 7 to 8 o'clock), but by pushing the ball with his hand toward the target. Where did you let it go? *Here* (12 o'clock). And if you turn the other way round? *You've got to let it go the other way round.* Where? *Here* (ball's trajectory from 6 to 12 o'clock).

ALA (4,10) starting without a target: If you let it go? *It goes straight* (that is, not in a circle). Where? *It goes everywhere.* Try. (Right rotation.) And the other way round? *The same thing.* With a target: success at the third attempt with release at 8 to 9 o'clock. And the other way round? *It's the same thing for letting it go.* (Despite this, he gets the ball in the box.) When do you have to let it go? *You have to let it go when it is . . . when you see the box.*

VOG (5,3) without target: *It would go everywhere, here in the corner.* (She points to the left in front of her, when turning to the left, which could be correct.) And if you went the other way round? (She releases the ball before answering.) *There* (to the right). Could it go anywhere else? *Yes, here* (to the left). Target beyond 12 o'clock: she misses. Why didn't it go in the box? *Because it turned.* Where did you let it go? *Here* (center of the circle, where her hand was). Where did it go to? *Here* (6 o'clock, thus near the child herself with the ball's trajectory again following the diameter of the circle). After some very near misses, she continues to designate 6 o'clock as the release point.

It does seem remarkable that these young children manage to get the ball into the box by finding, through trial and error, the right place to release it. It is difficult to analyze in this respect the part played by proprioceptive information and that played by sensorimotor regulations stemming from the results of the child's actions during the session. The subject's cognizance and explanation of his actions place more emphasis on his own position and the force he uses than on the observable features of the object, except for the unanimous opinion that once the ball has been released it does not continue to turn in the same circle but, no longer held by the string, goes off *straight* (ALA) toward the outside, that is to say, following a trajectory, unspecified but outside the circle.

Having said this, the first consideration concerns the trajectories that the subject predicts for both right and left rotations when there is no set target. Of course, the ball's destination depends upon the release point and the direction of rotation. Only subjects who have reached stage III can understand these objective trajectories. However, with no set target, right from level IB on, the child imagines that the ball will always go off to the left for a left rotation and to the right for a right rotation, landing in what might be termed "privileged zones"—that is, for a small number of turns the ball will go to the right or left of the subject (according to the direction of the rotation) and for a greater number of turns it may land behind him. These trajectories to the left or right of 12 o'clock will be construed as the result of a sort of throwing. At level IA, where the idea of throwing is more firmly embedded, these privileged zones in the "no target" situations are only rarely accepted according to the direction of rotation.

Generally, the subject is not concerned with the release point and forecasts, like TOM, either just one trajectory or (where there is a set target) a favorable trajectory for one direction of rotation and an unfavorable one (*too far*) for the other. VOG does not even take account of those results she herself has seen.

When the subject at this first level IA aims at a target and ends up by hitting it, his ideas about how he succeeded show some remarkable characteristics (a younger child would have no ideas at all). The first is the tendency to believe that for the ball to go into the box, the subject must be opposite it (like TOM, for example). This leads to a second reaction: when asked where the ball was released (or more simply, for a description of what has happened), the subject designates as the release point the spot nearest his own position (6 o'clock if the target is beyond 12 o'clock) as if the ball traveled straight across this diameter (6–12) to reach the target. LAU even maintains that there are two distinct actions: making the ball turn several times, slowing down near 6 o'clock, then throwing it from this point to the target beyond 12 o'clock. By contrast, TOM and VOG picture the ball's release after rotation, but their conceptualization still corresponds to LAU's two distinct actions. HER first thinks (like the slightly more advanced level IB subjects) that the release point (in fact at 7 to 8 o'clock) is at 12 o'clock, but, after rotating the sling in the other direction, he again points to the 6 o'clock position, which shows that for him the ball first has to cross the circle from 6 to 12. ALA, by contrast, thinks that the line that links the subject to the target does not start from where he is, but from the spot where he *sees the box*. This explains why some of the children at this level correctly consider the ball's release point to be at 9 o'clock, for instance, and not at 12 o'clock, as is subsequently the case when the child coordinates conceptually (and no longer only in his physical actions) the need to aim at the target, on the one hand, with the circular trajectory of the rotation, on the other, in order to judge the correct release point. When a subject sees someone else (either the interviewer or another child) in action, he is sometimes better able to determine the release point, since he is no longer solely concerned with his own action. The initially correct answers given by some of these young children (they subsequently become more involved and correspondingly less accurate) stem from a simplistic view of the task. Older children see far more problems.

Level IB

Although there is no real homogeneity in the reactions at this level, they clearly indicate a transitional stage between levels IA and IIA. The subject may no longer consider it essential to be opposite the target; or (without a set target) he may now predict that the ball will go off in the same direction as he has been turning it; or he may designate 12 o'clock, or some other point, as the release point. But a child at this level, unlike one at level IIA, does not grasp all three of these points.

Examples

BOR (4,7), with no set target, forecasts that with a right rotation the ball will go off to the right and with a left rotation *it isn't the same; it would go on the other road* (to the left). Still, when a target is placed and then moved, he always puts himself opposite it and in fact does get the ball into the box. He considers the release point to be 12 o'clock.

CAR (5,8) succeeds by releasing the ball at about 11 o'clock, but thinks that the ball left him opposite the target, at 12 o'clock. Without a target, he predicts that with a right rotation the ball will go off opposite or to the right, and that with a left rotation it will go off opposite or to the left; but when he tries again with a target, he releases at 9 o'clock and thinks that he has rotated to the left and not to the right, while admitting that he released before 12 o'clock.

CEL (6,0) first of all thinks that the ball will drop to the floor at the point where she releases it, then notes that *it goes far,* but without forecasting in which direction. Nevertheless, with the target opposite 12 o'clock she releases the ball at 9 o'clock, but thinks 12 o'clock is the release point. Rotating the sling the other way, she releases at half past two: Where did the ball go? (CEL goes through the motions of two rotations and then a release at 6 o'clock, indicating that the ball travels first to 12 o'clock and then on toward the box.) Could you aim at the box if you were turning the sling the other way? *Yes.* Where would you let it go? *Here* (12 o'clock).

REN (6,4) doesn't forecast the ball's trajectory in the case of a right rotation, but thinks that if you turn to the left, the ball will go straight forward from the 12 o'clock position or at right angles to the left. With a set target, she is immediately successful by releasing at 9 o'clock and agrees to change her position without insisting on staying opposite the target. However, after another success, she still thinks that the ball travels across the circle: 6 o'clock → 12 o'clock → target. Subsequently, she says that she releases *when I see that it's on the line* (from 12 o'clock to the target), but as the ball misses the box, *it was nearly there, but it turned before it got to the box.* Later, she announces that *if you turn this way* (right) *the ball will go to the right, and like that* (left) *it goes to the left,* then nine times she indicates 12 o'clock as the release point.

Progress achieved at level IB is thus only partial and varies from subject to subject without any clear pattern.

Level IIA

Examples

FRA (7,7) (who has not quite reached level IIA) is placed at 6 o'clock with the box opposite 12 o'clock: Where will you let the ball go? *There* (12 o'clock). Can you try? (The ball is released at 9 o'clock and almost reaches the left side of box.) *I ought to let it go a bit nearer here* (1 o'clock), so, had she corrected from the 9 o'clock position instead of the 12 o'clock one, her answer would have been right. In fact, she then releases the ball at 7 o'clock. Where did you let it go? *Here* (10 o'clock); *I made a mistake.* (She changes her own position to near 9 o'clock and successfully releases the ball at 9 o'clock as well.) Why did it go in? *I was a bit more there, to the side: like that, you can let it go a bit more like that* (ball going in a straight line from 9 to 2 o'clock) *and it goes there* (as if the ball had turned through a sharp angle at 2 o'clock to get into the box opposite 12 o'clock). The interviewer then moves the box and puts it opposite 6 o'clock, with the child staying opposite 9 o'clock. FRA successfully releases the ball at 3 o'clock: Where did you let it go? *There* (12 o'clock, as if the ball had to travel in a straight line from 12 to 6 before dropping into the box). The interviewer then suggests that he himself try it, following her instructions, that is to say, she must call out *go* when it is time to release the ball. The child then goes to the 6 o'clock position, with the target opposite 12. FRA says *go* at 12 o'clock (incorrect): Should I have let it go before or after? *Before* (points to 10 o'clock). Then FRA has another attempt herself and successfully releases at 9 o'clock, although again pointing to 12 o'clock as the release point. Didn't it go off from there (9 o'clock)? *No, there* (between 10:30 and 11 o'clock, thus an intermediate position between 9 and 12).

COR (7,6), starting without a target, correctly indicates that if you turn to the right the ball will go *over there* (to the right), and only to the right. Could it go anywhere else? *Yes, there* (points to the wall, moves so that she is opposite it, and indicates a trajectory perpendicular to it). Then she again points to trajectories on the right. How about trying to make it come toward me (interviewer stands near 12 o'clock)? (Successfully releases at 9 o'clock but points to 12 o'clock). *I let it go here* (12 o'clock—she then actually does this and misses the target). Where now? *There* (10 o'clock, which is a good correction). And if I go here (opposite 12 o'clock)? *There* (2 o'clock, followed by another accurate correction). And if I go here (7 o'clock)? *There* (7 o'clock—her first attempts are unsuccessful, but then she tries again and successfully releases before 8 o'clock for a left rotation and near 6 o'clock for a right rotation, thus clearly having good motor regulation). Where did you let it go? *There* (7 o'clock for her actual release point of before 8, and 7:30 for that of 6). She draws a curved trajectory starting off opposite the target and perpendicular to the tangent.

MAR (7,6), starting off with a set target opposite 12 o'clock (child positioned opposite 6 o'clock): *I've got to aim* (he releases at 8 o'clock: misses). What did you do? *I let go too quickly* (second attempt: releases at 9 o'clock, successful). However, he indicates a release point of 10 o'clock, then after another miss from 8 and renewed success from 9, he indicates 11 o'clock as the release point. The box is then moved to opposite 1 o'clock: Now where are you going to let it go? *There* (1 o'clock). In accordance with the interviewer's instruction, he marks the spot with a cross, but then goes on to release the ball after the cross. Now, I'm going to try it; you tell me where to let go. *Where the cross is* (the interviewer does this: misses). *It wasn't quite on the cross . . . You let it go right, but it won't work, because when it's going around, the ball keeps on going around.* The box is then placed opposite 10 o'clock, and the child makes several attempts so that he can really do it properly. On the sixteenth try, he releases at 8 o'clock for a right rotation and at 4 o'clock for a left rotation. How do you do it? *When you see that the ball is there* (10 o'clock), *you see that it's there, then you let it go.* After fresh attempts, he is asked to choose between 8, 9, and 10 o'clock: he points to 9 as a compromise between what he sees actually happen and what he feels should happen (conceptualization).

TON (8,6), with the box opposite 12 o'clock, lets go of the ball at 8 o'clock. (Miss.) *It went off to the left* (of the box) *because I let it go when it was there* (11 o'clock instead of 8 o'clock!). Where should you have let it go? *There* (12 o'clock, which she means to try to do, but in fact releases it at 8 o'clock). *It's gone again* (to the left of the target). Are you going to change where you let it go, or go on as you were? *Do the same, aiming better.* Can you aim at the target? *No.* What about me? *Yes.* You told me that you wanted to let it go here (12 o'clock)? *No, more there* (1 o'clock: she thus moves the release point in the right direction with respect to the supposed, not the actual, point of 8 o'clock). (She tries again, releasing at 8:30, but pushing the ball with her hand.) *It always wants to go somewhere else.* How come? *Because my aim's bad.* Try again. (Releases at 8:30.) Put this (small object) where you let go of the ball. (Puts it at 11:30, then successfully releases at 9 o'clock.) Good. Where did you let it go? *Here* (11:30). I'm going to try: you say *go* when I ought to let it go. (She says *go* at 12 o'clock and the ball goes toward the child.) *It's come to me!* Where did I let it go? *Here* (2:30! opposite the subject). This does not stop TON from continuing to say *go* at 12 o'clock, attributing her misses to the fact that the ball goes too slowly. She tries again herself, releasing at 8:30, then successfully at 10, but indicates the release points at 12 and 11 o'clock. She even changes the direction of rotation without realizing it and successfully releases five times at 2:30, then misses three times (at 1, 3, and 3:30). When do you get it in and when do you miss? *When I let go of it there* (at 2:30—so she does realize her mistake!) *I miss, and when I let go of it there* (12 o'clock) *I get it in.* Have a good look. (2:30—success.) Where did you let it go? *There* (1 o'clock). The drawings are at first almost correct (ball's departure virtually along a tangent, with the trajectory curved toward the box), but subsequent drawings match her conceptualization (trajectory virtually perpendicular to the box). Look: I'm going to let go there (successful release at 9:30). (TON is amazed.) *It went in the box.* Where did I let it go? *There* (12 o'clock). Have another look. (successful release at 9 o'clock.) Did I let it go at the right time? *No!* Are you sure? *Yes.*

VER (8,0) rotates to the left and successfully releases at 2:30. Where did you let it go? *There* (1 o'clock). *It went straight off and went in the corner of the box.* How did it turn? *Like that* (toward the right—incorrect) *around my hand.* When the interviewer successfully releases at 10 o'clock, she recognizes that it is the right place because it went in the box; but soon afterward, when she is asked to make a drawing, she draws a straight line from 12 o'clock to the box. But to be sure of getting it in? *There* (12 o'clock).

JOS (8,0), by contrast, having successfully released at 9 o'clock and almost reached the box from 8 o'clock, indicates that he released at 12, then at 11:30, then at 10, thus gradually bringing his conception nearer to true cognizance of the event and showing that he is close to level IIB; however, a moment later, when asked to mark the release point, he says, *If you put it more to the left the ball will go farther to the left, while if you put it more here* (opposite the target) *it goes into the target.* When the interviewer releases the ball at 3 (left movement), *You've done it right, but the ball went straight . . . sometimes it goes straight for a bit and sometimes it goes around for a bit.* (Fresh attempt.) *It kept on going* (on the tangent), *it didn't want to turn.*

ISA (9,2), starting without a set target, predicts the release points *there or there* on the correct side or opposite her. The box is then placed in position and she releases at 6 o'clock (thus opposite 12), at 8 o'clock, and twice successfully at 9. Where did you let it go? *Here* (at 12), and so on with slight variations between 11:30 and 12:30, while continuing to release successfully between 9 and 10.

COL (8,10 then 9,0) at the first session starts off with reactions similar to those of the preceding subjects; she attributes her misses to the fact that she was *not yet quite near the target, not opposite.* When the interviewer takes the sling, ISA suggests that he release at 12, then when the ball misses the box, recognizes that *you've got to let it go a bit before,* having clearly located the release point, which leads her to say: *The ball flies off to the side,* and so on. But after two attempts at releasing at 9 o'clock, she sums up from memory: *If I made it go from there* (12 o'clock), *it could go there* (a little to the right of the target) *or there* (in the box). During a second session she progresses to level IIB.

Thus, all the subjects initially questioned without a set target think it possible to predict whether the ball will go to the left or to the right according to the direction of the rotation, although they cannot specify the actual direction or, of course, the relevant tangential departure of the ball. Instead, they designate a sort of special area, with possible variations, but take no account of the release point. Furthermore, these subjects succeed in reaching the target regardless of their location or that of the box, without asking to be placed opposite the target. On two counts this provides us with evidence of decentration regarding the actual action, since in their prediction of the trajectories these children pay more attention than do those at stage I to objective characteristics. So no child, except momentarily the intermediate subject FRA (when the target is placed opposite 6 o'clock), now thinks that the ball starts off by crossing the rotational circle (going, for instance, from 12 to the 6 o'clock target) and thus providing a direct link between the subject and the box.

The most general characteristic of this level IIA is the very strong tendency of the child, despite his successes with the ball, to conceptualize the release point as being directly opposite the target, for example, at 12 o'clock if the target is opposite 12 o'clock, even though he had actually released the ball at 9. With some children, like TON (8,6) this tendency is so strong that the answer *12 o'clock* persists throughout the session, even when it is the experimenter who is using the sling. Others like MAR finally compromise between the actual release point and their original answer (the point opposite the target), although these children give the release point correctly when the sling is handled by the interviewer.

Of course, there is a contradiction between what the children say when there is no set target and the fact that they expect the ball to go off from the side and not from a point perpendicular to the tangent. If they took account of this, they would also indicate a release point at the side and not one that is perpendicular to the tangent and opposite the target, particularly since this is what they actually employ when they use the sling. Their conception of the location of the release point is thus contrary both to their own predictions before being presented with a target and to their own actions once the target has been placed.

However, the contradiction between the release point opposite the target and the previously predicted paths is not so great as it might seem and may simply constitute an insufficient form of coordination. When the subject swings the ball and then releases it without a set target, he thinks that the ball will go to the right or left according to the direction of rotation, so that the ball is in a way thrown as soon as the string is no longer held. However, once the target has been placed, the subject tries to aim at it, and generally speaking, when you aim a ball at a rectangular box (target), you seek a trajectory perpendicular to it. In the subject's action, the two successive motions (preliminary rotation and aiming at the target) are rapidly coordinated, thanks to his motor regulations, and the ball is released near 9 o'clock for a target situated at 12.

In the child's conceptualization there remain two points in time or two distinct actions (such as LAU at level IA still carried out: first rotation and then throwing). Hence we see the initial rotation, with release in the direction of the rotational movement as long as there is no set target, and then, with the introduction of the target and the consequent attempt to aim and throw the ball at it, the release opposite the target. The child appears to be untroubled by any apparent contradiction, but rather to coordinate by simple succession or juxtaposition two movements conceived as heterogeneous (rotation and aiming by throwing the ball from a point opposite the target), while not understanding that the ball will go off at a tangent to the circle described by its rotation: hence his conceptualization of a release at 12 o'clock.

On the other hand, there is complete contradiction between this erroneous conception of the action and the action itself with its good coordinations resulting from the sensorimotor regulations (and this as early as four years of age!). Here therefore is the central problem: why is this conception still so wrong (less so than at level IA, where the ball's trajectory was thought to cross the rotational circle along its diameter, whereas for these IIA subjects it simply forms an extension of a radius, but this is still a major residual error), even though, when he thinks about it, the subject is now forced actively to reflect upon his course of action instead of performing it more or less automatically as a result of simple sensorimotor regulation? As in all such cases, these subjects are "victims" of a pseudocontradiction that leads them to reject the evidence of their own eyes, however clear it may be. The pseudocontradiction in this particular case arises from the fact that when a mobile object goes off to one side, as happens when it is released at some point along a circular trajectory, the child thinks it cannot reach a target unless the path it has to follow goes straight to the target from a point opposite this target (the trajectory thus forming an extension of a radius, or being perpendicular to the tangent, at this point opposite the target). This incompatibility results, as we have just seen, from insufficient vector coordinations. Still, it is not any less significant at this level (in fact, it is even more so than at level IA where, as has been shown, some children like ALA are not far from a correct reading of the data, since they have not reached the stage of questioning what they see) and it leads to the remarkable phenomenon of these children's refusal to believe what they must see (release at 9 or 2 to 3 for a target opposite 12 o'clock and the like). In this case, what they actually see is considered impossible because of the pseudocontradiction and is rejected, just as an affective tendency can be influenced by a contradiction between sentiments (which can also be a pseudocontradiction).

Level IIB (Beginnings of Cognizance)

Examples

PED (8,8), with no set target, accurately describes the ball's trajectory for the two directions of rotation, but nonetheless maintains, when the target is placed in position, that to reach it the ball must be released at 12 o'clock. The interviewer then takes the sling and asks for instructions. PED says *go* at 12 o'clock, then at 9, then four times at 12, without the ball's actually being released. Finally, the ball is released at 12: when it misses, PED immediately says, *You've got to let it go here* (at 10). Then he tries himself, to the left, and releases at 2 o'clock. Where did you let it go? *Here* (7, thus almost diametrically opposite the target). The interviewer makes as if to release at 7 o'clock, and PED immediately says, *I bet it will go there* (correct trajectory). Subsequently, he correctly indicates his own release points.

COL (9,0)'s attempts during her second session are similar to those of her first: she successfully releases the ball at 9 o'clock, but declares that she released it at 12. By contrast, when she has rotated the sling the other way, she realizes that she released it at 2:30. And if you went the other way round, where would you let it go? *There* (at 10). But she draws an oblique line starting at 10 and going far to the right of the target, whereupon it makes a sharp turn (at an angle of about 120 degrees) and joins the box. *It can go straight or it can turn.* Her next drawing shows a bend instead of the angle.

GUN (9,5), without a target: *It would go on turning; it would go over there* (more or less tangential straight line). And if you turned the other way? *Here* (same), *because the ball goes to the side you release it from.* Then with a set target she draws curved trajectories and insists that the ball has to be released as 12 o'clock, but after a few attempts she finally indicates about 9 o'clock in one direction and 2 in the other. How did you find the spot? *It's almost straight across from the target.* However, when the box is replaced by a skittle, she declares: *You mustn't let it go here* (9 o'clock) *because it would go to the right. You've got to let it go here* (12 o'clock). After various attempts, she again indicates 9 and 3. However, when obstacles are placed along the edge of the path the ball has to follow, GUN imagines that *the ball will go around bends,* and she draws zigzags, or *a turn like that* (straight lines with an obtuse angle between them). At the end of the questioning she still maintains, after having released at 9, that she had released at 12 and draws a straight line perpendicular to the box; then she corrects herself and indicates 9 o'clock.

These subjects therefore still begin by thinking that for an actual release point of 9 o'clock they released the ball at 12 or

1, then they correct themselves. How does this correction come about? Clearly, it is not a question of simply observing what happens, since the younger subjects could do that. A certain inferential ability seems to remove the hitherto insurmountable contradiction that prevented the younger subjects from believing the evidence of their own eyes, so the answers of these level IIB subjects become progressively more accurate. This inferring can therefore only be of an operatory nature and is readily explained by the progress that generally takes place at this age when children first grasp the significance of direction and vectors in the construction of natural systems of coordinates.

However, our aim is not to explain new facts by old, but to interpret what is already known in the light of an analysis both of our subjects' practical actions and of their cognizance of them. Once again, the vital question may be stated quite simply: what causes removal of the pseudocontradiction that earlier had prevented the subject from accurately coordinating his actions, or rather conceptualizing them, in view of the fact that they were already coordinated at the sensorimotor level as a result of the relatively easy regulations? When the child has already admitted, without there being a set target, that after release the ball will follow a lateral trajectory continuing in the direction of the rotation, he needs only to discover that aiming at a target does not involve a new action distinct from that of rotating the ball, but simply one that is actually carried out during this rotation. Just as a baby needs to attain the "try and see" of the fifth sensorimotor stage before he discovers that to hit the ground with an object he needs only to let it go and does not have to throw it, so with concepts, it is not until this IIB level that children discover that the ball's lateral trajectory, following its release during rotation, is sufficient to make it hit the target without there being any need for a change of direction. Here the difference is that this discovery had already been incorporated by the subject into his action but not into his conception of his action. For the latter it can only be inferential, and with the discovery thus being incomplete, the child has to understand how to link two directions (that leading straight to the target and that of the ball's trajectory after its release during rotation); these must first be identified, then made the properties of just one movement. However, this operation is conceptually so difficult, despite appearances, that these level IIB subjects still regard the movements as separate. COL does draw an oblique line, but it does not go straight to the target; and she makes it turn through an angle of 120 degrees, referring to bends and curves. GUN does the same, and PED, who finally settles for straight lines, initially draws a trajectory reminiscent of the diameters of stage I (from 7 o'clock to 2 o'clock) in order to join the 2 o'clock point to the target opposite 12. These subjects not only find it difficult to generalize the oblique trajectory to the form of a unique straight line, but they are also unable from the outset to indicate correctly the release point. Unlike the stage III subjects, they therefore do not immediately see that the ball's trajectory cannot be perpendicular to the box.

Stage III

At this last stage, which generally starts around at about eleven or twelve years (although, as usual, there are a few exceptional younger subjects), cognizance of the requisites for success takes place immediately. A distinction must still be made between a level IIIA, where the children still draw trajectories with bends or angles, and a level IIIB, where these are truly tangential.

Examples (Level IIIA)

ROB (9,7), with no set target, thinks the ball would go to the right or left, according to the direction of the rotation. When the target box is in position, he starts by releasing at 12 o'clock (a level IIB reaction), but immediately corrects himself (*Oh! No, I'll do it again*) and indicates the actual release points of 10 and 2, depending on the direction of rotation. *The points where you let go must be in that half of the circle.* How did you see that? *By trying it* (active regulation). But his drawing shows a slight bend: *It turns toward the middle* (of the trajectory). *It goes straight, then it turns.* However, he subsequently corrects this as well and draws one straight line from the center of the circle to the release point and another (perpendicular to the first) from this point to the box: *That's an angle* (right angle), *it's an* ⌐. And in the other direction? *An L the other way around.*

BEL (10,2) immediately realizes that she has released at 9 and at 3 when she hits the target, but describes the ball's trajectory as *a curve.*

RIN (10,10) also correctly observes the release points at 3 and 9: *If I push it from there* (9 o'clock), *that will work as well.* However, he starts off drawing zigzag trajectories, although later drawings show steady curves instead.

STE (11,6): His reactions are similar to those of RIN and BEL. He comments, *It curves a bit* (after release) *because it turns* (before).

TIA (11,5): *It's thrown outside its usual circle; it goes in a curve . . . If it hasn't got a lot of force, it will make a bigger curve.*

KAB (12,6): *When the ball goes in a circle, if you let it go, it tends to continue its circle.* Yet when he sees what happens upon release at 3 o'clock (his correctly predicted release point), he says, *My calculation was wrong because it goes more in a straight line than I had worked out.* This does not prevent him from finally drawing a circle with trajectories starting from four equidistant points, but all having parabolic paths.

Interestingly, level IIIA reactions can be divided into two types. The trajectories drawn by some subjects (such as RIN) are reminiscent of those of level IIB in that they still contain

angles or zigzags. By contrast, the curved trajectories of other
subjects (although occasionally encountered also at level IIB)
clearly indicate that for these children there are no longer two
heterogeneous actions — that is, making the ball turn, then
when it gets to the release point somehow or other throwing
it — but just one movement (making it turn) which, inasmuch
as the ball was released during rotation, makes it continue in
a curve because, as KAB explicitly says, *it tends to continue its
circle* (see also STE and TIA). In the supplementary experiment
that takes place on the school grounds where the subjects can
rotate the sling in a vertical plane, the same prediction was
encountered in the form of hypocycloids.

Examples (Level IIIB)

These subjects are all between eleven and twelve years of
age except for one advanced child of eight whose exceptional
success could perhaps be accounted for by his having played
with the sling for a long time.

> BRU (8,6), with no set target, first correctly indicates
> four paths for the ball based on the direction of the
> rotation, then three more based on his own posi-
> tion. After this, he is asked where he should release
> the ball for it to hit an imaginary target slightly
> below that to which he has just pointed and he
> answers correctly by moving the release point a
> little farther forward. When similarly questioned,
> this time regarding another imaginary target
> slightly above, he selects a release point further
> back. Only after these tasks is the target box
> placed, whereupon BRU is immediately successful
> in indicating his release points. This advance over
> the level IIB subjects could therefore result from
> the gradually increasing difficulty of the initial
> questions; however, to the question, Can you make
> the ball go around in a circle? the child answers,
> *No, when you let it go, it goes completely straight.*
> He maintains this answer when the interviewer

suggests that the ball might be made to go around obstacles.

AIN (11,1) correctly indicates release points of 9, 6, and so on, according to the target's positions. *I look at the ball . . . sometimes at the target, and I go myself* (mentally) *where the ball has to go.* Does it go in a straight line or a curve? *In a straight line.*

MEL (11,2) also knows what he does and, furthermore, observes that *the longer the string is, the nearer the target we have to let the ball go . . . The string always makes a straight line and not a curve.*

ERI (12,7). *I see in my head the ball as it turns, then I picture where it goes . . . When I've got my thumb down, I can hold the ball better. If I hold the ball up, I can see better when I've got to let it go.* Where does it go? *It doesn't go like that* (from 12 to the box), *it follows the movement of the circle a bit* (he draws the tangent). What are the angles like? *There's a right angle* (between the tangent and the radius), *at the place where you let it go, it's perpendicular.*

It seems that it is not before the age of eleven or twelve (the success of the (8,6)-year-old was exceptional and we are not sure why it occurred) that the subject can free himself immediately of the pseudocontradictions that held back his cognizance of the release points at the first two stages and understand that the ball's release during its circular trajectory, and before it comes in front of the target, is enough to make it go inside the box. However, this understanding is clearly not complete at level IIIA, since these children (from BEL to TIA) do not yet consider the trajectory tangential, or at least not at the start of the session (ROB and KAB); it becomes so only after the subject has considered all facets of the situation, whereas the inferential composition (*my calculation,* as KAB calls it) is not enough. At level IIIB, on the other hand, this coordination by inference (*I go myself,* says AIN; *I see in my head,* declares ERI) is sufficient to deduce that the path is tangential.

Supplementary Experiment Involving Different Planes of Rotation

In addition to the experiment involving only the horizontal plane just above the floor, one group of subjects was also asked to use the string to get the ball in the box from an upright position. This generally led to their swinging the string like a pendulum; so the interviewer then added that it had to be rotated, but did not specify the plane—which thus could be horizontal, vertical, or oblique. With the vertical or oblique planes there is more than one possible release point, since the force used by the subject also plays a role; the trajectory can describe either a high or a low curve. The advantage of this technique is that it allows more detailed observation of the motor adaptations of the action and comparison of them with the conceptualized cognizance of the situation.

Clearly, the selection of the plane of rotation, and of the amount of force to be used, together with the variation in distance (the box is situated between 3 and 6 meters from the subject), demand more active adjustments on the part of the subject than is the case where the ball remained just above the ground. In addition, the relationships between the actions of making the ball turn and of propelling it into the box in the vertical and oblique planes are different from those in the horizontal plane. In the case of the vertical and oblique planes the child must first ensure that the target is in the proper plane and then take into account whether the rotation is overarm or underarm. These new factors can also modify the child's picture of the situation.

Examples (Stage I)

CAR (5,8) whose responses to the original ground-level experiment were reported in our earlier discussion of level IB, predicts in the horizontal plane (above his head) which side the ball will go according to the release point. When the box has been placed, he selects an oblique plane, correctly adjusts this for the target, into which he manages (after trial and error) to get the ball by means of an underarm rotation. When returning to a horizontal plane, he indicates the release point first at 9 (correct), then at 6 (diametrically opposite!), then at 12: *I let it go there.*

CEL (6,0—again see level IB discussion) begins in the vertical plane with an underarm rotation, which is, however, not correct for the target; he then adjusts the plane. Now above your head. (He does it well.) And if you let go? *It would go on the ground over there* (opposite). How about aiming? *Yes.* (He changes the direction of rotation and releases around 3 to 4 o'clock.) Where did you let it go? (The interviewer points to 12, 9, 6, and 3.) *More like there* (12).

So there is hardly any difference between his reactions regarding the horizontal plane above his head and those during the ground-level experiment. Still, when he rotates the string in the vertical plane, CAR knows that he has released near the bottom of the rotational circle.

Examples (Level IIA)

PHO (7,4) starts off by simply swinging the sling back and forth like a pendulum. *It goes better when you do it a lot of times.* His drawing represents a swing that reaches the box (about 3 meters away) rising in front of it; however, after watching the interviewer's performance, PHO draws a convex curve. For his rotations he generally selects oblique planes, but his drawing shows (because it is easier) a vertical plane with the release point at the base of the circle and not opposite the box (which is therefore correct), and a convex curve. *The ball goes farther and farther* (with the highest point near the middle) *and it falls down again into the box.* The conceptualization thus is correct for a vertical plane, although subsequently, after rotating the string in the horizontal plane near the ground, PHO

releases his ball at 10 and at 2, believing in both instances that it has been released at 12 o'clock.

LIP (7,6) begins his rotations in an oblique plane,
which he adjusts, making it slightly more horizontal. His drawing shows a release point at the top of
the circle with the ball going down to the ground
and bouncing up into the box, but when he is asked
if he can improve his drawing, he indicates the
release at the point on the circle nearest the target;
his grasp of the situation is therefore correct, while
his revised conceptualization elicited by the interviewer's question brings LIP back to the ideas generally held at this developmental phase in the original ground-level experiment.

LIN (7,6) begins in the vertical plane, but is badly
oriented in relation to the target and attributes his
failure to a very slight breeze blowing in the field
(Beaufort Scale, Force I). *It's because of the wind
that it goes off to the side.* So? (He changes his position.) *Here, I'll be right in front of it.* After a successful attempt, he makes a correct drawing with
release in the lower part of the circle and a curved
trajectory (convex) that ends up in the box. However, after a successful attempt in the horizontal
plane, he indicates 12 o'clock as the release point
even though he has released the ball earlier.

LIS (7,6) begins at ground level (unlike the preceding
subjects) and successfully releases at 10 or 2, but
thinks he let go at 12 and so draws the paths perpendicular to the box. The interesting feature of his
behavior is that when he is asked to repeat in slow
motion what he has done, he does it correctly, letting go at the right place. Nevertheless, when
giving a verbal description, LIS insists that he released the ball at 12 o'clock! Even when the interviewer demonstrates, he still maintains that *the
best way would be that* (pointing from the 12
o'clock position to the box). *You've got to let it go*

here (opposite). When it comes to the rotations in space (with the box 3 meters away), he naturally suggests that *you've got to turn it and release just before.* After adjusting his plane of rotation, initially slightly oblique, then very inclined, and then vertical, he succeeds and correctly indicates the release points (*the ball goes up in the air*); his drawings also are correct.

MAN (8,8) begins by rotating in space and reaches the target 3 meters away with a vertical plane of rotation. His drawings, showing the circle in profile, indicate a release point at the bottom of the circle and, on one of them, he starts by drawing a path perpendicular to the box (thus the equivalent of the 12 o'clock release of the ground-level experiment), then corrects it himself. At ground level, on the other hand, he points to 12 o'clock, having released the ball at 9.

PAT (8,11) starts by indicating a perpendicular path (12 o'clock for a horizontal rotation above his head), then corrects himself without being able to explain why.

Examples (Level IIB)

JAC (9,9) rotates in the vertical plane and misses. *You've got to let it go lower down.* (Fresh attempt.) *Not at the same place, higher. Sometimes it curves more and sometimes less.* His first drawing for the horizontal plane shows a release point more or less in front of the target; a second shows it to be at the side but with the wrong direction of rotation.

LOU (9,10) in the vertical plane: *I shot it too hard; I'll do it more gently.* The drawing shows a release at the top of the circle for a rotation in one direction and at the bottom, in the other. In the horizontal plane, *It's harder . . . Before, I let it go there*

(12 o'clock), *then here*, indicating 10 to 11, then 9 in one direction and 3 in the other. How will it go? *It will curve.* Where will it go? *Into a corner* (of the box). And if you want it to go in the middle? (Release) *a bit before.*

ANG (10,8) in the vertical plane first of all indicates a release point almost in front of the target, then at the bottom of the circle with the ball rising. In the horizontal plane (above her head) she immediately generalizes, showing on her drawing a release at the side (3 or 9 according to the direction). The trajectories are curved in the horizontal plane, as they were in her drawing for the vertical plane.

In the case of the horizontal rotations at ground level, the children clearly find it difficult in their conceptualization to coordinate the path leading to the target with the movements necessary to make the ball turn. In the case of the vertical or oblique planes, on the other hand, the problem of the path to the target is solved in advance through adjustment of the orientation of the plane: the subject then has to contend only with the length of the trajectory, which depends both on the momentum obtained through rotation and on the release point. However, as there can be several possible release points for one given direction of rotation, and the latter has already been taken into account by the plane's orientation, there is no longer a contradiction (or even pseudocontradiction) for the subject between the action of releasing or throwing in the direction of the target and that of making the ball turn. The subjects thus find it easier to picture the action, the more so because of the greater number of active adjustments that have to be made; they do not draw trajectories starting at the point on the circle nearest the target (except for LIP when he is asked to improve his drawing), but draw them starting near the top or bottom of the circle. In the horizontal plane (above the subject's head or in front of him) there remains the tendency, despite the successful releases at 9 or 3, to show the release point at 12 o'clock, opposite the target. When the horizontal plane is selected after the vertical or oblique planes, the subject sometimes is better able to conceptualize the 9 o'clock and 3 o'clock release points.

Concerning stage III, it is noticeable that although all the children's actions reveal a greater awareness than is the case at stage II, the subjects at level IIIA differ from those at level IIIB in their ideas regarding the shape of the trajectory. Initially, for rotations in a horizontal plane (not near the ground) the IIIA children draw curved trajectories, as they do for those near the ground. Subsequently, when the rotation is vertical or oblique and the trajectories have to be convex, these children sometimes draw them not as one curve, but as a series of loops (hypocycloid; a curve akin to the cycloid, described by a point on the circumference of a small circle rolling inside a large one and not along a straight line).[1]

Examples (Level IIIA)

JUA (11,4) selects a vertical plane and modifies its orientation. He next draws a trajectory formed by just one curve, which he then corrects by putting in three loops, as if the ball were still circling after it had been released.

ERA (12,8) also starts off with a simple curve, then introduces a twist, and finally four successive loops.

Example (Level IIIB)

DOM (12,3), for a vertical plane, draws the release point at the bottom of the circle but specifies that one can vary *the force of the throw:* whence four round curves, starting from the same point and ending up in the box at the same place, but each one

1. This combination of the supposed rotation of the ball along its curved trajectory does not appear to raise a complicated problem for the child at this level, since before constructing true cycloids on a horizontal path, the eleven- or twelve-year-old subjects studied earlier with Professor Bärbel Inhelder often started by drawing hypocycloids.

higher than the previous one. After rotating in a horizontal plane and getting the ball in the box, he immediately draws the release point at 3 o'clock (left rotation), although before this attempt he had been less sure about its position.

Thus the findings of this supplementary experiment outside the classroom confirm the previous results. In the horizontal plane (above ground level) the same tendencies were encountered as in the ground-level experiment, despite the subjects' success in getting the ball into the box—in other words, a pseudocontradictory conflict between the paths to the target and the preliminary action of making the ball turn. In the case of rotation in the vertical or oblique planes, there is no such pseudocontradiction, since there is no longer a problem regarding the paths to the target (because the children have already had to orient the plane); hence their better understanding of the events.

Conclusions

The results of this research offer a good example of a situation in which the cognizance, and of course the conceptualization on which it rests, remain distorted as long as the subject's actions (although successful, and even coordinated at the sensorimotor level) cannot be coordinated at the conceptual level because of the pseudocontradiction. The child is fully aware of what happens only when his conception is backed up by an inferential or operatory coordination drawn from the coordination of the actions themselves through reflexive abstraction. The remaining problem therefore is to understand why this happens so late, or in other words, to determine the basis of the initial pseudocontradiction that prevents conceptual coordination and delineate the logical processes through which the pseudocontradiction finally resolved.

(a) This initial pseudocontradiction is, in one sense, a real contradiction between two suppositions improperly limited by restrictive postulates, and thus bounded by reference frames that are too narrow. The children imagine that when the ball is released during a circular movement, it always goes off to the side, but only into what are perhaps best described as privileged zones (for example, within two conical beams, one on each side of the 12 o'clock position at which their vertexes meet), without relating these accurately to the release point. The other supposition is that to attain the target there is only one trajectory, or at least an equally privileged group of them, all starting from a point opposite, or more or less opposite, the box (perpendicular to its long side). Here is clearly a contradiction, since the ball cannot be released opposite the target and then go off to the side. This most primitive type of contradiction is between two actions and the schemes for them, such as there would be for an animal or a baby wishing to reach a desired object and having to set off in the opposite direction (hence the difficulty of the detour behavior), but it is none the less significant. This leads to the idea widely held at levels IA to IIA that to reach the target one has to interrupt the circular movements and make the ball go off in a straight line, forming an extension either to the diameter of the circle $(6 \rightarrow 12 \rightarrow \text{target})$ or to a radius. The fact that at the sensorimotor level the coordination is effected between the initial rotations, aiming at the target, and the releasing the ball, does not prevent the subject from subsequently picturing two distinct and successive actions.

(b) For the same reasons, the subject remains unconscious of the following real contradiction; if the ball always goes off to the side (left or right depending on the direction of rotation), its trajectory cannot be perpendicular either to the tangent or to these approximate tangents. The child solves his problem either, like LAU at level IA, by carrying out two separate actions (rotating the sling, then stopping and throwing it, a clear forerunner of the more advanced reaction of pushing the ball a short distance with the hand in the desired direction) or by imagining that there are in fact two distinct movements, of which the second does not prolong the first, but simply succeeds it — whence the absence of coordination.

(c) Having said this, it is easier to understand how far the subject still has to go before he can make an inferential coordination, since for each of the two suppositions given in (a) the reference frame must be enlarged through the construction of new relations founded on more accurate recording of the features (or what is observed) between which there appears to be no (or almost no) contradiction. As for the second supposition regarding the ball's trajectories, the subjects need to realize that no privileged areas exist, and also that the ball can be released at any point on the circle of rotation. However, the children must also relate (and this is only gradually achieved) the ball's flight paths to the release points and must understand that there is one possible trajectory for each specific release point—without the target being involved at all. The ball's trajectories after release must therefore be reduced to geometric terms, with all that this implies regarding frames of reference and coordination.

(d) To conceptualize the right path traveled by the ball from the release point to the target, the child must again be able to picture all those paths that are possible, since even at level IB or IIA he is well aware that, independently of the initial rotations, a box may be reached by oblique paths and not just by starting the ball off opposite it. The fact that the ball's path toward the target immediately succeeds the circular movements does, however, create a problem; but children quite soon stop sticking to a release point at exactly 12 o'clock and admit slight variations (11 or 1 o'clock), or even end up compromising between the actual release points and those figuring in their conception: for example, 10:30 between 9 and 12. Then the child has only to generalize the oblique nature of these paths to reduce the initial pseudocontradiction and so be on his way to coordinating the ball's circular movements and its trajectories after release.

(e) However, this conceptualized coordination is of a different type from the sensorimotor coordination that enables children from four years of age to get the ball in the box. The child starts off by making various attempts to reach the target. These attempts in fact correspond to a sort of set of possible solutions, but the child is not conscious of this and so does not picture them as such (consider, for example, the "extension" of a sensorimotor scheme of which the subject, who is centered on his own "understanding," is unaware; trial and error gradually leads to elimination of all the incorrect possibilities and thus to the correct solution). By contrast, conceptualization starts from one or two observations (correct or incorrect) and from limiting postulates (assumptions); it can be correct only if the subject has understood all the possible trajectories for the ball after release, regardless of any target, and if he has realized that the target may also be reached by oblique trajectories. Between the motor and the conceptual coordination there is therefore a fairly fundamental difference (in orientation): on the one side, there is unconscious selection through trial and error, of the correct release point from all those possible, and on the other side, gradual understanding of all the possibilities of the situation—and only subsequently, application of this understanding to the action that has been carried out, which may then be interpreted.

(f) Thus resolution of the initial pseudocontradiction and removal of the actual contradiction existing at the lowest levels may both therefore be explained by a progressive extension of the frames of reference, from the initial classes of limited observable features to those embracing all the possibilities. In fact, while the initial frames of reference, constituted by the class of oblique paths after the ball's release (whence the supposition p of privileged zones and so on) and that of the trajectories leading to the box (whence the supposition q), lead to reciprocal exclusion, that is, $(p.\bar{q}) \lor (\bar{p}.q)$, the final frames of reference (all the possibilities) include an intersection, that of the oblique paths culminating at the target. This intersection of the classes corresponding to extended p and q (thus to the classes of all the tangential departures and of all the trajectories, including the oblique ones, that lead to the target) gives rise to the most understandable system $(p.q) \lor (p.\bar{q}) \lor (\bar{p}.q)$, which eliminates all contradiction between p and q. Correction of the definitions of p and q follows naturally, that is, substitution of a relational point of view for the initial restrictive false absolutes (privileged zones in the absence of a target and the need for the ball's trajectory to be perpendicular to the long side of the box), and so the child is able to coordinate the two actions or movements, originally considered heterogeneous, in a coherent conceptual system.

(g) However, all this does not mean that inferential or conceptualized coordination is not drawn from the sensorimotor coordination of the actions through reflexive abstraction, since without success in action, the conceptualization would remain inoperative. In fact, the two fundamental and distinct characteristics of the "reflexive" property of such an abstraction here emerge clearly. On the one hand, there is a sort of projection or reflection in the physical sense (reflecting), consisting in transposing from the motor level (where it was already effected) to the conceptual level the unity of the two actions. On the other hand, there is reflection in the sense of a conceptual reorganization, since through inferential coordination a new and essential element is added to the sensorimotor coordination: that is, an understanding of how and why it exists, which involves insertion of the practical success as a particular case into the range of possibilities achievable under analogous conditions, and thus construction of a conceptual frame of reference of a quite different nature from the initial sensorimotor system.

These two characteristics of the reflexive property are linked developmentally in that their projection or reflection in a physical sense constitutes a correspondence (or morphism) between the sensorimotor links and the conceptual links that represent them. At the same time, the reflection in the sense of a conceptual reorganization consists in making these same links correspond to analogous ones intervening in the other possible cases, which also involves the construction of morphisms: the operation (or the function) intervening in the reflection, in the first sense of the term, thus becomes a particular case of the set of morphisms constituted by the reorganization in the second sense of the term "reflexive."

3 The Ping-Pong Ball (or the Hoop)

In the experiment described in Chapter 2, cognizance of the situation with the sling was hampered by the young subjects' persistent belief that they were themselves carrying out two successive actions (making the ball turn on the end of a piece of string, then throwing it into a box) that involved heterogeneous movements, whereas after its release the ball follows the same tangential trajectory regardless of whether it has been released on some point of the circle of rotation and with or without a set target. In the ping-pong ball experiment to be described in this chapter, back spin is put on the ball as it is projected forward, so that it returns to base. Here what delays cognizance is the failure to grasp that by pressing on the back of the ball, one is simultaneously carrying out two heterogeneous actions: projecting the ball forward with a push so it slides, and putting a reverse or back spin on it so that it returns once the forward motion stops. The spin, contrary to

With the collaboration of Androula Henriques-Christophides.

what young children think, is (right from the start) always in
the reverse direction.

At the beginning of the questioning, the child is asked if he
thinks it is possible to make a ping-pong ball go forward and
then come back without anyone touching it again, or without
the ball bouncing against a wall or the like. All the children
(including those who think it is impossible) are asked to have
a try — in fact, there is little difference between the responses
of children who have never seen this done and those who
have, except in the case of an advanced boy of (8,6) who had
tried it with a hoop. If the child does not manage to put
reverse spin on the ball, the interviewer demonstrates,
keeping his hand hidden behind a screen so that the child
does not see him actually press the back of the ball and only
the subsequent movement of the ball is visible. If the child
still cannot do "the same thing," the interviewer shows him
the whole process without the screen and asks him to try
again. The child is allowed several attempts, so that he succeeds at least once or twice (success is possible from age five
on and becomes more or less constant after six to seven).
    Later, the subject is asked for an accurate description of his
action. This can take three forms: a mime of the action
(young subjects generally do this spontaneously: *I did it like
that*; a verbal description; or instructions to the interviewer,
given step by step by the child, on how to carry out the action.
    Next, the interviewer asks the child to describe the ball's
movements, even if he has already referred to them when
talking about his own action. The interviewer uses such questions as, "What did the ball do?", followed by "That's all?",
and so forth, so as to try to avoid suggesting any answers. The
idea is to find out if the child thinks the ball simply went
forward without spinning (or *turning*, as they often say), or
slid, or spun, and if he thinks the trajectory is straight or
curves around a terminal point. It is particularly important to
determine whether the child thinks that the ball spins on
both the outward and the return paths and, if so, in which
direction (that is, in the same direction as the ball is traveling,
which we shall term "direct," as is the case on the ball's return path, or in the opposite direction to the one in which it
is traveling, which we shall term "reverse," as is the case on
the ball's outward path, regardless of whether it touches the
ground). To find this out, the interviewer asks a child who
recognizes a rotation to describe it by means of a demon-

stration with a larger object (say, a sponge held in the hand). If the child has clearly not grasped how the ball travels, then the interviewer carries out the same action on another ping-pong ball, this time one that is half white and half black, thus making it very easy to see the reverse rotation. Subsequently, he reverts to using the all-white ball and repeats the questions.

Finally, the child is asked to explain why the ball comes back, why it goes forward in the first place, and either why it stops (if the child expresses himself in this way) or why it slows down at the end of its forward path, and so forth.

Stage I

The four-to six-year-olds interviewed had never played with a ping-pong ball in this way or even seen anyone else do so. The interviewer therefore had to demonstrate. After several attempts some children were able to copy the action sufficiently well for success to be fairly consistent (our level IB, around six years of age), while for the remainder their occasional successes were still interspersed with failures owing to regulations that were not sufficiently selective (our level IA).

Examples (Level IA)

FRA (5,2) maintains that it is impossible to make the ball come back unless it hits the wall. The interviewer gives a demonstration (hand hidden behind screen). *It came back*. Why? . . . Try it yourself. (He takes the ball, get down on the floor, but does nothing.) I'll show you again (without the screen). Can you do it now? *Yes*. (First, he does the right thing but does not put enough reverse spin on the ball, so that it does not come right back, then he presses and withdraws his hand quickly, and so is completely successful.) That's very good. Try again. (He gazes at the ball under his hand, then withdraws his hand without putting enough pres-

sure on the ball: failure.) Look. (The interviewer
gives several demonstrations.) Have another try.
(Partial success.) Tell me how it's got to be done.
Like that (makes as if to press the top of the ball
down toward the back, away from the direction in
which the ball is to travel). Do you start there on
the top, or lower down? . . . Show me with your
hand. (Lifts his fingers from the ball so that the
palm of his hand stays, quite still, on top of the
ball, more or less parallel to the floor.) And what
does the ball do? . . . Like that (reverse spin outward path)? *No, it goes straight.* And then? *It
comes back.* When it's going straight, does it turn
as well? *No.* Show me with that (small box or the
like). (Indicates direct translation for both outward
and return paths, that is, →, then ←.) And with the
ball? (Direct rotation forward and back.) We'll try
with that ball (black and white). (FRA goes through
the same motions as before.) Did I make it come
back or did it come back all by itself? *All by itself.*
Why did it stop there? . . .

FLO (5,8) throws the ball against the wall to make it
come back. And if the wall weren't there, would it
come back? *Yes.* Someone else told me that it was
because it hits the wall—is that right? *No.* Why
does it come back then? *Because you threw it so
hard.* (She is given a demonstration, hand behind
screen.) Do you know how to do it? (Success: she
presses very hard on the back of the ball.) Where do
you put your hand? *Don't know.* On the ball or
under the ball? (She is shown.) *Under the ball.*
Under? *Yes.* And then? *You throw it.* Like that
(makes as if to throw it up into the air)? *Yes.* Try
again and be careful. (Two failures, then successes
and partial successes.) Did you put your hand on
top of the ball or under the ball? *On top of the ball.*
How? (She puts three fingers on top of the ball.)
And then? *I do this* (withdraws her hand). And then
what happens? *Don't know.* And the ball? *It goes*

and it comes back. Why? *Because I do it like that.*
How does it go? (Simple translation forward and
back.) Suppose there were an ant here, what would
it do? *It would always stay on top.* And this ball
(black and white), how does it go? *It goes around
and around* (rotates about all the vertical, oblique,
or horizontal axes, but the rotation, as was the
translation, is direct for both outward and return
paths). Have a good look at how it turns. (She indicates a direct rotation for the outward path, and
reverse for the return—an answer that is doubly
wrong.) Show me again. (Two direct rotations.)
Listen, I suggest there are two ways it could turn
when it goes forward: like that (reverse). *Wrong.* Or
like that (direct). *Right.* But why does it come back?
Because we throw it hard.

OLI (6,3), like FLO, having thrown the ball against
the wall, maintains that it would also come back
without it. The interviewer gives a demonstration
(hand behind screen). The child's efforts to do the
same thing meet with mixed results: failures, successes, and partial successes—but when asked why
the ball comes back, he just says *we caught it again*
or *it came back by itself.* He is given another demonstration and makes several attempts before succeeding. Why don't you tell me how it's done? *Like
that* (taps on top of the ball without pressing backward) *and it goes.* And afterward? *It comes back.*
What makes it come back? . . . Is there something
that makes it come back? *Yes, it comes back to get
back.* All by itself? *Yes.* You didn't do anything?
No. But how do *you* do it? (Hits it three times, then
presses on the back: success.) What did you do to
make it come back? *It came back all by itself.* Did
you do the same thing when it didn't come back?
No. What did you do more when it did come back?
*I threw it on the floor and it came back all by it-
self.* Show me how you throw it. (He puts his hand
on the top.) There or lower? *There* (top). And how

did the ball go? Show me with that (a larger object). (He indicates a curved trajectory[1] with no rotation of the ball.) Just now, FLO thought it was like that (direct rotation). *That's right.* And when it comes back? (Curve and return by simple translation.) Show me again. (This time direct rotations forward and back with two straight trajectories, thus with no curves but with inversion of the rotation for the return.) CHA thought it was like that (reverse rotation for the outward path). *That's right.* Try again. (Seven consecutive attempts, of which five end in failure and two in partial success.) How did it go? (Simple translations.) Would an ant stay on top? *No.* (Direct rotations forward and back.) Why didn't it continue going forward? *Because we threw it there* (toward the wall). But what makes it stop there? *The wall* (the wall has power to prevent the ball from actually hitting it). Then: *It's that* (the floor).

Examples (Level IB)

ART (6,3) maintains that it is impossible to make the ball come back without the wall. Look. The interviewer demonstrates with the screen. How do I do it? *Don't know.* Try. (Simply pushes it.) Did it come back? *No, because we didn't hit it.* Have another look (without the screen). *You placed the ball and you hit it, and you slid your fingers.* Try. (Correct action: failure, then partial success, followed by several successes.) Try again and tell me what you are doing. *I put my fingers on the ball and I slide them.* How? *You've got to slide them onto the floor, it's got to fall on the table.* Where do you press, there (on top) or there (at the front) or there (at the back)? *Lower.* And afterward, what

1. By "curved trajectories" or "curves" we mean trajectories that start off straight, then become curved, so that the ball makes a round trip and in the child's view never actually stops.

does the ball do? *It rolls.* How? (Translation.) Does
it do anything else while it's going along? *It turns.*
(Again shows a translation, then a direct rotation.)
Is it like this? (The ball is simply thrown forward).
No, it rolls. (Simulates a direct rotation.) What
makes it go forward? *My hand.* And come back?
The wall. Look, is it the wall? *No . . . the wall
which hits* (and which the ball avoids). *I can do it
myself.* (Renewed success.) Is it you who make it
come back or does it come back by itself? *Me, I
made it slide.* And why did it change direction?
Don't know. Look. (The interviewer makes the ball
go forward with a reverse rotation, then with direct
rotation.) Is that the same? *Yes.* Someone else told
me that it went like that (forward with reverse rotation). *No, because it can't.*

BER (6,9), after the demonstration with the screen,
simply throws the ball, then after a second demonstration without the screen, imitates correctly: partial, then complete, success. How did you do it? *I
put my finger like that.* (Shows how to push the
ball downward.) You've got to let it go like that. Do
it again. (Several successes.) *You've got to pull, like
that.* (Presses with his fingers, but does not take his
hand away.) And the ball? (He indicates two translations.) It only did that? *Yes.* One boy told me that
it turned? *Yes.* (Curved trajectory.) Another one
told me it was like that (rotation). Is that right? *Yes.*
(Indicates a direct rotation for both outward and return paths.) Do it again. (Success, then indicates a
translation with a curved trajectory.) Doesn't it
turn? (Interviewer indicates a rotation.) *Yes.* (He indicates a reverse rotation forward and back.) (The
interviewer shows him the two ways the ball can
rotate.) Which is right? . . . Try again. (Success
but again only indicates a curved trajectory.)

The level Ib children, around six years of age, thus can copy
the interviewer's action when his hand is not hidden behind

the screen and can repeat this success without further demonstration. So the six-year-old can press down on the back of the ball and then pull his fingers back, projecting the ball forward and simultaneously making it turn backward (reverse rotation). Of course, these children require an initial period of trial and error, indicating the presence of sensorimotor regulations—which are, however, sufficiently selective for subsequent success to be more or less consistent. The level IA subject can achieve some partial successes (the ball does not come right back) and even some complete successes, but the lack of consistency of their successes indicates the presence of similar but less selective sensorimotor regulations.

By contrast, when it comes to conceptualization of this action, or rather of this double action (projection and reverse rotation), and even when considering only awareness of what happens and not the understanding of why these things happen, it is clear that at stage I conceptualization of the action lags far behind the ability to carry it out. Generally speaking, four levels may be distinguished with regard to the child's verbal description of the action and not his success in copying or simulating it: (a) no reference to pressing, pushing, sliding, or the like; (b) such actions mentioned, but no reference to "pulling back"; (c) mention of the latter, but no allusion to two simultaneous actions of pushing and pulling backward; (d) a distinction between these two conjunct aspects.

The level IA child's description of his actions does not go beyond the first of these four levels; no allusion is made to the act of pressing or pushing, and the nearest any child comes to it is OLI's *I threw it on the floor,* which, it must be admitted, is fairly inadequate. Of course, these children can already mime their actions: *I did it like that* (simulating the action) and so on, but clearly in the case of an already successful action the fact that the children can reproduce it in such a way hardly implies a conscious conceptualization, and as has often been apparent in other studies, such correct autoimitation (imitation of one's own action, which is in fact more difficult than "heteroimitation," the imitation of someone else's action) is frequently accompanied by a contradictory verbal conceptualization. FLO even starts by maintaining that she put her hand under the ball (to throw it) instead of at the back of it, and, like others, FRA thinks she put her hand on top of the ball.

The level IB child's conceptualization has reached the second of the four levels, and ART, for example, says: *You hit it, and you slid your fingers,* then, *I put my fingers on the ball and I slide them . . . onto the floor.* The third level is not reached by any of these stage I subjects, as none of them talks of pulling his hand or the ball backward; only BER uses the word *pull,* but with no idea of pulling back.[2] However, the level IB subjects do know that they put their fingers behind the top of the ball.

These subjects' conceptualization of what happens to the ball, as opposed to what they themselves do to it, is no better and remains analogous to that existing at levels IA and IB. None of them suspect that by pressing on the back of the ball they make it spin backward, and if, on any occasion, reference is made to such a reverse rotation it is not the result of a temporary and exceptional flash of insight but, on the contrary, to a failure to pay attention to the direction of rotation, such that at that particular moment they do not remember that a ball which generally goes forward (except in our experiment) rolls with a direct rotation. In fact, other variations of this common observation were also encountered: some children think that the ball has a zigzag path or turns about a vertical or oblique axis (like a top but moving forward), or (and this is the most common variation) that the ball's trajectory is curved.

Finally, there is no causal explanation of the ball's return: it comes back *all by itself* (FRA and OLI), *because you threw it so hard* (FLO), or because it must not hit the wall (ART has this idea at one point and then discards it, and OLI ends up with it).[3]

2. Here the author explains that for French children of this age, the word "pull" (*tirer*) is often synonymous with "throw" (*lancer*) as in the French expression *tirer un coup de pistolet* = "fire a pistol shot."

3. Interestingly, in earlier experiments on children's understanding of the effects of the impact of a ball against the cushion of a billiard table, subjects at this stage often think that the ball's trajectory is curved when it approaches the cushion, so that the latter does not make it stop dead.

Level IIA

The novelty at this level is that, having given numerous incorrect descriptions of his action and the ball's movements, the subject finally talks about withdrawing his hand, which is sometimes thought to be instrumental in the ball's return; but without the child's understanding, in the case of the white ball, that when he pulls it backward he makes it spin backward while going forward.

Examples

GER (6,9) (intermediate case), during the demonstration with the screen: *I know how you do it: you push it a bit and then it comes back. Do it.* (Correct action but with insufficient pressure toward the back, thus partial success, followed then by success.) How do you do it? *I put my fingers here* (on the back). Tell me with words how you do it. *You put the ball at the end of your fingers.* Like that (hand on the ball but parallel to the floor)? *No, like that* (hand sloping). And then? *You throw it.* How? *Like that* (pressing downward); *you let it go and then it comes back.* Why? *Because you made it go forward. You push it and it comes back.* Do I do it, do I make it come back? *No, by itself.* I have nothing to do with it? *No.* Try again. (Three partial successes because of insufficient spin, then two successes.) Is it you who make it come back? *Yes.* How? *You do that* (simple forward and back translations). Does it do anything else? (He tries again, with success, again indicates simple translations.) Doesn't it go like that (rotations)? *Yes.* (He shows direct rotations forward and back.) Look again. (New success and same description.) Why does it come back? Do we do something to make it change direction or does it do it by itself? *It's us.* Look. (The interviewer shows him with the black-and-white ball). How does it go? (Again direct rotations.) But when it goes off, does it turn like that (direct rotation) or like that (reverse)? *Like that* (reverse rotation). And that one (white ball)? *Like that* (direct rotation). Show me with that (large object)? (Reverse rotation.) Why does it come back? *Because you make it go behind, you push it and it comes back.*

ANO (7,2) has consistent success, after only a few tries at imitating what she was shown, but cannot explain how she did it. The interviewer asks her to tell him what do do. *Like that* (tips of the fingers on the back of the ball). *You've got to take these two fingers and put them on the ball.* And then? *You've got to push.* Like that (forward)? *Yes.* (The interviewer tries this.) It doesn't move. *You've got to press.* (The interviewer presses on the top.) It doesn't move. (The child does it again and succeeds.) *You've got to put your two fingers on the ball.* And then? *Make it go forward.* Show me. (Correct action.) And now describe it. *You put two fingers on top and you push on the ball.* Like that? (forward). *No, you push back and then you press.* Show me again. (Success.) It's right, but why does it come back? Do you know what makes it come back? *Because you push it backward.* Well, why does it go forward first? *Because you push it forward, and afterward it comes back.* So what makes it go forward and what makes it come back? Do it again and explain it to me. (Success.) *It went forward and then afterward it came back.* The session continues without getting any further, and the child is seen again two months later. She starts right off with a partial success (the ball does not come back) followed by success. Why did it come back? *I don't know.* Show me with that (sponge) what it does. (Direct rotation, then circular path without change of rotation.) How did you do it? *I took two fingers and pressed on top.* (The interviewer presses on top of the ball.) *I pull my fingers back and it goes off and comes back.* With the

sponge she then shows direct rotation in both directions. The two-colored ball makes no difference: *It
rolled, jumped, and rolled back.*

REN (7,2), after failing, succeeds (without having to
be shown how). *You've got to make your hand
slope* (instead of parallel to the floor); *you've got to
push it, press on it, and then it goes.* (The interviewer puts his hand as suggested so that it touches
both the top of the ball and the table.) It doesn't go;
what do we have to do? *I don't know, press a little
bit.* You do it. (Three successes.) *You pull and you
press.* How did you do it? *You roll it backward and
then it comes back.* How do you roll it? *You've got
to take the ball, push it back, and then off it goes.*
But how do you push it? *You push your hand.* Like
that (forward)? *No, you push your hand, you pull it
back, and the ball goes forward.* What makes it
come back? *I don't know.* Two months later:
immediate success. *It rolled and it came back.*
Show me with that (sponge). *It rolled like that*
(direct rotation forward). *It stopped and it came
back like that* (again direct rotation). What makes
it come back? *I don't know.*

RIE (7,7): *You put two fingers on the ball and you
push. You press on top as you . . . You put your
fingers a little bit behind and that makes it go,
then it comes back all by itself.* What makes it
come back? *I don't know.* Try again and have a
good look. (New successes.) *It came back like that.*
Why? *That I don't know. It's because you press
like that, then it goes* (forward). Tell me exactly
what I must do. *You put your fingers on the ball at
the back and you push.* Like that (forward)? *No,
you push on top.* What does that do? *It goes and
then it comes back all by itself.* Why? *Because you
put your fingers on the top and then you press.* Do
you just put your fingers there and press? *No, you
bring your fingers back a bit to make it go.* What

makes it go forward? *It's because you do it like that and then you push it.* Tell me again? *You put your fingers on the ball, you move your fingers back a bit, then you press, and then it goes.* And why does it stop? *I don't know.* Why does it come back? *Don't know.*

CRI (7,4) was questioned for a long time about a similar task with a hoop, without being able to do it herself (because of the difficulty in keeping it upright); however, she remarked that to make it come back *the man rolled it a bit forward and a bit backward.* She concluded that in the case of the ball *you put your hand on top and you push backward: the ball goes forward and then comes back.* Why? *Because you nearly throw it and you press on top of it. It's a bit like the hoop.* Good. And why does it change direction? *Because it turns: like that* (direct rotation forward), *then like that* (again direct rotation).

RAP (7,1): *You move it* (your finger) *down a bit. You've got to go a little bit back and do it like this* (oblique position of his hand). For the ball and the large objects he first indicates a simple translation, then a direct rotation. And why does it change direction? *Because* (when it gets to the end) *it goes backward.* What is it that makes it . . . *You do.* What do I do to make it come back? Two-colored ball: RAP indicates a direct rotation, *first the purple bit and then the white bit.* Why does it go forward? *Because you push it.* Why does it come back? *All by itself.* Why does it change direction? *Because it comes back* (curved trajectory without change of rotation). Show me again. (RAP tries again and succeeds.) Does it turn like that (direct rotation) or like that (reverse rotation) when it's going forward? *Like that* (reverse). And what about this (large solid object)? (She indicates a direct rotation.) And when it comes back, does it change direction? *Yes, because it comes back.* The interviewer takes the white ball again and demonstrates the two possible ways for it to go forward: RAP again selects the direct rotation.

JOE (7,2): *You've got to push it back like that* (downward), but in fact he makes it go forward with a direct rotation.

GEN (6,9). *When you make it go like that* (by pressing on the back instead of simply pushing it forward), *that makes it go farther and that makes it come back.* And what makes it stop and come back? *It stops to get enough push to come back.*

AMB (8,3): *I hit the ball here* (indicating a point right at the back), *and off it goes, and it comes back* (three consecutive successes). Why does it come back? *Don't know.* What does the ball do? *It rolls and it turns quickly* (direct rotations). Does it turn like that (reverse rotation forward)? *No, because it would go backward* (!).

JEN (9,4): *You put your hand on the ball and press like that* (moving it back), *you press on it, pulling it back.* Why does it come back? . . . And before that? *It rolls like that* (direct rotation) *and it slows down.* Why? *To come back.* How does it turn on the way back? *The other way* (direct rotation).

ARE (9,5) has the same reactions. He indicates only direct rotations, even with the two-color ball and the sponge.

NAN (9,5) starts off by pinching the ball between her thumb and forefinger with the idea that *that will make it turn.* How? (Shows it rotating about a vertical axis like a top.) Do you think that will make it come back? *I'm not really sure! Look.* (Several successes right away.) *It also turns when you do it like that.* How does it turn? *Like that* (again like a top). Show me with that (sponge). (She presses on the top and sees that it turns around.) *I press on the top and it goes backward.* And the ball, how does it start off? (She indicates a reverse rotation.) And afterward? (New attempt.) *It turns very fast. then it slides* (direct rotation for both outward and return paths. And what happens when it stops? *It turns on the spot* (like a top, then direct rotation reversing itself on the spot at the end of the outward path). But what makes it come back? *It's always got enough push . . . it stops.* Try with that one (black-and-white ball). *It starts like that* (reverse rotation). *But how can it go forward?* How? *It's because it slides on top* (just above the ground while turning), *but I don't know what makes it come back . . . When it's got push, you could almost say that it flies, and that gives it a bit of spring* (hence the bounce back in the opposite direction!).

GIS (9,11): *I press on the ball and pull my hand backward.* Why does it go forward? *You give it a bit of bounce with your hand . . . It jumps a bit.* And afterward? *It's as if someone pushed it back and then it comes back.* What makes it come back? *The bounce. I'm also wondering about the floor . . . There's something in the floor, and it comes back.* GIS indicates a translation and a direct rotation for the outward path, then *it jumped. When you hit it, afterward, it bounces back* (cf. NAN).

Level IIA sees the beginning of concrete operations, with a grasp of the concept of reversibility in general, of the transitivity relationship, and, in the realm of causality, of the mediate and semi-internal transmission of movement. It might therefore be expected that, since the subjects have at long last come to realize that when they press down on the back of the ball they carry out a withdrawal movement (with their fingers), they would immediately conclude that this made the ball spin backward even as it was projected forward, and that the reverse rotation caused by their action would explain why the ball comes back. In fact, this is not at all the case and they continue systematically to distort observable features of the object. Why is this so?

With regard to their observation of the action, all the subjects are clearly aware of how they press down on the back of the ball and pull their fingers away. The intermediate subject GER (at 6,9) is not absolutely clear about it, but when he says at the end, *you make it go behind, you push it and it comes back*, the expression *make it go behind*, while remaining halfway between denoting pressure on the back and withdrawal of his hand, does indicate an action considered to be the cause of the ball's return—although the child has not grasped the concept of reverse rotation in the case of the white ball. For ANO, on the other hand, the withdrawal movement of her fingers is clearly conscious, or rather it becomes so after numerous attempts (as always, our account of these has had to be abridged): *you push back*, and above all, *I pull my fingers back*, but again, she indicates a direct rotation. What REN means by *you pull* is made clear by his words *you roll it backward* and *you pull it back*, which makes his assertion that the rotation is direct appear even more paradoxical. RIE has the same argument: *you bring your fingers back a bit.* CRI is more subtle: *the man rolled it a bit forward and a bit backward*, then *you push backward* and *the ball goes forward*, hence a direct rotation, and JEN even gets the formula completely right: *you press on it, pulling it back*, while insisting that the rotation was direct. Briefly, while all these subjects naturally realize that the ball was projected forward, they also note that they withdrew the pressure of their fingers from the ball (withdrawal movement), probably because of the more active nature of the action and particularly when the interviewer's detailed questions about what happens lead them to pay careful attention to this aspect.

This being the case, why do these same subjects find it so difficult to observe and comprehend what happens to the ball? They all continue to "see" a direct rotation when the white ball goes forward. Some, like ANO, even say that the black-and-white ball rotates in this way despite the very obvious reverse rotation; others, like RAP, eventually come to recognize a reverse rotation in the case of the two-color ball, but continue to think the all-white one goes forward with a direct rotation. Why is there this surprising gap between the incorrect observation of the rotation of the ball (that is, the object) and the clear progress of the observation of the action, a gap that is even more remarkable when one recalls that a direct rotation clearly contradicts the child's own description of how he pressed and *pulled* his fingers and the ball *backward?* In fact, although this causal relationship between the action of withdrawal and the reverse rotation seems clear to us, in the child's eyes there is another even more obvious causal relationship — namely, that if a ball goes forward, it must turn in the direction in which it is traveling; hence there must be direct rotation. This is what AMB clearly says: if there were a reverse rotation, the ball would not go forward, *it would go backward* — a curious objection because it is precisely what the ball does do on the return, but it appears conclusive to AMB since on the outward path it goes forward! Similarly, when NAN sees the black-and-white ball going forward with a reverse rotation, she exclaims: *But how can it go forward?* However, she then correctly answers her own question: *It's because it slides on top (just above the ground),* but then, strangely enough, she no longer understands how the ball comes back, as if the reverse rotation were not conserved and, because of this, became a direct rotation on the way back! Her hypothesis of a bounce is an attempt to reconcile the two ideas.

To sum up, at this level children systematically distort their observations of the object (the ball) by "seeing" a direct rotation for the white ball (and sometimes even for the black-and-white ball, where one would have expected the direction of rotation to be obvious); once again their reading of what they see is a function of their understanding of the situation and not of pure perception in those cases where what they see contradicts that they think they ought to see. To resolve this contradiction, the child must first observe the object more accurately: when the ball goes forward it does not really roll, it slides a fair distance (as NAN momentarily realizes). Secondly, the child must recognize the significance of this improved observation and coordinate it with the reverse rotation. This involves a complete causal model with a return to the mechanism of the action itself, pushing and pulling at the same time, thus making the ball slide along forward while turning backward. Even when some of the subjects (GER at the end of her session, RIE, and others) think that the ball comes back because of the pressure they apply at the outset (like most of the children, though, they maintain that the ball comes back *all by itself* or say that they do not know why it comes back), they do not reflect on it sufficiently deeply to be able to grasp its twofold nature (in other words, its two component parts) and really to understand what happens. The apparent causal relationship does not at this level go beyond a direct apprehension of the fact that a physical law is involved: hence the supplementary hypotheses on the bouncing, the part played by the floor, the walls, the air, and so forth.

Level IIB

Subjects at this level manage, but only after many contradictory statements and hesitations, to understand that pressing on the back of the ball makes it go off with a reverse rotation.

Examples

PHI (8,2), after his first success: *I pressed on the ball and it slid, then it came back.* How did you do that? *I pressed with my hand, not quite in the middle, a bit toward the edge . . . and at the end the ball jumps all by itself* (when I let go of it) *and off it goes.* Why does it come back? *Because it slid.* How? *It turns on itself* (in the air), *then it goes forward because it's turning on the ground.* Despite this, he indicates a direct rotation. So it's turning like that that makes it come back? *Yes, because you press and a bit later it comes back.* Can you show me how it slides? (This time he demonstrates a reverse rotation.) Does it turn like that? *It doesn't stay flat* (on the table), *it jumps a bit.* Does it slide or turn? *It does both.* At the same time? *It turns first.* How? (Again a direct rotation.) And then? *It starts off sliding. It turns and then it slides.* And what makes it come back? *It's because it turns, that makes it come back.* And why does it stop? *Because it slides and then suddenly it's no longer sliding* (on the floor) *so it comes back.* Explain it to me once again. *You pull your hand a bit back, it slides, it turns, but not really like when you kick a ball.* What happens when you kick? *It goes like that* (direct rotation). And when you press on a ping-pong ball? *No, it jumps a little bit and then you pressed, so you first made it turn the other way* (reverse rotation). Show me. (He actually demonstrates a reverse rotation.) But this precocious understanding is so unstable that at the end of the session PHI reverts to indicating direct rotation for both outward and return paths. It is as if the reverse rotation at the start simply produced, after a suitable lapse of time and at the end of the outward path, the change in direction that caused the ball to come back.

ACO (8,6) continues to think for some time that the ball starts off with a direct rotation, saying simply: *I put my finger on top of it* (back), *I pulled, and then it turned and came back.* Do it again. (Three new successes.) *I put my finger on the ball, I pulled like that* (back toward himself), *and the ball turned.* How? *Like that* (direct rotation). Show me with the sponge. (He indicates a brief reverse rotation followed by a simple translation.) And how does the ball go, like that (translation) or does it turn? *It went off straight.* Didn't it start off turning? *Yes, it turned but not at the same time.* What does it do first? *It turns.* And then? *It goes forward, it turns, and it comes back.* It goes all by

itself? *No, my finger does it* (correct action). And
what makes it come back? *It turns.* It's because it
turns that it comes back? *Yes.*

JEA (9,6), who prior to the session had already been
shown by someone else that it is possible to make a
ball come back, starts with reactions that appear
close to those of stage III but turn out to be not
quite so advanced: *You put your hand on top and
you push back, you press on top.* Are you still
pushing when you press? *Both at the same time.*
And if I push and then press afterward? *That's O.K.*
And then? *When you push backward, it goes backward. When you press as well—no, when you press
on top—it goes forward.* How? (Indicates a translation without rotation.) *It goes when you push. It
goes forward and it's still got the push behind it, so
it comes back.* Show me with this sponge. *You
push backward and you press on top.* (Indicates a
simple translation.) That's all there is to it? *No, it
turns in the air* (reverse rotation). And the ball? *It
does this* (same rotation). What makes it go forward? *It's when you push it.* What makes it come
back when it's going forward? *It's also when* (that
is, because) *you've pushed it.* Why does it stop?
Because there's no more push behind it. What
push? *The one that makes it slide forward.* And
to come back? *There's still the push to make it go
forward, so it comes back.* Where does this push
come from, to make it come back? *It's also when
you pushed it.* Black-and-white ball: *Same as the
other one. It turned backward.* And when it
stopped? *It was still turning a bit, and with the
push that made it go forward it came back.* How
was it turning on the way back? *Backward, a bit in
all directions, because it's not that* (black part)
that's going to tell me how it was turning. But
why does it come back? *Because it wasn't turning forward but backward, so it comes back.*

It didn't turn forward? *Yes, backward, but in all directions.*

GAB (10,5): *You push a bit on the side* (back), *lower on the round bit, and you push forward.* After three perfect successes: *It went off with little jumps and only afterward did it really roll, then it came back.* How did it roll? (Direct rotation.) What makes it come back? *Don't know. It must be us: you do something to make it go off and at the same time to make it come back.* What? *When you press, at the same time that makes it go and come back.* Try again. *The last little jumps are right near the floor; it almost rolls when it goes forward, and when it comes back it rolls properly.* Show me with the sponge how the ball turns. (Hesitations: reverse rotation, then direct, then finally reverse rotation from the start.)

So, more accurate observation of what the ball does has nearly led these subjects to complete understanding; the fact that some inaccuracies remain results from insufficient coordination of observations of the object with those of the action. This is why, although PHI begins well by saying that on its outward path the ball first *slides* or *jumps* before starting to roll on the ground, then because it spins he feels obliged to say that there is a direct rotation; later he briefly recognizes the reverse rotation (outward path) but then reverts to the direct. When asked to explain the return, he gives a valid explanation: when it slides the ball turns as well, but in reverse rotation—and this is why when it finally touches down it comes back. However, since he is not able to relate this discovery sufficiently to the two aspects of his own initial action (propelling and reverse rotation), he ends by dismissing his correct explanation and again introducing a phase of direct rotation between the reverse rotation caused by the withdrawal of his fingers and the start of the ball's return journey.

In the case of ACO, this lack of coordination between observations of the object and the action is even clearer: he is well aware that by pulling the ball toward him while propelling it forward, he makes it spin backward (which he demonstrates with the sponge). However, since he pictures two successive actions, and not two simultaneous aspects of this double action (*yes, it turned but not at the same time* as *it went off straight*) he dissociates the rotation from the forward translation and so continues to think that the ball goes forward in direct rotation, while declaring that it comes back because it turned (he clearly imagines that the effect of the ball's spin is delayed rather than continuous).

By contrast, JEA's almost complete initial coordination between his observation of the object and of the action, would have brought him just up to stage III: *you press on top,* which sends the ball forward, and *you push back,* which causes the reverse rotation, and you do *both at the same time.* His *that's OK* in answer to the interviewer's suggestion that he could push and then press afterward reveals, however, that he is not quite there. Furthermore, although he recognizes that the ball continues to *turn in the air* in a reverse rotation, he refuses to attribute this reverse rotation and the forward projection to two separate forces (or *pushes*), as is the case at stage III, and he ends up with this contradictory interpretation: *there's still the push behind it to make it go forward, so it comes back and with the push that made it go forward it came back.* Having thus mixed up, through trying to simplify, a situation that was clear at the beginning of the session, JEA ends up by doubting the reverse rotation itself—even, paradoxically, in the case of the two-colored ball. He tries to get around the problem by attributing to this ball a polyvalent rotation: *yes, backward, but in all directions* (thus like a top as well as a ball).

Like the level IIA subjects, GAB starts off by saying that the ball goes forward in direct rotation. Then, when it comes to explaining why it comes back, he comes near to the correct interpretation: having noticed from the outset that the ball *went off with little jumps* and only afterward *really rolled,* he then simultaneously appreciates the reverse rotation on the outward path and the two effects of the action of pressing, but his final hesitations show how unstable this appreciation is.

Stage III

The stage III subject understands from the outset that by pressing on the back of the ball and pulling his fingers away from it he is in fact simultaneously carrying out two hetero-geneous actions: he is propelling the ball forward and making it spin backward and so return. The average age of this level is eleven to twelve years, but, (as is usually the case in our experiments) there are one or two more precocious cases, including that of the 8½-year-old, who admittedly was already aware of the phenomenon, having previously tried by himself to make a hoop come back.

Examples

DIL (8,6) succeeds right away. *I didn't press this way but the other, and when it came back down to the ground that made it come back. I've already done it with a hoop, but it doesn't always work.* What do you mean by 'the other way'? *I press backward; it's sent off in the other direction.* Why does it come back? *Because the force that it's given like that* (toward the back), *that makes the ball come back. You give it some force to make it go off, then by pressing on it you make it come back. You give it two forces: one to go off, the other to make it come back.* What is a force? *It's a hit you give it to make it go forward for a longer time.* How do you do it? *First by pressing like that, that makes it go off, and at the same time, when you do it, you make it turn like that* (reverse rotation): *you make the ball turn the other way from the way you send it off. When it hasn't got any more force for going* (forward), *it comes back.*

CEL (10,4): *I squeeze it to make it go forward, but by making it turn backward . . . You don't push very hard, but so that it slides and then it comes back.* When it goes off, what does it do? *It turns backward, then it stops and comes back.* Why does it stop? *Because it doesn't have enough force to go forward any more. It runs out.* All at once? *No, little by little.* Why? *Because the force to go backward gets stronger and stronger.* Does it increase? *No, it doesn't run out.* And where does it come from? *From our hand when we make it turn backward.*

JAC (10,6): *It's sent forward while it turns backward. It goes like that* (reverse rotation) *until it's got no more force and then it comes back like that* (continuation of reverse rotation). What makes it come back? *Because it turns in the opposite way* (from the outset). *After a while it hasn't got any more force, so it stops while still turning on itself, and it comes back.* Does it always turn the same way? *Yes, on itself.* And does it come back by itself? *No, with the new force.* Where does this force come from? *From the fact that it turns in the direction where it's got to go back to.* And what makes it turn in this way? *Pushing with your hands. First it was sent forward while it turned like that* (reverse) *so that it comes back. After a bit it hasn't any more force* (to propel it), *it turns on itself, always the opposite way from where it was sent, and so it comes back.*

MEL (11,0) thinks it is impossible to get the ball to come back, but as soon as he has seen the interviewer do it, he is himself immediately successful. *I'm trying to make it turn like that* (reverse rotation). What makes it come back? *When you press, that makes it turn* (the opposite way) *and it goes off.* Does it go forward because it turns? *No, because it slides as it turns.* And why does it stop? *Because it hasn't got any more force to go forward and because instead of turning like that* (direct rotation) *it turns like that* (reverse), *so it comes back.* Where does the force run out? *On the way: it's used twice as much force because it turns like that* (reverse rotation). *If it turns like that* (direct), *it's only got to go around once to go forward once; when it turns like that* (reverse), *it's got to go around twice to go forward once.*

ALI (11,0): *you press* (explanation) *and that makes it go off turning on itself like that* (reverse rotation) *and not like that* (direct). *When it's gone, it's got force because you've sent it off, and when it hasn't got any more force left it comes back toward us.* Why does it come back? *It's got some backward force because it's turning on itself. There* (on the outward path) *it's got more force, and when this runs out there's a second force because it's turning on itself and that's why it comes back.* Because there's a second force? *While it goes, it's got two forces, but there's one that runs out.*

MAN (11,7): *You press on it to make it turn backward, it goes off and it comes back.* Why? *When it stops going straight, it comes back because it's turning backward.*

RIC (12,2): *I'm trying to make it jump by making it turn the other way.* Why does it stop? *It brakes in the first bit because it's turning the other way.*

So the stage III child understands why the ball comes back, because—thanks to an inferential coordination—he is able to relate what he sees the ball do to what he observes regarding his own action, with both sets of observations at last—again thanks to the inferential coordination—completely objective. The child accepts the reverse rotation on the outward path, which explains why the ball comes back without there being a need for the rotation to change direction in order to become direct on the return path. Furthermore, he immediately admits that when it goes forward the ball does not really roll, but slides while spinning backward. With regard to the action, he realizes that he simultaneously projects the ball forward and makes it spin backward toward himself.

How does the inferential coordination referred to above enable the child to understand what happens? It involves comprehending two distinct transmissions or conveyors of movement; since one of these is by nature unobservable, the two together are *a fortiori* also unobservable. As DIL says: *You give it two forces; one to go off* (projection), *the other to make it come back* (reverse rotation from the outset). Despite DIL's attempt to define his *force* in terms of what can be observed (*It's a hit you give it to make it go forward for a longer time*), it is clear that between this *hit* and the duration attributed to its effect, there is transmission of something, with the dynamic element that is transmitted no longer perceptible. When asked for a definition of these two forces, most of the subjects simply describe it without seeking the reason for it: force I (projection) *runs out*, while force II (reverse rotation), which exists from the outset and which ALI qualifies as opposite to the first force, then asserts itself independently (JAC and ALI). CEL says a little more: having said that force II, that is, *the force to go backward*, becomes *stronger and stronger*, he corrects himself by specifying that this force is simply conserved (*no, it just stays, it doesn't run out*) and so gets stronger only relative to force I, which *runs out*. MEL and RIC do better still by trying to explain why, if force II is conserved, force I *runs out:* it is, RIC tells us, because the reverse rotation (thus force II) *brakes* it. MEL specifies that the braking of force I is caused by the fact that on the outward path, the ball *used twice as much force:* when *it turns like that* (direct rotation), *it's only got to go around once to go forward once*, while in reverse rotation (outward path) *it's got to go around twice to go forward once* — that is, the distance of a reverse rotation plus the distance that it would go if the rotation were direct.

Undeniably, therefore, the child's progress in operatory development has resulted in an impressive set of inferential coordinations. It is such coordinations that stabilize his reading of the observable features by making them intelligible and by enabling him to relate completely those of the object with those of the action itself, since he now sees a reason behind what would otherwise remain simple connections involving a physical law.

Conclusions

The alternating action (dialectic) of the two categories of observations (object and action) on each other and the need for inferential coordination

The five levels just described clearly provide a typical example of development through equilibration. Level IA subjects often succeed in making the ball come back, whereas it is not until stage III that there is a complete and stable conceptualization of this action: as will be shown below, the successive discoveries marking the five levels appear to be governed more by an endogenous process of relating the various observations than by empirical encounters with new facts.

(a) The first task is to check the consistency of these levels. The following table (in percentages of each age performing at a given level) shows the results of the experiment carried out with about fifty subjects (nearly all of whom were questioned on two separate occasions).

| Level | Age | | | |
	5–6	7–8	9–10	11–12
1A	50	0	0	0
1B	37	0	0	0
IIA	12	78	45	0
IIB	0	14	40	25
III	0	7	15	75

Although (except for levels IA and IB) a wide age range is represented at each level, the *maxima* of the percentages for each do follow a chronological order if we take IA and IB together: 87 (50 and 37) percent of the five- to six-year-olds at stage I, 78 percent of the seven- to eight-year-olds at level IIA, 40 percent of the nine- to ten-year-olds (as against 14 percent at seven to eight years and 25 percent at eleven to eight years and 25 percent at eleven to twelve years) at level IIB (being an intermediate level, this one is the least consistent), and 75 percent of the eleven-to twelve-year-olds at stage III.

(b) Most of the research on cognizance has seen continuous interplay of the two categories of observations (object and action), with this reciprocity increasing from one level to the next, and with the subject initially obtaining the greater part of his information on the nature of his action from the results of this action on the objects. On the other hand, in the ping-pong ball experiment it seems that, except at the first and final levels, the subjects do not relate one category of observation to the other so rapidly: at level IIA the subject's new (or rather, more accurate) observation of his action does not immediately lead him to improved observation of the object, and the reverse happens at level IIB.

As usual, level IA offers numerous examples of a lack of differentiation between the subject and object, thus of partly distorted interactions between the two categories of observations: OLI thinks that the ball returns all by itself to *get back* to within reach of his hand, while FLO thinks she makes it come back simply by throwing it a little *harder* (at the beginning of the session, she is even unaware that she puts her hand on and not *under the ball*), and so on. Clearly, therefore, it is the child's observation of what happens to the ball when it comes back, or does not come back, that will tell him what he needs to know about his action, since the sensorimotor regulations involved in the latter are not in themselves sufficient to ensure its cognizance. This becomes clearer from level IB on, and even more so from level IIA, where the more active adjustments, that is, those involving true choices and not just automatic corrections, lead the child to realize first that he presses on the back of the ball (level IB: ART and BER), and then, most importantly, that he pulls his hand away (level IIA).

Why is there such a wide age range at this substage (or level) IIA (one or two six-year-olds, 78 percent of seven- to eight-year-olds, and even 45 percent of the nine- to ten-year-olds)? Firstly, how does the subject discover that he pulls his hand away? Secondly (as has already been stressed), when he has discovered this, why does it take such a long time before he correctly observes the result of this action on the object—in other words, the reverse rotation on the outward path?

Certainly the child discovers the action of his fingers on the ball; instead of the earlier sensorimotor adjustment, there is now active adjustment according to whether the ball comes all the way back or only a little way back: thus observation of the object throws more light on the analysis of the actual action. It then is even more surprising that as soon as the child has correctly observed his initial action of making the ball spin, he does not immediately become aware that it spins backward. The reason for this is doubtless that from the time the active adjustments intervene in the interactions between the two categories of observations (object and action), these adjustments lead to coordinations with an inferential coordination that bears on the objects, constituting a causal relationship: it is therefore in trying to explain to himself why he makes the ball spin that the subject comes to discover what he actually does. It is only because the link between the two categories of observation has thus become causal that he also feels the need to understand how the ball moves forward once it has left the hand that made it spin. This is why a contradiction becomes inevitable as long as there is no differentiation between the two effects of the action itself (projection and rotation): the child continues to think that if the ball goes forward, it is because it is spinning in direct rotation, even if the action of pulling away his hand might suggest a reverse rotation. As a result, although the more accurate observation of the action is a result of the child's improved observation of the object, it does not lead reciprocally, between seven and nine to ten years, to his discovery of the reverse rotation on the outward path.

So it is not until level IIB that this reciprocity of the two categories of observations (pulling the hand away and reverse rotation on the outward path) is finally grasped, and the subjects quoted at this level show us clearly how the action of pulling away their hands finally leads them to an understanding of the ball's reverse rotation. This occurs only after some time and numerous hesitations on the part of the subjects, since, for the situation to become causally clear in their eyes, there must be reciprocal influence of this observation of the object on that of the actual action, that is to say, they must recognize the latter's twofold nature: it causes both the forward projection of the ball (sliding, without spinning, straight along the floor) and the reverse rotation while *making little jumps.*

This complete coordination between the two categories of observation (object and action) is in fact not encountered until stage III, and so, judging by our results, it is grasped by about 75 percent of eleven-or twelve-year-olds. The interactions between these categories of observations take place over several years and in three main stages: at level IIA through a predominant influence of the subject's observations of the object modifying those of his actions; at level IIB through the reciprocal influence of the latter on the former; and at stage III through a final synthesis, which logically could have occurred as soon as the subjects became able to relate adequately the information obtained from what was observed (or glimpsed) at the beginning of level IIA.

The Hoop

This experiment, really a simple variation of the ping-pong ball experiment, is interesting because, while making a hoop go forward and come back requires more muscular strength and, above all, more skill (to keep the hoop upright) than snapping the ping-pong ball, it is simpler to understand what happens. It is easier to see the reverse rotation, firstly, because the hoop is far larger than the ball and, secondly, because it resembles a wheel, which rotates in only two directions, unlike the ball, which can spin like a top.

(a) The subjects at the first level (including, however, some seven-year-olds) do not manage to make the hoop come back nor, when this is demonstrated, do they notice the reverse rotation[4]; but they generally note that the hoop goes up in the air as it goes forward (sort of a swinging movement):

4. Direct rotation is considered as rotation in the direction in which the hoop is traveling and reverse rotation, rotation in the opposite direction from the one in which it is traveling. In fact, in order for the hoop to come back there must be reverse rotation on the outward path and direct rotation on the return; until level IIB, subjects generally think that there is direct rotation on both the outward and the return paths.

CRI (7,7) just throws the hoop forward. Have a good look. *It's coming back! Oh! Because I had to throw it high and afterward it comes back.* What makes it come back? *Nothing. Nothing makes it come back.* (Fresh attempt.) *Because you shot (= threw) it hard and because it was standing up, so it comes back.* But why does it change direction? *Because it hasn't any more force to go forward, afterward it comes back.*

At level IIA, the reactions more closely resemble those encountered in the ball experiment: the subjects successfully imitate the action required to start the hoop off in reverse rotation, but this success does not extend to conceptualization, and they continue to think that the rotations on both the outward and return paths are direct.

Examples (Level IIA)

ANA (7,6), after several failures, swings the hoop up in the air, then—imitating what he has just seen—throws it so that it makes a half-turn. The interviewer shows him again and asks him to specify the hoop's movements: *It went over there and it turned there.* How did it turn? (He indicates direct rotations in both directions.) *First like that and then like that.*

STE (7,10): Did you watch carefully what I did? *Yes, very carefully.* What makes it come back? *Hey! I can't tell you that.* Did it turn at all when I threw it? *Yes, like that* (direct rotations in both directions). *What's always so funny is that it turns around* (at the end of the outward path) *and I'll never in all my life get that.* Have another look. *I see. I can explain just the turn around to you now: at the turn-around, there was the hoop which had turned properly for a bit* (indicates reverse rotation at the end of the outward path) *and then it came back.* Turned properly? *Yes, it turned properly* (indicates direct rotation). Show me with that (a sponge). (He indicates direct rotation in both directions with inversion at the end of the outward path.) Why does it change direction there? *Because it comes back: if it didn't do that, it would go straight on. It's really the turn-around that I find very funny.* Is there a trick? *I don't think so. It's like a spring: first you pull it and then bing!* (indicates return). *It's the same principle.*

MAR (7,4): And what do you have to do to make it come back? *You have to throw it.* Is that all? (The interviewer does it again.) *You put your hand back a bit.* Would you like to try? (Partial success.) She then describes the movement of the hoop as like a large arc of a circle with direct rotation both forward and back.

EM (8,2), after a demonstration, makes the hoop start off by doing a half-turn backward. He is shown again: What must you look at to be sure how you've got to do it? *You've got to look at the hoop because that's what's doing it!* Well then? *It goes forward some and comes back.* When it goes forward, does it turn? *It's got to turn* (indicates a direct rotation).

JEA (8,9) has the same partial success. Show me with the hoop. (Direct rotation both forward and back.) *Like that.*

These reactions in many ways are directly comparable to those encountered in the ping-pong ball experiment. Of course, the action is more difficult to carry out, and few subjects at this level manage to get the hoop to come right back to them. However, correct observation of the object seems easier the bigger it is, and it is on the object that the child centers his attention: *You've got to look at the hoop because that's what's doing it,* says EM, thus disregarding (like the subjects at the same level in the ping-pong ball experiment) the causal role of the action of *putting your hand back*

(MAR). However, this focusing on the object has two negative consequences: it leads the children to think that the
hoop comes back to its starting point all by itself (*like a
spring*, says STE) and then they get the idea (EM) that *it's got
to* go forward in direct rotation, an assumption that is contrary to what they can clearly see happening.

(*b*) At level IIB, intermediate reactions are encountered that
are similar to those described for the ping-pong ball at this
level.

Examples (Level IIB)

> DAN (9,0) admits to having already played at trying
> to make a hoop come back. How do you make it go
> off? *By making it turn backward.* And how would
> it come back? Turning the right way. DAN thus
> seems to have understood everything, and he gives
> correct instructions (accompanied by appropriate
> gestures) to the interviewer on how to make the
> hoop come back. Yet when he is asked to say in de-
> tail what the hoop did, he indicates direct rotation
> both forward and back. He shows what he means
> with the sponge: *It went like that* (direct rotation)
> *up to there and there* (stop); *it turned around once
> as it slid* (inversion of the rotation) *and came back
> like that* (direct rotation on the return path). How
> does it slide before it comes back? *Because it's still
> got a bit of the force that makes it go forward, so it
> slides and goes off again* (back). It's the same force?
> *Yes, it got it at the same time, because you give
> two forces at the same time, and when it touches
> the ground it goes off forward; it's the ground that
> gives it the force to go off* (forward) *because when it
> gets there it does that* (inversion of rotation fol-
> lowed by return again in direct rotation). But then
> does it change direction to come back? *Because it
> doesn't have enough force to go on, it comes back.*
> And where does it get the force to come back from?
> *When you make it come back* (by throwing the
> hoop).

CAR (10,1): *There's a way of throwing it that makes it come back.* He starts by simply swinging the hoop backward and forward, then says, *Now I do this* (rotates his wrist). When asked how the hoop comes back, *It gets into that position* (up in the air on the outward path); *that makes it brake, afterward it gets straight and comes back.* How? *It's difficult. It comes like that* (direct rotation on outward path), *then it does this* (rotates on the spot), *and it comes back* (direct rotation).

FRE (10,1): *It went* (direct rotation) *and it turned on itself* (like a top).He does not make the hoop come right back and says: *You pulled your arm farther back than I did,* which he considers to be the cause of the hoop's return.

LAU (10,9) manages by himself to make the hoop start off with a half-turn backward: *It went forward then backward.* Show me how it turned. *Around* (direct rotation for both outward and return paths). *When it comes back, it's the same.* Why doesn't it go on? *Because I pressed on top of it.* What does that do? *You press, then it comes back; I press to make it go back a little; it goes forward* (direct rotation) *and it comes back.* Why? *Because there's a sort of force.* Explain. *It's your pressing on it; it gets a bit shaken, and then it goes like a boomerang.* From then on, he understands that there is reverse rotation on the outward path: it comes back *because* (when it goes forward) *it goes back; that stops it going any farther—I mean it rolls.* It goes forward and rolls back: is that the same movement or two different movements? *No, when a tank goes forward its wheels go forward.* And what happens with a hoop? *It doesn't do it right.*

So all these subjects have grasped that the hoop comes back because it is pressed backward at the beginning, and so the return is caused by the action of the thrower. As in the case of the ball, this is not enough to make a child understand the whole process nor even to make him analyze accurately what he sees happening to the ball, since he sees what he thinks should happen—for example, LAU's *right* rotation of the wheels of a vehicle.

(c) At stage III the subjects accurately observe both the action and the object, and the inferential coordinations are at last correct; these children are generally about eleven or twelve years old, with one advanced nine and some ten-year-olds.

Examples (Stage III)

XAV (9,4): *When you swing it, you do that to the hoop so that it turns the other way and then it comes back.* And then? *And then that's all: because when you throw it the hoop turns like that and it comes back.* Why doesn't it go any farther forward? *The force that makes it turn like that* (reverse rotation) *makes the hoop stop and it comes back.* Is it still moving enough to come back? *It's moving less but just enough when it stops, and afterward it goes on like that* (return).

CLA (10,10): *I throw it as if I wanted to make it come back toward me: I make my hoop turn backward a bit. I made it slide* (forward), *but I make it turn backward at the same time.* Why doesn't it continue going forward? *Because it slides when it's turning backward, and when it starts to stop it turns backward* (on the floor) *and comes back.* Is it like something you push that stops? *No, because it turns backward and that brakes the force that makes it go forward.*

FRA (11,5): *You have to send if off pushing a bit on the other side and making it turn the other way.* What does that do? *First it slides, and because it turns the other way, when it stops sliding it comes toward us.*

ANT (12,2): *You've got to pull backward with your hand to make it turn backward.* Why does it stop going forward? *Because it grips the ground, that makes it skid. As soon as the power gets too fast, that makes it come back.* What power? *The power it has when it turns.* Where does it get it from? *From your hand.* Is that the power that makes it go forward as well? *No, it's only when it turns backward: you don't throw it very hard (forward)*

The developmental patterns emerging from these two experiments are thus on the whole very similar, despite the fact that, in one case, the action is more difficult (making the hoop come back) and, in the other, it is harder to see exactly what happens to the object (the ping-pong ball). In both situations the slow rate of progress stems from the essential factors involved in understanding the situations, whose importance far outweighs the perceptive or motor conditions of the solution to the problems, even when apparently simple findings are involved.

4 The Slope

All children like sliding things down slopes—or having a slide themselves—and even our four-year-old subjects were proficient at this. However, do they know how to make something slide down a large inclined sheet of cardboard along a predetermined path? In other words, can they correctly orient the cardboard so as to achieve this, or arrange bricks so that a sheet of cardboard placed on them will be tilted the right way? The aim of this research was to determine how and why children's physical skill in this area evolves, and then to study their cognizance of the problem. Thus we hoped to find out how the children progress to the stage of saying, like one of our twelve-year-olds: *It always goes down to the lowest side* (= finds the line of greatest slope), revealing a grasp of the principle of extremum.

More than sixty subjects (there is of course space here for only a few extracts of the protocols) took part in this experiment. At the beginning of the session, the interviewer shows the child a rectangular piece of cardboard (the lid of a large box), as in Figure 2, and asks him to make a counter move,

With the collaboration of Anne-Marie Zutter.

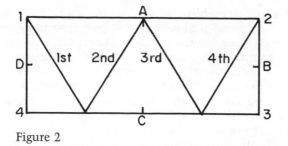

Figure 2

without touching it, on the cardboard along various paths.
(The child discovers for himself that he must make the
counter slide downward.) These paths may be perpendicular
(from point D to point B or, with the cardboard the other way
around, from A to C), diagonal (between corners 1 and 3 or 2
and 4), or just oblique (from A to B or A to 4, from D to C, and
so on). Then the child is asked to describe what he did, say
where the counter started and where it went, and explain why
it went that way (or whether it could have gone another way).

Subsequently, the interviewer takes a chalk and draws a
large W on the cardboard starting from 1, then going to a
point halfway between 4 and C (first stroke), from this point
to A (second stroke), from A to a point halfway between C
and 3 (third stroke), and from there to 2 (fourth stroke). The
child is asked to make the counter go along the W and then to
say what he did (partly to find out whether the child realizes
that for the first and third strokes corner 4 must be higher
than corner 3).

Next (but the order of the following tasks may be varied),
the child is given a large sheet of cardboard (this time completely flat and not like the lid of a box) and asked to place his
hands in the right place to catch a marble that the interviewer
is going to make slide down the inclined sheet. The child
must therefore determine (and everything happens so quickly
that this demands an ability to make correct inferences in addition to an ability to read the data accurately) where the
marble will end up (B to D, A to C, 3 to 1, plus various
oblique trajectories), judging from its starting position.

Another task involves a similarly inclined sheet of cardboard, but this time a screen masks the whole of the center
and only the peripheral area is exposed. The interviewer
makes a counter slide the length of the diagonal 2-4 and the
subject is asked to reconstruct this path, based on where the
counter started and the orientation of the cardboard.

In yet another task, the interviewer gives the child a six-point star and asks him (at the beginning of the session) to make a counter travel along various paths, some of which are straight and some bent, and then questions him on how he went about it, which points he touched and in which direction, and so forth.

In a final task, later abandoned, the questioning is similar to that of the initial session, but instead of a cardboard box the child is given a slate and asked to make a drop of water travel along certain paths.

Although all the subjects are not necessarily given all the above tasks, they are all given an inclined sheet of cardboard resting on bricks and asked to make the counter go along the diagonals 1-3 or 2-4 simply by altering the positions of the bricks; they are not allowed to pick up the cardboard with their hands. The child must therefore put the greatest number of bricks under the starting point (the highest) and the smallest number (or none at all) under the finishing point, not forgetting to support the rest of the cardboard. Finally, the subject is asked to explain his actions.

As these tasks are of varying degrees of difficulty, a comparison of responses to them throws light on the evolution of both the subjects' physical actions and their cognizance of the situation, and reveals the various conceptualizations lying behind the different interpretations — or caused by them, in the case of inferential coordinations.

Level IA

Examples

PHI (4,5) correctly lifts the short left side at D to make the counter slide from D to the short right side at B. How did you do it? *Like that.* (Mimes his action without touching the box.) What did you lift? *The box.* Where? *Here* (correct). And the counter? *It slid there.* Why? *Because I made a slope.* And if you'd lifted there (side 1-2 at A)? *It would have been there* (to C—correct). For an oblique path from A to B, he grasps the box at A and inclines it sideways toward B, revealing a spon-

taneous motor adjustment (of height and side) to
comply with the new instruction. However, when
it comes to the *W*, which implies a more active adjustment involving deliberate choices, for the first
stroke he just raises the box at *1* and makes it lean
toward the long inside edge *3–4*, which sends the
counter to *4*. Where is it now? *Here* (*4*). But we
want it to go there (between *4* and *C*). (He starts off
as before, but this time simultaneously runs his
other hand down the chalked path. Then, having
placed the counter between *4* and *C*, he raises the
box at *C* and tilts it toward the whole side *1–2*.)
Will your counter go the right way like that (second
stroke of the *W*)? *Yes, it's going to do that.* (He runs
his finger along the chalk stroke.) Despite the repeated failure, he does the same for the third and
fourth strokes of the *W* and starts the task again in
the same way when the counter is replaced by a
marble. When questioned concerning the relative
heights of the parts of the cardboard in the case of
the last stroke (right) of the *W*, he correctly indicates corner *2* as having to be *the lowest corner*,
but shows the whole side *3–4* at the point *C*, and
not corner *4* as being *the highest corner*. Still, when
the cardboard is masked by a screen and he sees
only the starting point and orientation of the slope,
PHI correctly reconstitutes the diagonal *1–3*: How
do you know? *Because I heard.* However, when it
comes to placing bricks under the cardboard in
order to make the counter travel diagonally from *2*
to *4*, he puts one brick under *2* and then another
under *4*. Do you think it's going to go down? *Yes.*
But there's no slope! (He moves the brick at *4* and
puts it under *3*, making the heights of *2* and *3* the
same.) What will the counter do now? *That* (*2–4*).
And why not *2–1*? (which it must do under these
conditions). *Because it doesn't go down.* Doesn't
it? *Because there's no line* (chalk!). Try. (Failure.)
No. He then puts a brick near *B* and another under

3, which together make the diagonal path impossible, then a little one between 4 and C, which would send the counter back toward 1. When presented with the star, PHI succeeds for the straightline paths (opposite arms), but fails in the case of the bent ones: for paths between adjacent arms, he takes the star by the two points and lifts it very high to make the counter go straight toward the opposite side. Why? *Because you can't make it go here* (that is, bend around to the adjacent point). Nevertheless, he succeeds with certain other bent paths by adjusting the orientation of the star as the counter moves along the path.

FLO (4,6) raises the box at *D* to send the counter toward *C*, and so on in similar fashion. How did you do it? *I tipped it* (and he indicates the path). He is immediately successful with the diagonal *1–3* by holding the box with one hand at *D* and the other between *C* and *4*, simply saying, *I did it like that*, and indicating the path. In the case of the star, he is successful with the bent paths by holding it by the two selected points, moving them in various ways until he gets the counter to go to the right place. But what do you do with your hands? *I did that.* (He indicates the arrival points.) And what do your hands touch? (He indicates various points at random.) *They make it roll here* (a point which the counter had, in fact, not reached). How? *Like that.* (He stands the star up on one point.) As for the cardboard box, he merely mimes the movements he carried out. In the marble-catching tasks, he succeeds for the paths parallel to the long or short sides (perpendiculars) but fails for the oblique ones such as *3–D*.

PAO (4,10) reacts like PHI for the *W*. Under the screen, for a *1–3* diagonal, she imagines a bent path *1–4–3: Like that.* Couldn't it stop here? (*C*). *No, because it's got to go like that* (from *1* to *3*, according to the plane's orientation). Why didn't it do it? *Because it doesn't know its way.* After that she arrives at the diagonal solution *because I heard it in my ears.* As for the cardboard on bricks task, PAO puts a line of bricks under the long side *1-2*, imagining that this will make the counter go the right way, along the diagonal *2-4*; then when it does not, she puts another line under the short side *1-4*. In the marble-catching task, PAO is successful with the perpendicular paths, but with the oblique or diagonal paths, she expects them to be perpendicular.

DOM (5,6) is immediately successful in getting the counter to move from *D* to *B* (parallel to the long side). *I lifted at the back; it went down the road,* but for the left stroke of the *W*, he merely raises *1-2* to make it higher than *3-4*, then does the opposite for the second stroke, and so on. Finally, he lifts corner *1*, but without making sure that both corners *3* and *4* do not touch the table—in other words, without lifting *4* less than *1* and more than *3* (which remains on the table). Why do you lift like that (toward *3-4*)? *That's the right way.* In the screen task, he looks at corner *1*, which is raised up higher and higher, and correctly concludes *it went there* (3), but he indicates a bent path, descending from *1* to *C* and then parallel to the edge from *C* to *3*. How was the box? *Like that* (resting on *3*), but he still shows the same path. In the cardboard-on-bricks task, when asked to make the counter again travel along the diagonal *1-3*, he puts one brick under *2*, then another under *3*, and two more under *1* and *4*, hence a horizontal plane. Do you think the counter is going to roll? *No.* (He takes away the bricks under *4* and *1*.) And if I put the counter here (*2*)? *It will go there* (*4*, wrong prediction of a *2-4* diagonal). After fresh attempts, again ending up with a horizontal plane, DOM this time removes the bricks under *4* and makes corner *2* higher than *1* and *3*, which is right.

BOL (5,6), in the screen task, correctly *guessed* the path *1–3 because I knew it was going there.* How did I lift? *Like that* (toward *2–3*, which would have sent the counter to *2*). In the case of the *W*, BOL makes the same mistake: he lifts first one side (*1–2*), then the other side (*3–4*), and continues in this way. What are you thinking about? *I'm wondering how to get it there* (obliquely and not the perpendicular path that it in fact took). In the cardboard-on-bricks task, when asked to make the counter go from *3* to *1*, he puts a big brick under *2*, then a whole row of bricks all the same size under the side *2–3*. When this does not work, he is temporarily successful by placing unequal-sized bricks in such a way that corner *3* is higher than *2*, which is higher than *4*, which is higher than *1*, which is on the table; but then he reverts to incorrect constructions (making perpendicular paths). Can you tell what's going to happen? *No.* In the marble-catching task, he succeeds when the marble goes down parallel to the sides, but fails in the case of the oblique paths. Could it have gone there (opposite)? *Yes, to either corner* (inconsistent).

ANT (5,6) behaves like the preceding subjects in the *W* task, but correctly predicts the diagonal in the screen task. In the cardboard-on-bricks task, however, when asked to make the counter travel along the diagonal *2–4*, he puts a row of bricks of the same height under this path and so ends up with a horizontal plane. He then replaces these bricks with a brick under each corner. Finally, he puts just one brick under *2*, but without bothering about the heights of *1* and *3*, hence a bent path. To remedy this, he puts two bricks under *2* and *1*, thus making

the path almost perpendicular to the side *1–2*.
When he is shown (without bricks) a sheet of cardboard oriented so as to give a path *1–C*, he predicts
1–3.

The most striking characteristic of this level 1A appears to
be the contrast between the effect of the almost automatic
sensorimotor regulation and that of the active adjustment
with deliberate selections (and, consequently, a sort of elementary conscious deliberation), with one child sometimes
displaying both—not of course simultaneously—in the course
of the same task. Thus the active adjustment through which
the child comes to grasp what actually happens (and eventually arrives at a correct conception and so true cognizance of
the situation) leads at this level to success in the case of paths
parallel to one of the long sides of the plane. As soon as
oblique, bent, or even diagonal paths are involved, the subjects are not yet quite able to picture the great variety of possible orientations of the sloping plane. By contrast, the motor
regulation successfully masters all the required actions, except that of the *W*, through the very simple process of lifting
that point (of the box or star) which is opposite the target
higher than all the others—no attention being paid to the
heights of the latter.

The failure of motor regulation in the *W* task certainly
results from the fact that because there are four linked
oblique paths, involving three different directions, the subject
does not dare act without first thinking; each of the oblique
paths taken separately could be found through automatic regulation. The subject PHI, for example, having explained how
he made a *slope* from *D* to *B*, manages to make the counter go
along the oblique path (*A* to *B*), but without the same explanation. In the *W* task he fails with the oblique paths; each
time, he lifts the whole side opposite the target and thus fails
to make the second adjustment of height (which is required in
the case of a nonparallel path) that he had managed for the
A–B path in the earlier task. While he correctly indicates the
lowest point (the target), he points to the whole of the op-

posite side as the highest point. However, he correctly guesses the path of the diagonal in the screen task simply by looking at the highest and lowest parts of the plane that are not hidden by the screen; the fact that he does not understand the principle is demonstrated by his failures in the cardboard-on-bricks task.

In the star task, the contrast between PHI and FLO is significant: PHI starts off by thinking carefully about the problem and maintains that the bent paths are impossible, while FLO, who immediately passes to action (as in fact PHI does subsequently), is successful by lifting the first two selected points, then the adjacent ones, and so modifying the counter's path as it goes along. However, in this case, FLO remains incapable of indicating which points he had lifted.

The cardboard-on-bricks task appears to be the most difficult one at this level, as it inevitably involves the greatest number of active adjustments; for each oblique path the child has to decide on the height and position of the bricks under at least two, and generally three, of the four corners of the cardboard. Some of the subjects do not manage to make a slope by varying the heights of the supports and thus even fail to make a path parallel to the long sides of the rectangle. Subjects incapable of making any slope at all are clearly, when it comes to conceptualization of the situation, at the lowest point in the lengthy evolution that finally results (but not until stage III) in the grasp of the concept of a path always following the line of greatest slope.

Finally, in the marble-catching task, subjects at the IA level succeed in the case of perpendicular paths, but fail with diagonal or other oblique paths, since the latter must be inferred from the orientation of the slope (cf. FLO and BOL). This provides further evidence of the most general characteristic of this level—that is, the failure to understand, at this lowest level of conceptualization, the orientation of the cardboard when the path is not perpendicular to one of the sides (although, as we have said, the subject who does not reflect upon his action sometimes succeeds, thanks to sensorimotor regulation).

Level IB

This is an intermediate level in that the subjects succeed, through trial and error, in those tasks that are mastered immediately at stage II.

Examples

CRI (5,6) makes the counter slide from *B* down to *D*. Why this way? *Because it had to go there.* If you did the same thing again, could you make it go here (corner *1*)? *No, because that would have been wrong if it had been there.* And to go from there to there (*1* to *3*)? (He lifts the side *1–4*, but higher at *1*, and succeeds.) What did you do? (He demonstrates by again raising side *1–4*, but this time the highest point is at *4*.) And if you lifted like that (*1* and *4* raised to the same height)? *It would have gone there* (*B*). In the cardboard-on-bricks task (for *1–3* diagonal), he puts two bricks under *1* and *2*, then puts one under *3*. *No, that won't make the slope.* Then what will? *Leave it like that.* (He tries, the counter slides down to *4*, and he adds a brick under *4*: the counter arrives at *3* but falls at this point.) What have you got to do? (He places other bricks at various points and then inclines the slope with his hand to find the right orientation, puts a large brick under *1*, two small ones under *4*, tries various bricks under *2*, and ends up succeeding with two large ones under *1*. Why have you got these two here? (*1*). *Because here* (*1–3*) *that makes it seesaw this way. And it went down there.* Could it have gone any other way? *No.*

TAN (6,8): *To make it go down I did that* (raises *D*) *and the coin went there* (*B*). Why there? *Because if I lift like that, it's got to go straight.* Why? *Don't know.* For the *W* task, she holds *D* and *B* and tilts the cardboard toward 3, which is correct. Should the whole side be on the table (3–4)? *That's OK too.* (Tries.) *Oh no!* What's the difference between lifting like that (toward 3) and like that (toward the whole side 3–4)? *Don't know.* For the second stroke she lifts toward 2, but holding the side 4–1 too high: Are you sure that's right? (She then lowers this side. For the third stroke she tilts the cardboard toward 4 but without 4's touching the table.) Shouldn't it touch there (4)? *No* (but hesitates and checks). *If it touches there, it'll go straight.* In the screen task she immediately deduces the diagonal path, but in the cardboard-on-bricks task for a 2–4 diagonal, she puts the same number of bricks under 3 as under 2, hence a 2–1 path. Before doing this, she had been sure that one had to have corners 2 and 3 *the same* (height). In the marble-catching task she succeeds for the perpendicular and diagonal paths, but cannot make up her mind for the oblique ones.

ANT (6,6), for the first task, limits his explanations to *I lifted like that,* demonstrating with the cardboard. In the W task he tilts it toward 3 for the first stroke. For the second, he aims toward 2, for the third, he lifts it toward corner 3, and too high, then succeeds right away with the last stroke. In the screen task he gets the diagonal right without any hesitation. In the cardboard-on-bricks task (diagonal 2–4), he gets the counter to D and for the 1–3 diagonal he gets it to C. As for the star task, he has no difficulty with the bent paths, but cannot show how he went about it.

PAT (6,8), in the W task, starts by tilting the cardboard toward the whole side 3–4, then corrects herself. For the second stroke, she lifts toward 2 and says that the box is leaning *only on this side,* but for the third stroke she leaves 2 and 3 on the ground. In the screen task, she correctly indicates the diagonal *1-3*, but says that the highest points are *these corners* (*1* and *4*), *no, the highest is* 4 (while again indicating the path *1-3*). Could it have gone to *2? No, only here* (*1-B*) *and there* (*1-3*). Her solution to the cardboard-on-bricks task is similar to ANT's. In the marble-catching task, she is successful with the perpendicular paths, but predicts diagonal paths for all the ones that are actually oblique (*1-C* and *A-B*).

RIS (6,3), in the first stroke of the *W* task, tilts the cardboard toward the *3-4* side: Does the whole side touch the ground? *No.* Where doesn't it touch? *There* (*4*—correct); *it mustn't touch, otherwise the coin would fall down* (would go from *1* to *4*). For the second stroke he tilts it toward the side *1-2*, then corrects himself, and so on. In the marble-catching task, RIS succeeds with the perpendicular and diagonal paths, but in the case of the oblique paths he expects the marble to come to the corner nearest to the actual point of arrival.

Again, it is the difference between what these level IB subjects actually do and their conception of the situation that is interesting, despite the fact that this contrast is less marked than at level IA—there being virtually no change in the former (actions), while the latter (conception) progresses to a point halfway between levels IA and IIA. Generally, however, while in their action these subjects constantly seek the line of greatest slope for a given incline of the cardboard, in their conceptualization they do not express this requirement and differentiate poorly between the cardboard's position when it is tilted with the lowest side horizontal and its position when one corner is lower than the other three—and even more poorly between the relative heights of the intermediate and highest corners.

This contrast is evident in CRI's response in the case of the diagonal *1-3:* he lifts corner *1* more than the rest of the side *1-4*, but his repetition of the action is inadequate and, when asked to explain why the counter took the specific course, he can only say that any other course *would have been wrong*. Similarly, TAN maintains that a path has *got to go straight*, but says she does not *know* why.

In the W task, these IB subjects generally tilt the cardboard so that the lowest point is corner 3 (or 2) and no longer (as at level IA) so that corners 3 and 4 (or 1 and 2) are the same height. However, PAT and RIS still start the strokes of the W by making the level IA mistake, then correct themselves and aim at one corner. TAN, however, immediately aims at corner 3, but when the interviewer asks if the whole side 3–4 should touch the table, she replies, *that's OK too*. When she discovers this is not so, she does not know why.

In the star task, these subjects have no difficulty with the bent paths (cf. ANT), but are no more successful than level IA subjects when it comes to describing their actions and saying which points they lifted (except, of course, for the straight paths).

In the marble-catching task, this level sees the correct prediction of the diagonal as well as of the perpendicular paths, but not yet of the oblique ones. PAT and RIS, for example, think that the latter end up at the corners, which shows that these two subjects are not really aware of the relative heights of the various corners. Similarly, in the screen task, they have no trouble reconstituting the diagonal 1–3 (as at level IA), but PAT still thinks that the highest points are 1 and 4, then changes her mind and says, *no, the highest is 4* (which would result in a path 4–2).

Finally, the cardboard-on-bricks task is (as we saw at level IA) the most demanding task with regard to conceptualization, since it requires the greatest number of active adjustments, which are impossible without accurate conceptualization. Whereas at level IA some subjects failed to make a slope at all, all those at level IB end up with slopes (although at one point CRI's path is horizontal, but he immediately says, *No, that won't make the slope*); the orientation, however, is usually incorrect (oblique instead of diagonal paths for instance). What is particularly interesting is that this is not always the case: at one point CRI stops moving the bricks, picks up the cardboard, and places it in the right position with his hand (simple sensorimotor adjustment, no longer one involving his conception of the situation), and then simply uses the bricks to hold the cardboard at the correct angle. Furthermore, accurate conception of the difference between a slope obtained when the cardboard is tilted with the lowest side horizontal and one where one corner is lower than the other three, sometimes appears easier when the subject instructs the experimenter on what to do (rather than carrying out the actions himself), because it is then only a matter of interpreting the observable features of the object (as in the screen and marble-catching tasks) and no longer demands an inferential adjustment of the child's own action.

Level IIA

Although several seven- and eight-year-olds remain at level IB, the majority grasp the difference between a slope obtained when the cardboard is oriented toward one corner and one resulting from two corners resting on the table. In other words, they can differentiate between the various possible orientations of the cardboard and so have a more accurate conception of the situation. These subjects are therefore well on the way to understanding the concept of the line of greatest slope.

Examples

MOS (7,5), in explanation of the counter's paths in the first task, says, *Because it was going down.* Could it have gone another way? *Only that way, only one way.* But why there? *If you didn't lift like that, it would go somewhere else.* He has no difficulty in making the counter follow the right path in the W task, but simply says, *I aimed it at the corners* (3 and 2 alternately). But why did it go there (first stroke)? *Because this side's higher* (points to the relevant side) *and that pushes it there.* In the

marble-catching task, MOS is successful every time;
to explain one particular oblique path (say, 2–C), he
says that he found it *because there's the same distance here and there* (between the nearest corner
and the marble's starting and finishing points)
— that is, because of the symmetry inherent in
this oblique path. Furthermore, he can reproduce
the same results at will. In the cardboard-on-bricks
task, however, he cannot obtain a 2–4 diagonal and
manages only a bent path 2–D–4.

WUT (7,10), in the marble-catching task, is initially
successful for various oblique paths, then misses
one, expecting a 3–1 diagonal: *There were three
possibilities: it would either go there* (between D
and 1, which is what happened), *or there* (diagonal),
or there (between 1 and A); *I thought it would go
straight* (= 3–1). The interviewer asks the child to
try again himself and then to make the marble go
from 1 to 3. After immediate success: How did you
do it? *I didn't tilt it toward 2 or 4 but toward 3.*
Why? *It can't climb up the two sides so it stays
like that.* He definitely has the basic idea of the line
of greatest slope; what WUT calls *climbing* to the
left or right of the diagonal (see his three possibilities above) would constitute less inclined slopes,
and he does not consider changes of direction toward the back, nor deviations along the path (of 90
degrees or so).

PID (7,2) is immediately successful in the W task
and when he aims at corner 2 for the last stroke
says that the highest points will be 4 and C. In the
screen task, in order to explain the diagonal path
under the screen as opposed to a parallel path from
1 to 2, he says that *the 3, the B, and the 2 are the
same* (for both paths), *the 1, the D, and the 4 aren't
the same.* In other words, he clearly judges the relative heights of the three points on the raised side,
but not on the lowest side. His initial response to

the cardboard-on-bricks task is similar to that of
MOS, then, proceeding by trial and error, he finds
(rather by chance) the diagonal.

TZE (7,5), in the star task, succeeds with a series of
bent paths from one point to the next. How did you
do it? *I moved like that* (shows that he lifted the
points, once to the left, then once to the right, and
so on).

PES (7,11), in the star task, makes the counter go
from one point to the opposite one (straight line)
simply by lifting the first point (which he subsequently indicates), and then makes it follow a
bent path, this time showing how he made it tilt
first to one side and then to the other.

VER (7,2) is immediately successful in the W task
and shows how she does it (compromise between
tilting toward the *4–3* side and the *1–3* diagonal for
the first stroke). In the screen task she explains that
it goes *there* (*3*) *because you lifted there* (*1*). In the
cardboard-on-bricks task, she misses the diagonal
and ends up with oblique paths. In the marble-
catching task, she has some successes and some
near-successes.

GAL (8,10) for the W task: *I tilt it* (toward *3*), *the
corner 1 goes up, then it goes down; I tilt here*
(toward *2*) *and it goes to* A, and so forth. In the
screen task, she explains her success with the diagonal: *I saw the box sloping.* Couldn't it have gone
here (*C*)? *No, you would have had to tilt it that
way* (toward *3–4*), *then there* (*3*).

TRI (8,5), in the first task, can make only *one path.
The coin can't go up.* For the W task, he tilts the
cardboard toward the side *3–2: That's only
touching on this side, so it will have to go there*
(oblique). For a *1–3* diagonal path, in the cardboard-
on-bricks task, when asked about the relative

heights of the corners, he says that corner *1* will be the highest, then *2*, then *4*, and *3* will be the lowest.

BAR (9,1), in the cardboard-on-bricks task, is at the same level as the preceding subjects: when trying to get a diagonal *2–4*, she ends up with *2–D*, and so on.

With regard to the action, the *W* task is completed successfully from then on without hesitation or mistakes. In the marble-catching task these subjects are successful not only in the case of the diagonals but also in that of the other oblique paths, which are in fact often at the same angle as the strokes of the *W*. Since these two sorts of actions both imply differentiations and coordinations between tilting toward the front and tilting toward the side and thus call for a deliberate selection (the diagonals are easier because of the opposite corners — that is, either *1* and *3*, or *2* and *4*), clear progress has been made in the child's conception of the situation (cf. MOS: *I aimed it at the corners*, and *There's the same distance here and there*).

The more advanced level of these subjects' conception is first apparent from their realization of the existence of only one possible path: *Only that way, only one* (possible) *way* (MOS); and from the fact that WUT, for example, in the *W* task realizes that if the cardboard is tilted in the general direction *1–4*, there are various possible paths according to how the sides *2–1* and *3–4* are lifted. In particular, this improved conception is subsequently revealed by the first idea of the law of the line of greatest slope: *It can't climb up the two sides*, says WUT about the marble, *so it stays like that*.

This progress does not necessarily lead to success in the cardboard-on-bricks task. While the subjects are well aware of height differences between the highest and lowest points (and are able to differentiate between a slope obtained when the whole of the lowest side is horizontal and one obtained when one corner is lower than the other three — in the case of the *W* the sides *1–2* or *3–4*, or the corners *2* or *3*), they do not always judge the heights of the intermediate corners correctly.

Level IIB and Stage III

Level IIB subjects successfully complete all the tasks including, by trial and error, the diagonal in the cardboard-on-bricks task, but unlike those at stage III, they cannot formulate the law of the line of greatest slope.

Examples (Level IIB)

RUG (9,1) says that *only one road* is possible in each of the initial tasks and succeeds right off with the W. In the cardboard-on-bricks task, for the diagonal 2–4, he first puts three bricks under the corners *1, 2,* and *3,* but *2* is not high enough, which he quickly and successfully corrects. *It goes to the lowest one* (of the four corners, but he does not discover the general rule). For the diagonal *1–3,* he foresees the need for three bricks under *1,* two under *4,* and one under *2* (correct solution).

OLA (9,5) comes to a similar conclusion in this task through trial and error. What are you looking at? *How it's leaning, because the marble can't go up much, so it goes to the side that slopes to the bottom; if you know about the heights, you can see it better.*

NIC (10,4) in this task reacts similarly, but he uses bricks of various sizes. *It will go from 1 to 3; no, more to C. Then? 1–C–3; before, it went from 1 to 3; the box wasn't leaning so much* (toward C).

Examples (Stage III)

VEN (11,0) is completely successful in all tasks. In the initial ones, he says if you tilt it a bit *you can't be quite sure, the coin could go off course.* And what happens if you tilt it a bit more? *If you tilt it enough it's bound to go straight: the coin can't go off course because it's heavy; once it's on course it stays there.* But why that particular path? *Because of the slope.*

CHA (11,6) explains: *It can't go in any other direction because there's one side lower than all the others.*

MOR (11,3) says, *It can't go there* (to the side) *Because it's tilting* (more) *toward there and the marble is pulled more toward the bottom.* Can you hold the box in several ways for one path? *No, there's only one way. There'll be only one possible path.* Why? *If that bit was lower, it couldn't go down when the slope is . . .* (less), *it's always got to go down.* And there? *If that bit had been the lowest, the marble would have gone there.*

RIC (12,4), for the last stroke of the W, says, *It'll go there* (2), *it always goes down the lowest side . . . , it always goes in the same direction.* Which direction? *It goes opposite.* Opposite what? *That depends. If you want it to go to 2, you put it* (the box) *right on 2. If you put it like that* (indicates the point *opposite* — that is, halfway between 3 and C — which must be higher), *it's got to go in the corner.*

TIS (12,6) explains, *I'm sure because I'm looking at the highest point and the lowest point: the marble will go along there.* For the W: *I'm lifting like that because it will be pulled over there; if I put it like that, it pulls it here,* since *these sides* (no clear difference in height) *aren't the same, there's always one that is lower . . . I look* (as well) *to make sure the slope is a straight line . . . not a curve.* And to make a curve? *You have to move the box to change the slope while the thing is going down.*

Level IIB sees success (although after trial and error in some cases) in the cardboard-on-bricks task, with accurate adjustment of the heights of the intervening corners and, generally speaking, accurate ordering of all the heights involved. This implies some concept of the line of greatest slope, but one that at level IIB always remains linked to a particular case; in other words, the subject compares the arrival point with the other parts of the cardboard (for example RUG's *to the lowest one* applies to one of the four corners as compared to the three others). The novelty at stage III, however, appears to be the idea that at each of the successive spatiotemporal points of the path, the object is continually forced to descend the line of greatest slope: the marble must *always* go down, says MOR, because it is *more pulled toward the bottom*; and if there had been an even lower point, *the marble would have gone there*, since it will only go down the steepest slope. Similarly, RIC says, *it always goes down the lowest side* specifying *always . . . in the same direction.* There is the same preoccupation with continuity in TIS's words, *it will be pulled over there*, and other similar phrases.

Conclusions

This is therefore the end of the long evolution of the child's conceptualization of the situation, which begins at about age four (level IA) with the idea of a simple "descent" and leads at around twelve years to the concept of the line of greatest slope. Between these two, there is the idea that if one wanted a marble to leave its straight downward path it would *climb up the two sides* (cf. WUT at level IIA), then another idea that, of all the possible points of arrival lower than the starting point, the actual one has to be the one that is *lowest* (RUG at level IIB); finally there comes the generalization of this to the idea of the line of greatest slope all the way to the bottom (stage III).

The subjects' responses from level IIA on therefore clearly reveal the existence of an inferential coordination that both goes beyond and facilitates the correct reading of the experimental data. Two aspects may be distinguished. Firstly, as was stressed in our discussion of level IIA, there is the realization that only one possible path exists. Of course, stage I sub-

jects already say *that must be the way*, but at level IA this
embodies both a deterministic view of the descent and a more
or less moral feeling of necessity resulting from the child's
inability to differentiate between the physical law and a sort
of social obligation (*because there's no line*, says PHI for a
path that was not taken; *because it's got to go like that*, and,
when the counter does not take this path, it is *because it
doesn't know its way*, says PAO). At level IB the child is mo-
tivated by a simple legalistic viewpoint (that it *would have
been wrong if it had been there* is sufficient explanation for
CRI; *it's got to go straight*, maintains TAN without knowing
why, and so on). However, by stage II, a grasp of the second
aspect of this inferential coordination is becoming apparent:
the child begins to relate the effects of tilting toward the front
and toward the side in order to determine the exact point of
arrival (for example, side *1–4* may be raised in such a way that
side *2–3* is horizontal, or such that either corner *2* or corner *3*
is lower than the other three). In the case of the oblique paths
other than diagonals (which are easier) this coordination of
the two ways of tilting the cardboard is really understood only
from level IIA on; it is the grasp of this coordination that
leads to the inferential necessity that is attributed to the
uniquity of the path.

   However, it is the subjects' actions that provide one of the
most interesting features of this experiment. In the case of the
straightforward paths (as opposed to the disjointed paths involving active selections in the *W* task, and to the more
complicated problems of the marble-catching and cardboard-
on-bricks tasks) even the level IA subject is capable of coordinating the two ways of tilting the cardboard through the
immediate sensorimotor regulations: at (4,5) PHI successfully
makes the counter travel from *A* to *B* and go from one point
of the star to another, while, in the latter task FLO makes the
counter go just where he wants. So here is still another example of a remarkable time-lag between the accomplishment
of an action and its conceptualization. Furthermore, in this
experiment it is particularly clear that the time-lag is not
caused by any contradictions arising between what the child

observes and his preconceived ideas about what should happen (as is the case for the release point in the sling experiment described in Chapter 2), but results quite simply from the natural time-lag described in the stage I discussion, which separates the ability to select consciously a course of action, and so make active adjustments from the more or less automatic sensorimotor regulations.

In fact, when the child himself handles the cardboard box and is asked to make the counter move down sloping paths between specific points, regardless of whether the paths are perpendicular to one side of the box, diagonals, or obliques such as *A–B*, he needs only proceed step by step, constantly correcting the movement of the counter. He starts off by tilting the box forward and then, if the counter deviates to the left or the right, he corrects the path by tilting the box sideways, without needing to understand exactly how the counter is moving and simply describing his action by the words *I made a slope* or the counter *slid there* (PHI). There is nothing to call his attention to the respective heights of the four corners of the cardboard or make him compare the slopes at various points along the path, let alone formulate a law of the line of greatest slope.

By contrast, when the interviewer's questions require a breakdown of the movements (*W* task) or predictions (marble-catching and cardboard-on-bricks tasks), the sensorimotor regulations described above are no longer sufficient; success requires the active adjustments that result from the conscious selection possible only with full cognizance of the situation—hence the delay in the solution of these problems. When these are mastered, the correct reading of the observable features of the situations and the inferential coordination between the two ways of tilting the cardboard lead to conceptualization of the notion of slope, and the progressive discovery of this particular case of the principle of extremum (the law of the line of greatest slope). So, while the four- and five-year-olds (level IA) are able to make simple, but purely praxeological, application of this necessary condition for any descent of the counter, it is not until stage III, and an average

age of eleven or twelve years, that the law becomes formulated, as a result of the gradual improvements in the child's conceptualization apparent at levels IIA and IIB. These improvements result from his growing grasp of what actually happens — in other words, his increasing cognizance of the situation.

5 Building a Road up a Hill

The actions needed to build something simple, as in this experiment, differ markedly from those that deal with a moving object, since the static material handled by the child in the former instance plays a purely passive role: in such a case, cognizance of his own action appears to occur so effortlessly in the youngest subject that if the constructions are easy, one might expect to find no progression in the development of the actions, or, above all, in the cognizance of the actions. This is far from the case, as we shall see clearly in the very elementary behavior chosen for discussion in this chapter: the children are asked to use small strips of wood and bricks to build a sloping road leading from a given point to the top of a "mountain" represented by a box.

The materials comprise either a small doll or a toy car, a parallelepipedic box (chosen because any other shape such as a cone might from the outset have suggested the idea of a

With the collaboration of Madelon Robert.

slope), nine bricks (one thin one, a taller one, a cylindrical one with grooves, and six small cubes), and several strips of wood. The latter are between 15 and 25 cm long, with the exception of one of 50 cm — which by itself almost provides the solution of a sloping road reaching the summit of the mountain M, starting not far from the point of departure of the doll or car.

In the doll variation of this experiment, the interviewer places a small doll about 50 cm from the foot of M and asks the child to build a road from it to the top of the mountain. If a child simply makes towers of bricks at the side of M or uses the long strip (and the latter is suggested when appropriate), he is asked to find other solutions. A week after this initial session, the subjects are asked to recall what they did and to make a drawing of their solution (without being shown the materials again).

In the car variation, the interviewer places a toy car about 50 cm from M, explaining to the child that there is a "lake" between the car and M into which he can put islands, and asking him to build a road to the top of M. The lake can be crossed by means of a bridge (bricks on the islands and strips of wood on the bricks); there is sufficient land around M for the children to put what they want (including the towers of bricks favored by the young ones), even though the problem involves a toy car, and not a doll which presumably is able to climb vertical slopes.

Twenty-one subjects were questioned using the doll variation and the same number (age from five to twelve years) using the car variation.

Stage I

Examples (Level IA)

ERI (5,3) (Doll): He puts three bricks one on top of the other, reaching half way up M, makes a second tower right next to the first, then puts the long grooved brick on top of one of the towers. And will the doll get there? *No, she's too small.* So? . . . What about using the wood strips? He lays the short strips horizontally on top of the bricks and puts the long one on top of the short ones, again horizontally, then removes the long one because it tends to fall off. And could you make anything with this long one? (He puts it almost vertically against *M* and makes a tower of bricks in front of it which goes higher than *M*, takes one of the bricks away, and seems satisfied.) *If I don't put that* (long strip), *it's too low. If it isn't there, you've got to bring everything closer together* (simple tower). And what if you just had the long one? (He places it sloping, and when it slides he wedges it with two bricks.) Why is that OK? *Because the bit of wood is lying* (sloping). And before? *If it isn't, the doll couldn't climb up.* And if we didn't have this piece of wood? He takes two smaller pieces which he tries to make into a slope of 90 degrees, then makes a tower preceded by a single brick on which he puts a short piece of wood, first almost vertically and then sloping only very slightly. After this, he wedges the latter with a brick in order to make the slope steeper, and then because it collapses he reverts to the simple tower. Finally, he takes into account the starting point (50 cm away), puts two strips of wood flat on the ground, and leans the third against the tower, so that it is almost vertical. A week later he recalls: *There was a doll who had to climb onto a box* (indicates a slope with his arm). How did she do it? *There was a bit of wood almost lying down* (slight incline), *but it's upright* (the drawing shows an almost horizontal strip of wood). What did the doll do? *Afterward, she jumped . . . After that I didn't need the wood any more, so I took the bricks away* (drawing of simple tower).

BOS (5,9) (Doll): Starting from the doll's point of departure, he lays out three horizontal strips of wood in a line, followed by two towers covered with a small strip, making a very slight slope, on which he puts another three bricks to get to the top of *M*. When asked to use just the long strip, he starts off by putting it up almost vertically against

M, then inclines it so that it leans against a new tower (between the three first and two last elements), again places it almost vertically, then puts an end about three-quarters of the way up M before finally placing it correctly. When the long strip is removed, he tries to fix a sloping strip onto a vertical strip (without wedging them in any way). A week later he recalls that there was *a ladder so that we didn't slip* with bricks and the two strips, which in his recollection were placed like T instead of like [.

SAN (6,2) (Doll): He starts off by making a tower, then a staircase with two bricks of different heights and a strip of wood stuck vertically against M. After making another tower he says, *You've got to make staircases*, but fails. The interviewer offers him the long strip, which he refuses because it doesn't have steps, but still keeps it in mind and stacks the little strips one after the other against the middle of M.

Examples (Level IB)

These subjects' initial reactions are similar to those at level IA, but their final solutions are approximately correct.

SYL (5,2) (Doll): She starts off with a tower and puts a vertical strip on top of it. She then makes two towers of bricks, side by side, and lays two strips horizontally on top (toward the middle of M). Next she puts the long strip on top of the other two, reaching the mountain, and tops that with a brick that brings it to the same height as M; she then adds another strip, making it slope up to the first tower from the starting point. Finally, after trying a few other solutions, she places the long strip so that it bridges the gap between the starting point and the first of her two towers.

BER (5,10) (Car): He builds towers and the like even though he is supposed to be building a road for a car! The interviewer points to the long strip, which he then leans against M, making a very steep slope. And without using the big one? *A road.* (He lines up the little strips end to end, horizontally.) But how's the car going to get up? (He takes two strips, which he makes into a slope, holding them together with his hand.) How are you going to make them stay together? (He puts bricks in the lake, makes a bridge with the last bit resting on two bricks, and, using a strip of wood, makes a slope between these two bricks and M.) A week later, his first drawing (from memory) shows a long sloping line going over the lake and ending at M (thus a simplification of the final solution), then he draws a bridge—the first three pillars made up of one brick each and the last one of two bricks. This final picture shows a fine solution to the problem, but one that bears no relation to the material in the experiment: an unbroken road resting on three bricks—a small one, a medium-sized one, and a large one.

JAC (5,7) (Car): He starts off with the long strip and places it obliquely against the side of M, then looks for something to put behind it, particularly since it is standing in the lake. He takes a small strip in his hand and leans it up against the top of M; he tries unsuccessfully to lengthen this road by simply putting another strip immediately following the first. He then remembers the car's starting point and makes a bridge to M, but it is horizontal. Is that all right? *No, you've got to put a bit of wood so that it can go up.* He does this, but the wood is too short and he tries to complete the road by adding a thin brick (tall side up) to the top of the second bit of wood, reaching the summit of M, thereby reverting to a sort of tower solution. He then takes two strips off his bridge and puts two bricks one on top of the other beyond the remaining piece. Then he makes one strip lean up against a brick and holds in his hand a second strip, which ends up resting on the two bricks. That gives him the idea of constructing a completely sloping bridge, which he extends with a new strip resting on three bricks. From there, a fourth strip extends to the top of *M*, which provides a correct solution.

GHI (6,4) (Car): She also starts by taking the long strip, making it slope, and noting that it *goes down*. The interviewer suggests that she use something else and she takes the two shorter strips, which she tries to join — first end to end, then at right angles. She next makes a tower of six bricks by the side of *M*, then a little farther away, and links the top of this to the summit of *M* by a thin brick, thus making a bridge. On being reminded of the car's starting point, she makes one strip lean against a pillar and slope down the other side, then puts a second pillar so that this strip is horizontal, and finally adds a third going toward *M*.

It is important to distinguish the three facets of this problem. First of all, the children have to relate the horizontal ground at the starting point of the car or the doll to the vertical mountain, *M*, on top of which is situated the arrival point — that is, they have to find the solution of the slope. Secondly, they have to discover the possible relationships between this slope and the objects proposed as intermediaries. And thirdly, they must determine the possible relationships among these objects and decide whether these have a direct link with the first two types of relationship. In fact, since the children act on their grasp of these relationships before they can depict them on paper or describe them, the interesting feature at level IA is that these actions are polarized on the goal to be attained and that the first part of the relationship is thus forgotten or neglected in favor of the second.

The notion of a slope is certainly not unfamiliar to four- and five-year-olds, and they even have a natural intuition about it before they begin to understand the relevant relationships between length and height. However, since here the child has to imagine the slope without actually seeing it and since the starting point is some distance from the goal, he forgets or even deliberately ignores the former and concentrates on the height to be attained: hence the vertical towers with no thought of what should lead to them. When the level IA subject sees the long strip, or its use is suggested to him, he does not immediately make it slant (as do subjects at level IB, who see in it right away the possibility of making a slope), but initially either puts it almost vertically so that it directly reaches the summit of M (ERI and BOS), or declines to use it at all because it cannot be employed with the towers of bricks to make a staircase (considered possible at this level).

As for the relationships between the intermediaries and the goal, two findings are noteworthy. Firstly, level IA subjects (unlike those at level IB) often forget that these objects are intended to act as intermediaries—hence the frequent appearance of all sorts of adventitious constructions, of a merely functional nature, which it would serve no purpose to describe here in detail. Secondly, since the subject's action is initially centered on arrival at the summit of M and not on the starting point of the doll or car, he pays no attention to those objects that are unsuitable for making his towers and the like; when he is reminded of the starting point and begins to build a road or a bridge, he places them horizontally and forgets to make them climb.

Finally, in addition to the permissible relationships among the objects themselves, the children try inadmissible ones (two strips held together by hand to make them reach M) or, on the other hand, adequate ones that have no relevance to the target (towers of bricks side by side serving no purpose, and so forth).

Briefly, children at these elementary levels find the problem so difficult, not because they have not grasped the concept of a slope (they are already familiar with it), but because they cannot interrelate the various factors; the ability to do this is developed only gradually, with level IB seeing the first approximately correct solutions. It is doubtless this very gradual grasp of the connections between observable features, always subordinate to specific actions, that accounts for the excellent cognizance of the successively executed actions that is revealed by the children's recollections after a few days.

Stage II

Subjects at stage II no longer make isolated towers of bricks, but start off with the intent (conserved, in fact, throughout the session) of trying to make a slope. This does not mean that seven- and eight-year-olds never build towers: even nine-year-olds sometimes build them, but this is a throwback to level IB, since the developmental stages determined by the subject's level of practical intelligence are chronologically far more elastic (while retaining their order of succession) than those determined by his understanding of the problem (operatory stages). At level IIB, subjects no longer make the mistakes in building their roads that still occur at level IIA.

Examples (Level IIA)

MAU (7,4) (Doll): He first leans a strip against the side of *M*; since this is too short, he puts the thin brick (tall side up) at the end of it, then immediately replaces it by a second strip that slopes more steeply than the first, and that slides. He discards it and supports the first strip with the long grooved brick, which then gives him the idea of making a staircase; but he covers this up soon afterward with the long strip (at a 45-degree angle). In his subsequent recollection he describes his initial attempts: *I had put it like that, quite straight, because if you put it leaning it didn't hold.* Then: *I put it sloping because it was better; you can't climb straight up like that.*

GEM (7,8) (Car): (She puts an island in the lake, then makes a slope with the long strip.) And what if we didn't have that one? (She puts a vertical strip at the edge of the lake, then lays a strip horizontally along the top of it.) *There's a bit missing.* (She puts the whole construction on the island, holding the second strip by hand, and then adds a strip at the beginning. To wedge the horizontal strip that she wants to make reach *M*, she moves it back a little and puts a brick to counterbalance it at the other end.) *It's to hold here.* Since this construction is not stable, she finally builds a support against *M* and adds the thin slanting brick as the last step up to the top of *M*—in sum, two slopes linked by a horizontal plane.

DIM (7,8) (Car): He first builds a sort of road made up of islands placed side by side and at the far end puts a sloping strip up to *M*; this is, however, too short and comes only to the middle of *M*. He replaces this strip by the long one, but leaves its other end in the lake. He then builds a staircase by the side of the lake (near the starting point), but the bricks are not adequately wedged and the staircase immediately collapses. He then puts one brick on an island with a strip linking it to the shore and another directed toward *M*. His final solution consists in three islands in the lake: the first has one brick, the second two bricks, and the third three bricks. On these rest the strips of wood, thus making a sloping road from the start to the top of *M*.

RIA (8,6) (Doll): She starts off by making a staircase, but some distance from *M* (showing that she is taking account of the starting point). She then replaces this staircase by a horizontal strip on two bricks; she puts another brick on top of this strip halfway along and tops it with a second horizontal strip (clearly trying to make a staircase with the strips making the horizontal sections). On being reminded of the existence of the long strip, she immediately places it correctly, then, when asked not to use it, she makes supports of gradually increasing height and puts first two, then three, strips resting on top of them. In her recollection a week later, she says, *We had to be careful to make sure that it wasn't always the same height; it had to climb higher.*

SPA (9,9) (Doll): He starts off a fair distance from M with a sloping strip resting on a brick, then tries to link this to M by another strip, which is too short. Next, he adds more bricks to his first one (making a tower), which he links horizontally with a strip to the summit of M (but with no means of access to the top of the tower, since the first strip is too short and only reaches the first brick). As the incline is too steep, he puts a sloping strip on the other side of the tower, then moves the tower near to M, lowering the horizontal strip by one brick—which does not solve his problem. He then tries using the long strip and, after several unsatisfactory attempts (inclines still too steep), finds the solution of one road from start to finish made up of three sections resting on supports of increasing height.

So, with regard to their actions (as opposed to their understanding of the problem), these subjects no longer start off by centering their attention on the goal to the exclusion of the starting point and consequently of any idea of a slope, but they take both ends of the road into account throughout the session. Because of this, they try to make a slope and do not simply pile up bricks in towers.

Is this improvement regarding the action the cause or an effect of the progress of the concept? Subjects at stage I already possess this concept of slope, but in an undifferentiated form—that is to say, without analysis of the links between the height and the length, while level IIA subjects obviously have begun to relate the two dimensions. Is it then progress in understanding that leads them to attempt to relate the two factors, or is it because in their actions the subjects are concerned with all facets of the problem, retaining them simultaneously, and so are led to these new ways of relating the data? The question may seem pointless, since the action linking the observable features and the relating of these in the child's mind may appear to constitute one and the same thing. However, there is a *tertium quid*, which is the cognizance of the actions: one must take account of the stages, or areas, of conceptualization of the effective action that occur between the preoperatory and the operatory structuring of the concepts. The specific actions carried out by the subject in this experiment are perfectly retained and described without any real distortion (and this is frequently not the case in the other studies); but what the stage I subject does not tell us, because he simply is not aware of it, is that when building his towers right up against the mountain M, he forgets the starting point of the doll or car, and it does not dawn on him to wonder how they would climb such a very steep incline.

In other words, these subjects correctly observe each facet of the situation in turn, but once each has been so observed it is either forgotten or simply put aside—so the result is virtually the same as if the observations had been incorrect. In this case, the successive actions consist in corrections and regulations, linked together according to the results obtained (that is, the failures and partial successes); and while the child is clearly conscious of each individual action, he is not conscious of all the facets of the problem at the same time. If he were, he would be able to work out the complete solution in advance (the interdependent predictions and retroactions that occur at stage II) instead of simply adjusting his construction after each individual action. In other words, as emerged from my research with Professor Bärbel Inhelder regarding elementary logical structures, while the understanding of operatory relationships results from the combined effect of predictions and retroactions, the latter also constitute an extension of the conceptualized cognizance of the action itself with the child now able to picture each individual successive action, plus all the actions required to solve the problem, including the reasons for any mistakes and subsequent corrections.

Even though the level IIA subjects are sufficiently aware of the positions of both the start and finish of the required road to realize the need to make a long slope, they still make numerous mistakes in the details; the strips are too short, there is no link between them, the slopes are too steep, and so forth. This shows that despite the realization of need, they are not yet able to interrelate the bricks and strips so as to fashion the required slope. The IIB subjects introduce a greater degree of order in the succession of attempts.

Examples (Level IIB)

SMI (7,6) (Doll): (He starts off by putting the long strip against M, and in front of it puts a little strip representing the flat road before the slope. Asked not to use the long strip, he replaces it by two small ones linked together on a pillar made of two bricks; he then introduces numerous variations on this same theme, even using four strips and three pillars with a short horizontal road in the middle.) And suppose we want a smooth slope? *A bigger one* (pillar), *a middle-sized one, and a little one.*

BRU (8,7) (Doll): Although he gives this same type of solution (road-climbing in sections with pillars supporting the strips) he concentrates most of his efforts on constructing two types of staircases starting some distance from M: he either places strips on top of one another or overlapping, ending up with a stable staircase that uses six overlying, staggered strips, the last one holding a sloping strip that reaches the summit of M. His recollection contains instructive remarks about the method he had worked out and consciously followed: *I thought of all sorts of things and I tried this and that. If you've got to use the long piece it's more of a nuisance, because with the little ones you've got to put them for example here* (a ways off); *if you start*

*the building near the mountain (M) with the long
strip that's OK, but with the little ones it isn't.*

JIO (9,1) (Doll): She, by contrast, starts with a long
horizontal road; at the end of it she places a fairly
steeply sloping strip resting on bricks. She then
increases the number of bricks to reduce the incline
and ends up with a road that climbs from the start
in two, then three, sections with adequate pillars.

PHI (9,10) (Doll): He starts with too steep a slope,
then reduces the incline by increasing the number
of sections to three (held by pillars, one of two and
one of four bricks). However, in his recollection a
week later, he draws a gradually sloping road
(which is not what he built) with five sections and
with supports ranging from two to seven bricks!

KAS (10,5) (Car): He starts with a series of islands
and puts the long strip on the second one. Asked to
find another solution, he starts with too steep a
slope in the second section of his road, tries three
sections, but with one pillar too many, which looks
rather like a tower and which he removes with the
comment: *The strips are for the car to go on, the
bricks are to hold up the strips.*

FAV (10,6) (Car): She starts off by making a small
staircase at the edge of the lake to support the
beginning of the road. When she realizes that this
will not work, she sketches a solution to the
problem: a constantly sloping road in three sections
supported by pillars of increasing heights. She then
constructs the road.

The progress of the anticipatory scheme is clear. BRU
explicitly notes that if you want to avoid mistakes, you have
to start at the bottom, that is, at the beginning of the road and
not at the mountain. As soon as she has given up the idea of
making a staircase, FAV sketches her proposed road and then
builds it. So these subjects no longer make any fundamental

mistakes and only need to correct minor errors regarding the incline.

Reactions at stage III are more or less the same as at level IIB, except that the children pay more attention to the accuracy of their solutions (for example, the location of the pillars, wedging of the bricks and strips, and weight of the road in relation to the strength of the pillars). This has no bearing on the processes leading to cognizance and its possible links with the retroactive or anticipatory regulations involved in the preceding findings.

Conclusions

It is interesting to compare a construction problem such as this one that may be solved (with varying degrees of accuracy) at any age, with a question involving the use of mobile objects, where the degree of practical success is also relatively constant. Of course, there are two important differences that closely condition cognizance of the actions and of the objects involved. Firstly, in the case of the construction, the objects are static: they are offered to the subject in an immobile state. In this experiment the bricks and strips of wood are selected by the child at will and he moves them only to arrange them in specific ways, whereupon they again become immobile; the solution of the problem is not dependent on the kinetics or dynamics of these movements, but only on the child's final arrangement of the objects. By contrast, when mobile objects are involved, it is their movements that are important, and the solution is largely dependent on the subject's skill in making them move and in adapting their movement to the goal. Secondly, and this is equally important, when the objects are mobile, the sequence of the subject's actions is relatively brief and dictated by the way the objects move, which very young subjects sometimes hardly notice, but which increases in importance in the subjects' eyes as they become more advanced. In the case of the constructions, on the other hand, the subject is free to combine the materials at will, as far as this is feasible, which results in a great many possible constructions. Consequently, the sequence of actions is far longer and more diverse—an essential dimension of the behavior that is the history itself of this sequence, including the reasons for the adopted order.

If we consider the subject's cognizance of the situation, the first of the above differences may give the impression of radical opposition. When the object is mobile, the subject does not immediately know how he succeeded: he needs a long analysis of the results of the action (observations of the object) in order to understand the movements that he has carried out and their interactions with those of the object (pressure on the ping-pong ball, direction taken by the sling, and the like). But when he is making something, the subject always knows what he wants to do with the object and can do it, or at least, if he cannot (strip too short, insecure staircase, and so on), he sees why immediately. So with the immobile objects there appears to be perfect cognizance at all levels, while with the mobile objects this is achieved only by stages, and the levels of achievement of cognizance differ one from the other to a far greater extent than do the levels of achievement of the action itself.

The situation is quite different when it is the sequence of the subject's actions in each case that is compared, since what has just been said concerns only each specific action and not the successive links, which may be more or less systematic or may be devoid of any internal order. When mobile objects are involved there is no problem, since the sequences are rapid and merely constitute a simple adaptation to the object. However, in the case of the constructions, the children's responses clearly point to a fundamental finding: when the subject passes from one action to another, the fact that he knows what he wants to do and sees the result of his action (failure or success) does not mean that he knows the method he has followed or the reasons for all the changes he has made in it. In fact, the more the subject's actions are governed by an overall strategy, the higher his level of cognizance will be, because such an overall strategy can result only from sufficient conceptualization from the outset of what the problem is all about. In the case of haphazard trial and error, however, the subject becomes conscious of the fact that he has gone wrong and knows what he is going to try next, but does not know where it was that he went wrong (whether he misunderstood the question or incorrectly set about answering it).

In this respect, it is instructive to compare the recollections after a week at the different levels. At level IA, ERI simply says, *There was a doll who had to climb onto a box.* He forgets his starting point and is unaware of the reasons and consequences of this oversight. BOS, even though he started from the right place, recollects only *a (vertical) ladder so that we didn't slip* and horizontal strips of wood. At level IB, BER's drawings show some good solutions, although these are in no way comparable to the towers he built initially; he makes no attempt to find out where he had gone wrong at the beginning of the session. At stage II, on the other hand, it is striking to witness the subjects recalling from memory the reasons for their actions (MAU in IIA), the precautions observed (RIA, IIA), and finally the method (BRU, IIB), which reveals a far more advanced level of cognizance of actual sequence of the actions.

Briefly, in the situations described in this chapter, a distinction must be drawn among the four possible areas of cognizance and of conceptualized observation.

(a) There is conceptualization of the question and the relevant data. It could be maintained that these are levels of understanding and not of cognizance. However, when you say to a child that a doll or a car must start from a particular place and go to the top of a mountain M, he has no difficulty understanding the instruction. Thus when ERI says, *There was a doll who had to climb onto* [M], forgetting where he is supposed to start and so the fact that the road has to go between the starting point and M, this reveals a process consistent with a cognizance initially centered on the result of the act, rather than one embracing the preliminary conditions also. Of course, it is indeed possible that a child may not understand the question, and as Seymour Papert said during a discussion at our Center of Genetic Epistemology, "The child always correctly answers the question he has asked himself," but why does he see no difference between the question he is asked and that which results from his distorting assimilation? In this respect the problem stated in the instructions and the objects forming the experimental materials are comparable to observable features, of which the subject at first retains only certain aspects (bricks useful for making towers but not pillars, and so on), and this therefore constitutes the first area of cognizance and conceptualized observation.

(b) The subjects' various ideas on how the problem may be solved must be considered.

(c) His successive ways of carrying them out are also significant. Both (b) and (c) give rise to cognizance of the particular action and to clearly grasped observations, even though the links between them, the formulation of the actual problem, and the assimilation of all the other items of pertinent information have yet to be established. (It is because of this that the subject cannot know why he has gone wrong.) However, cognizance in areas (a) and (d) eventually leads him to realize why he made a particular mistake.

(d) There is finally the realm of cognizance of the connections between successive actions and the reasons for their variations. Here lies the crucial point in the conceptualization of the constructions, and examination of it will lead to solution of the problem outlined above in stage II. The young subjects' first consideration is how to climb to the top of M, and they forget all about the first part of the road (just as in experiments involving the use of scales, young children often try to use just one of the pans, forgetting all about the other) — hence a series of haphazard trial-and-error solutions when they have to link the finish to the start. At level IB, the subjects are eventually more or less successful (but only after a similar process), while from level IIA on, children consider the relationship between the start and the finish from the outset, revealing the beginnings of an understanding of the concept of slope as a link between height and length.

How does this come about? The first clear difference between these reactions and those of the less advanced children is that the latter carry out an action, note its failure or partial success, correct it, and then establish new relationships as a function of these corrections. Although a stage

II subject may go through the same motions, he performs them in his head before actually doing anything with his hands, so his corrections are more or less complete before he starts building the road. Subsequently, these interiorized trial-and-error attempts themselves become unnecessary and the solution is predicted as soon as the problem has been understood. However, while these interiorizations appear natural, we still do not know under what conditions they take place. The fact that the interiorization of the actions in the child's mind presupposes cognizance of the actions is obvious, since this cognizance itself constitutes a conceptualization. However, another condition is necessary before the child is able to progress from interiorization of actions to immediate prediction of solutions; the cognizance must cover not only each individual action, but also the sequence of these actions—what appear to be the most haphazard trial-and-error procedures are, to some extent, already directed not only from the outside by the law of effect, but also by the relationships that the child establishes between the results of his successive interpretations of the situations. It is this progressive cognizance of the connections between successive actions and the reasons for their variations (item d) that is observed throughout the stages described above; while this variety is different from that which characterizes the second and third areas of cognizance, it is no less essential when it comes to actions involving construction.

6 Tiddlywinks

When a child has to carry out a fairly complex action in order to solve a practical problem, his cognizance of the situation proceeds fairly systematically from the periphery to the center, that is, from the results of the action to its internal mechanism. If the action itself is simple but the subject has to use a device of perhaps greater complexity, he has to make a series of successive interpretations linked to the successes or failures of his practical intelligence; from these interpretations he must extract the relevant law.

The first such interpretation by the subject naturally consists in an answer (we shall call it solution A) to the question of knowing "why" the target has been hit or missed. The second occurs in the subject's subsequent attempt to delineate solution A—in other words, his progression from the "why" to the "how." This distinction may remain completely relative, and his preoccupation with the "how" may consist simply in seeking the "why" of A, thus the "why" of the "why"

With the collaboration of Catherine Dami.

or the cause of the cause (our solution *B*), which is tantamount to extending the problem or, more precisely, to extending the relevant field of causality by introducing the articulated question. Clearly, sooner or later will come the "how" (thus still the "why") of *B*, resulting in solution *C*, which refines or throws more light on *B* and *A*; one could go on ad infinitum. This is not specifically applicable to errors or to corrections or regulations pertinent to *A*, *B*, and so forth, since the general process remains the same, with the passage from solution *N* to solution *N* + 1 almost always resulting from both refinement and correction.

However, the problem is to establish whether the order of succession of the interpretations (or solutions *A*, *B*, and *C*) obeys a law. As the *A* solution is only the reflection of the more direct and global relation between the action and the goal to be attained, it would seem that the *B* and *C* solutions must go behind it to the preliminary conditions determining the possibilities of *B*, then of *C*, and so on, in the sense of an analysis of the internal mechanisms characterizing the interactions between the objects and the subject's acts. In the case of the action, this would constitute a general process extending the passage from the periphery to the center, which is not surprising since in its causality the latter already obeys physical laws. However, it constitutes more than this general process, since the greater the distance from the periphery, the greater the distance from the observable features of the situation, and the closer the child to a grasp of the coordinations; as for the action itself, it involves the general coordinations characterized by logicomathematical links. If such a law exists, then an essential dimension must involve the translation of reality into logical and mathematical, or at least geometrical, terms.

The research described in this chapter concerns a well-known children's pastime, the game of tiddlywinks, where the idea is to take one counter and press it on the edge of another, to make the latter jump. Because this is extremely simple, the research centered less on cognizance of the movements actually carried out and more on conceptualization of the action in general and, above all, of its results on the object. This experiment therefore provides a suitable framework for consideration of the problem outlined above.

The subjects are given one large and one small counter and a fairly wide box and are instructed to make the small counter jump into the box. As soon as the child has done this (and on a carpeted floor subjects succeed fairly rapidly), he is asked to describe the event in detail: his hand movements, point of pressure of one counter on the other (subsequently referred to simply as pressure point), positions of the counters when the box is directly in front of the counters and when it is moved to one side (in their drawings young children frequently do not alter the relative positions of the two counters), path taken by the small counter to the box, and so on. The interviewer requests a verbal description, and the child generally illustrates this by miming and by drawings.

Subsequently, the counters and the box are placed on a table; the child is asked to predict what will happen when there is no carpet and then to try it out for himself. Of course, the counter does not jump, but slides, and when he has described this, the child is asked to explain the differences in the two situations and so determine the role of the carpet. He is again encouraged to draw the respective positions of the two counters at the moment of pressure (both on the carpet and on the table). The idea is to find out whether the subject observes that the counter makes a slight dent in the carpet and, if so, what conclusion he draws from it (care is taken to avoid any suggestion or interpretation of this dent on the part of the interviewer).

Finally, the child is presented with two boxes of matches (one the normal size and one smaller), a pawn from a game of chess, and a role of adhesive tape and asked to predict, through analogy with the tiddlywinks situation, what would happen if he were to press on the edge of these objects (with his finger). After his attempt, he is asked to describe what happened and explain why the matchboxes and the rest fall over backward instead of being propelled forward like counters. In particular, the interviewer tries to ascertain (through drawings and the like) how the child pictures the movements and resulting positions of the matchboxes.

The older subjects are questioned also about the ping-pong ball (see Chapter 3) to see whether they show any sign of connecting it with the problems described in this chapter.

Stage I

Examples (Level IA)

FLO (4,6): Try and get one of the pawns (her word) into the box. (She puts the small counter on the large one and then presses down on the former, with all her attention on the movement of her hand and none on the target.) Where did it go? *Onto the table.* And what about the box? (She first misses it and then gets the counter in it.) How did you do it? *I pressed very hard.* Can you do it on the table? (She tries.) *No, because it slides.* What does it do on the carpet? *It jumps up high.* Why? *Because the table isn't soft.* Her drawing of the counter's trajectory on the carpet shows a horizontal line, rising slightly as it reaches the box. The counter's trajectory on the table is again depicted as a horizontal line, but this time it stops in front of the box. The interviewer then asks FLO to try the same thing with the matchbox. She tries. *It fell because it doesn't go into the box.* What about that one (small matchbox)? *It's going to jump into the box.* Why does it go backward? *It's not flattened* (= thin). Her drawings of the counter situation show the pressure point with the two counters juxtaposed instead of superposed, and the relative positions of the counters are not changed when the box is moved to one side.

SYL (5,0) first uses her finger to push one counter toward the box. The interviewer suggests she use a second counter. *I took a middle-size one, then I went right around like that* (as if running her finger around the edge of the counter were tantamount to pressing). After succeeding in making the counter jump, the interviewer asks her what the counter did. *It jumped. I took a middle-size one and I made it jump.* Try it on the table. (Shows surprise.)

It doesn't jump, it just goes along. What does it do on the carpet? *It jumps better.* What does the carpet do? *It makes it jump a lot better.* Can you do the same thing with the matchbox? *It will jump too.* (Tries.) *No, it turns.* How about those (two five-franc pieces)? *That will be like the little tiddly-wink.* (Tries.) *No, it spins around and around also.* Why? *They aren't all the same.* In her drawings, the trajectories are straight, the pressure point is marked by juxtaposition instead of superposition, and she cannot indicate the relative positions of the counters when the box is moved to one side.

Examples (Level IB)

SEV (5,0) immediately takes one counter and uses it to propel the other, but without aiming properly at the box. (When the counter goes too far, she alters the angle of the active counter, to make it a right angle, and gets it nearer the target.) And what if you had only one counter? *I pressed with my finger, that works.* Where do you press when you use another counter? *There* (edge). *You can also put it there* (up to the middle). How? *It's hard, but you can still do it.* I'm going to try. Will you tell me what to do? *You press there* (edge) *with the big one.* (The interviewer presses in the middle.) *No* (that won't work), *it's because you're putting it in the middle.* (The interviewer holds the big counter the other way around, so that it points in the opposite direction.) *No, it will go to the other side.* Can we put another box between the counter and the box we've got to reach? (The interviewer does so.) *You can't, you'd have to go around it.* (The obstacle is removed.) *It's difficult because it's so far away.* (Succeeds.) *I've pressed very hard.* (In her drawing the trajectory is shown as a straight horizontal line, which rises steeply near the box and drops over the edge.) *It can go like that as well* (correct mime of a jump). After trying on the table: *No, it doesn't jump very well, because the carpet is all soft and the table isn't.*

SEV is questioned again at (5,4): Where do you press? *There* (edge). And there (in the middle)? *No, that's too far.* Will it go on the table? *Don't know.* (Tries.) *No, it slides.* Why? *Because the carpet isn't slippery, it's fatter and thicker.* After trying with the matchbox: *It goes the wrong way around, it isn't round and it's heavier.* (And then with the large pawn.) *It comes back; I don't know why—it's thick—it stays back.* In her drawings the trajectories are shown as horizontal lines; in the case of the carpet, there is a more or less vertical rise just before the box, then a dropping down over the edge; in that of the table, *the counter stays on the floor.* The pressure point is correctly marked by superposition and intersection, and the relative positions of the counters are correct when the box is moved to the side.

CHA (5,6) has initial reactions very similar to those of SEV. When a second box is put halfway between the counter and the target box, he fails to get the counter into the latter *because you've got the box* (obstacle) *here,* but he succeeds when a larger target box is placed at the same distance. *It's easier because it's opposite.* How did you do it? *I made it jump high; I made it go farther.* Can you make your hand go the way the tiddlywink went? (Horizontal trajectory, followed by a steep climb into the box.) *It's near the box that it climbs up and gets inside.* Interestingly, when it is the interviewer who makes the counter jump, he draws the trajectory correctly as a wide curve, but when it is he himself who activates the counter, the drawing conforms to the preceding mime.

CLA (5,9): *I put this other one on top and then it jumps.* Where did you press? *At the edge: it slides and then it jumps.* How about on the table? *It won't go; it goes below the box.* Why? *Don't know, it's harder.* (He comments on his own drawings.) *It goes straight* (horizontal) *and then it jumps* (into the box). (The pressure point is correctly shown as an intersection. He explains what happens to the matchbox.) *It goes backward because it's too big.*

PRI (6,6) has the same reactions, but her drawings are splendid. She draws in the counter at the start of the trajectory, then puts it in again at the base of the box (with a horizontal line connecting the two) then again on the top edge of the box (vertical line connecting these last two), then finally inside the box at the bottom of the same side (vertical line connecting the relevant counters). In the case of the table, the trajectory is the same until it reaches the box, where it stops. The pressure points are depicted as intersections: *The tiddlywinks touch each other, then the big one goes a bit above the little one.* The relative positions of the counters are correct when the box is moved. When asked to try the same thing with the matchboxes and other materials: *It turns over because it isn't round, it's too heavy,* and so on. The ball, on the other hand, is round, but *I don't know why it doesn't jump, it rolls. The tiddlywink jumps because it's flat and round; the ball is round and not flat.*

MAR (7,0) still aims badly when the trajectory is not straight in front of her (box moved to the side). He draws a horizontal trajectory, which rises sharply on reaching the box. The pressure point is correct *because at the edge it jumps.*

DUR (7,4): *I've put the big one right at the edge, then it* (the little one) *jumps in the air and falls into the box. If you press in the middle it goes up a little bit but not a lot . . . if you do it hard it spurts in the air.* Nevertheless, her drawing first shows a trajectory near the ground rising sharply close to the box. Then, having seen what happens on the table (horizontal trajectory), she correctly draws the trajectory in the case of the carpet and so reaches level IIA.

So all these subjects make the counter jump and realize that it jumps because of the action of pressing, but their cognizance of the situation remains inadequate. At level IA, conceptualization of the pressure itself remains relatively undifferentiated from that of the simple push, even though the relevant actions are clearly different and this difference is noted verbally (*I pressed very hard*, at four and a half years). In fact, SYL's mime does not show the partial superposition (intersection) of the active counter on the passive, but only a contact of the first with the edge of the second, and in their drawings FLO and SYL mark the pressure point by a juxtaposition of the counters. From five years on, however, the level IB subjects have no difficulty in representing the partial superposition by a small intersection of two circles. At level IA, the children cannot alter the relative positions of the counters when the target box is moved to the side, whereas at level IB subjects not only succeed in this action, but also are able to depict it on paper.

The most remarkable finding at both levels IA and IB concerns the subjects' conception of the counter's trajectory between its start and its arrival in the box. They all picture this trajectory as a more or less horizontal line, clearly revealing their continuing inability to differentiate, when it comes to conceptualization of the action, between pressing on something to make it jump and simply pushing it along: however, they know it must jump because it clears the edge of the box; hence they imagine the counter's sudden rise as it reaches the box. It is not that these children find it difficult to draw a curve: when CHA is asked to mime the trajectory he gives the same response, and CLA (like CHA) even specifies verbally *it goes straight and then it jumps*. Furthermore, CHA draws a fine curve when asked what the interviewer's counter did, but reverts to the straight line when it comes to his own counter's trajectory. This clearly shows that he assimilates his own action as a sort of push, while as a mere spectator to the interviewer's motions, he has fewer preconceived ideas about what must happen and thinks the adult capable of more complicated actions. Thirdly, SEV and CHA either refuse to try, or else fail, to get the counter into the target box when an obstacle is placed between them and the box, but succeed at the same distance when it is removed.

This conception of a straight trajectory, which rises suddenly in front of the box, indicates a difficulty in understanding (and so conceptualizing) an action effected by the subject himself and recalls two other sets of findings relative to the action of pressing. The first concerns the experiment conducted by Professor Henriques (Chapter 3) in which children are asked to press on a ping-pong ball to make it go forward and come back. It was found that even children far older than those classified at level IB in this experiment think the ball rolls forward and then rolls back: in this case the translation is not wrong (sliding), but the children do not see that it is combined with a rotation, any more than they see here the need for a curved trajectory. Secondly, in the case of the catapults that we shall discuss in Chapter 10, until level IB the projection of the object is also conceived as a translation, because the part played by the rotation of the bar responsible for the projection is not understood. Briefly, in all these cases, a successful action leads to an adequate cognizance only to the extent that the conceptualization remains in conformity with the preconceived kinetic or causal ideas, which govern the subject's understanding of what in fact he carries out differently.

It might be argued that the movements of the counter, of the ping-pong ball, or of the plasticine ball in the case of the catapult, are no longer dependent on the subject once the action of pressing has been accomplished, and that it is then a question of observing the object and no longer one of cognizance of the actual action. Nevertheless, were the subject to differentiate better between the actions of pressing and pushing, he would not make these mistakes. Generally, it is his observation of what happens to the object as a result of the action that leads the child to cognizance of the action itself. If, in the three particular cases compared here, this awareness is not heightened, then there must be something preventing it (for example the part played by the preconceived ideas).

As for the role of the carpet in the projection of the counter and the backward somersault of the thicker objects, these subjects simply refer to the differences in texture or shape: the table is not *soft* (= it is hard), the boxes are *not round* or *too heavy*, and so forth, but without any causal understanding even when the thickness of the boxes is appreciated.

Stage II

At level IIA (achieved by some six-and-a-half-year-olds, but generally speaking from seven to eight years of age) the trajectories of the counter are conceived and drawn as curves.

Examples (Level IIA)

GRA (6,6): *It doesn't jump immediately; you've got to press first, on the edge of the little one; it stays in the air for a bit.* And if you do it on the table? *It doesn't jump, it slides; the table's smooth.* He takes two pieces of cardboard representing enlarged counters and simulates what happens with the counters: on the carpet you press on the edge of the counter and first it goes up a few millimeters remaining horizontal, then it goes off along a straight incline until it gets to the top edge of the box and falls inside. On the table, when you press it, it doesn't jump, it moves forward horizontally. When asked if it is possible to do the same thing with the matchboxes, he says, *No, they would have to be round and completely flat.*

MOS (6,3 advanced) succeeds after a few attempts. And on the table? *It won't jump.* Why? *The table's hard while the carpet's soft; on the table you can't press: it doesn't jump.* (Tries.) *It slides because the table's hard.* Does the carpet help it to jump? *Yes, you press on the carpet.* And the counter? *It's got to be hard to jump.* And if you press in the middle? *It stays where it is, the carpet gets a little bit squashed.* And when you press on the side of the tiddlywink? *The little one goes up the side where the big one isn't.* (He draws the big tiddlywink flat and the little one slanting.) And what happens on the table, does it go up as well? *Yes, a little bit, then it slides.* He tries with the matchboxes and when *they all go backward,* says, *they go back over my finger because they're heavy.* His drawing of the counter situation shows two successive curves, as if the counter touched the ground halfway along and bounced back up toward the box.

GUR (7,6): *I pressed on top and it went off.* How? *It slid and it went off. When you press, it goes like that* (incline from the horizontal position). Does the carpet help in any way? *No.* And on the table? *It's going to go off.* Will it go into the box? *Maybe.* (Attempts.) *It doesn't work, it slides.* Like on the carpet? *No, the carpet helps it and the table doesn't, because the table slides and the carpet doesn't: it sticks and it goes with the tufts of the carpet as if there were a brake.* Does it just brake? *Yes, the table's hard and the carpet's soft.* With the matchbox, GUR says that it can fall forward or backward *because there's a little corner* (angle), *it's not rounded.* In the case of the ping-pong ball: *It's going to roll* (forward) *and sometimes it will go backward.* The counter's trajectory is drawn as a splendid curve.

GIS (7,11): *First you press: it waits until you press before it's sent off, it goes up in the air a little.* And on the table? *It can't go; it mustn't be smooth.* Does the carpet do something? *Yes, it helps the little one because it's rough. That makes it go up; while if it's smooth, it slides.* With the matchbox:

It's heavier, it turns over, it's also because it's rectangular. Which is more important? *The shape and thickness.* With the ping-pong ball: it rolls forward, *then it comes back backward . . . it turns back on itself; there are the tufts of the carpet that stop it.*

KAU (8,6) tries on both the carpet and the table: *On the carpet it jumps, on the other it slides.* What use is the carpet? *I don't know.*

PUG (9,0) compares the two surfaces: *It slides* (on the table) *and it doesn't make it. The carpet's rough.*

Thus these subjects all understand that when you press down on one side of the counter, the other side rises and goes off at a slant, with its path forming a curve to the box. There is then the question of why this is possible on the carpet and not on the table. A level IIB subject sees the reason and can depict it on paper: the pressure of the counter results in compression of the carpet pile in such a way that the counter is sent off at an angle and so rises; the table, on the other hand, resists the pressure and the counter slides horizontally. The preceding subjects, although approaching the idea that the edge of the counter sinks into the carpet (the carpet is *soft*) do not yet picture the situation correctly and simply credit the carpet with the dynamic role of prolonging the pressure to which it is itself subjected. This complex role consists simultaneously, as GUR says clearly, in *helping* the counter to jump and to *brake*—the significance of the braking being to prevent the counters from sliding and so allow the large counter to press on the small one without the latter's immediately escaping, before it is lifted and sent upward. The youngest subject, MOS, who comes nearest to realizing that the fact that the counter sinks into the carpet is significant for the direction it takes, nevertheless still sees the carpet's major role as that of allowing the counter to be pressed down without its sliding away. When he says that the carpet is *a little bit squashed,* he is describing the case where the counter is pressed in the middle and stays put, while he appears to think that the big tiddlywink, when it is pressed down on the side of the little one, is solely responsible for the rise of the latter, no part being played by the dent in the carpet. GRA (the least advanced subject) even thinks that the resistance of the carpet enables the counter initially to rise while remaining horizontal before going off obliquely. GIS, like GUR, sees the carpet simultaneously as a help and a brake: it is *rough* and enables the counter to rise without sliding. KAU and PUG have similar ideas.

Between this complex scheme of projection with braking, or the slightly more advanced one of retention allowing the counter to rise, and the accurate pictorial representation of the situation (level IIB), are all the intermediate cases — hence the absence of a clear boundary between levels IIA and IIB, although the extreme cases in each are, of course, very different. The following subjects exemplify the transitional cases where, unlike the level IIA subjects, the children refer to the counter's sinking into the carpet, but interpret this in various ways.

> PEI (7,7) says, *On the carpet, it's soft, the tiddlywink jumps; on the table it doesn't jump, it goes forward.* Why does it jump on the carpet? *Because the carpet's thick and soft, it sinks in.* And on the table? *It goes forward, it isn't soft.* So does the carpet help it to jump? *Yes, it sinks in.* What does it do then? *Nothing.* However, the box is *too heavy, it comes back backward.* The ping-pong ball *rolls, you press, then it comes back.*

> ISA (8,3) tries to make the counter jump on the table: *Some day I'll do it. At the moment, I can't.* Does the carpet do anything? *On the carpet you can make the weight and the tiddlywink sink in and because it's sunk in, that makes the tiddlywink jump . . . the table's too hard, the tiddlywink slides.* As for the matchbox: *It falls back because it's heavy and fat; the most important thing is that it's fat.*

Examples (Level IIB)

LAU (7,11) (classified as IIB despite his doubts): What did the counter do? *It goes up a little bit, it's the big one that makes it go up and jump.* And on the table? *It'll jump.* (Attempts it.) *No, the table's smooth, the carpet's soft.* What does the carpet do? *It helps, it gets flattened* (= becomes indented). *The table stays straight, it's more solid, the tiddlywink doesn't jump.*

DAM (7,5 advanced): *When I press, that gives it force and makes it go up; the carpet makes it press a bit more.* How? (He draws a V-shaped dip.) *There's a place on the carpet that's squashed, then when the button goes, it* (the carpet) *goes back flat again.* Does that help the button? *Yes, on the table, that gives it force, but it doesn't make it jump. On the carpet the tiddlywink slopes, on the table it doesn't.* With the matchbox: *If I press, it puts it upright and it makes it turn when you give it a bit of a push.* The ping-pong ball *just rolls, then after a bit, it comes back again; I don't know why: it stopped, then came back.*

SLA (8,1): If you press in the middle, it doesn't go up, but *if I press down, the little tiddlywink will go up because you press and the carpet's soft. On the table, if I press, it slides instead of jumping because the table's fixed. You can't make the table go down.* With the matchbox: *It sinks in there and the other end goes up, because it's heavy and thick.*

WAR (8,2): With the counter on the table *it's harder, it can't get up . . . , bounce up.* And the carpet? *It's a bit elastic, it's more supple.* But why does it jump? *It sinks in and it's better; it makes a sort of little slope and it goes off. There's a bigger hollow in the carpet.* And why does it go off? *It's because you press on the table it goes off like* → *and not* ↗. With the matchbox: *It doesn't work. Perhaps it's because it's heavy; when I press, it rolls over back-ward.*

CAR (9,9): *It's hollow, it goes in* (draws a slope). The matchbox *turns over on the way, it turns,* because of its weight and square shape.

BLA (10,7): *The carpet goes in and after the pawn's gone off, it comes up again: it helps the tiddlywink to bounce up,* but the drawing ∨ shows a dent as opposed to that of the table situation where he draws a ＼＿. He says the matchbox *won't work because it is too thick.*

SAS (11,11) has the same reaction and similar drawings. The matchbox *will go anywhere, it'll stand up.* Why doesn't it jump? *It's too heavy, too fat.* (The ping-pong ball rolls as it goes forward, then comes back) *because the carpet's rough, it stops the ball and it comes back.* Why does it come back? *Because it's round.*

PUR (12,10): *It goes in, slides* (on the slope), *and goes off,* while on the table *it goes along the ground and just slides.* But the matchbox comes back because it's *bigger and heavier,* and the ping-pong ball *comes back; it could be in the air.*

So although the subjects at the intermediate level, PEI and ISA, talk about the counter's sinking into the carpet, they do not seem to have grasped why the resulting dent helps the counter to jump. They make a connection between the dent and the jump, but cannot define it and explain its causal nature. The level IIB subjects, on the other hand, are more specific, in that they refer to the sloping side of the dent in the carpet resulting from the pressure of the counter. LAU speaks clearly on this point when he contrasts the carpet which *gets flattened* with the table that *stays straight,* with the former forcing the tiddlywink to rise. DAM and WAR are even more explicit when they talk about the *slope* down which the tiddlywink rolls in the dent or the *little slope* that governs the direction it takes. The other subjects reveal their understanding of the situation through their drawings, and although BLA and SAS add a bounce, they clearly mark the wide V-shaped dent in the carpet in contrast to the $\searrow\!\!\!\!\_$ representing the counter's departure on the table.

This change in interpretation of the carpet from something that simultaneously pushes and brakes the counter (preventing it from sliding as it would do on a table) to the correct interpretation of the V-shaped dent in the carpet that forces the counter up at an angle is interesting. The younger children think that the curved trajectory from the carpet to the box results simply from the pressure put on the small counter by the large one, so the significance is purely dynamic. For the more advanced subjects, the parabolic trajectory constitutes the extension of the *little slope* (WAR) caused by the dent—that is, a geometric and directional representation has now been added to the dynamic interpretation that naturally remains necessary. The progress resulting in the child's conception of the counter's trajectory as a curve, owing to its starting off at an angle because of the dent in the carpet, is reminiscent of the similar change in interpretation encountered in the catapult experiment to be reported in Chapter 10.

However, again as in the case of the catapult, children find it more difficult to picture the rotations than the curves: so these level IIB subjects who have an adequate conception of the counter's angled departure on the carpet are still rather hazy about the rotation of the matchboxes and the rest, the backward somersault remaining rather difficult to interpret. Of course, they all point to the part played by the thickness of the matchbox, but they also mention its weight and shape, and above all cannot portray the rotations adequately in their drawings—it is not until stage III that subjects manage this.

Stage III and Conclusions

Examples

DEV (10,10): The counter *goes up because you press on top of it and that makes a little hole* (he points to the slope). (He predicts that the matchbox will turn over backward because of its thickness.) What's the thickness got to do with it? *When you press, it touches there* (back) *and it turns over backward.* His drawing shows the progressive incline of the short back side, and the stages of a complete rotation; but there is a mistake in that the eighth position is identical to the first, with respect to both shape, which is true, and location, which is not. Of the ping-pong ball he says: *It will go forward then backward. When you press, the ball goes like that* (backward rotation) *and because you push, it goes forward.*

GIL (10,4): *When you press, the front of the counter goes up, the carpet goes in a little bit.* The matchbox, however, will not go forward *because here* (short back side) *it goes up* (= it's high) *and if you press the front here* (the other end), *it will go higher; the box will go up and stay upright.* (Attempts it.) *It comes back: here* (bottom of back side) *the bottom sticks, it doesn't slide, it sticks to the carpet and goes backward.* When he is asked to demonstrate this rotation of the back side, he uses his hand to hold the bottom of it and shows its progressive incline leading to rotation of the whole box. Of the ping-pong ball, GIL, like DEV, says that if *you press here, the ball turns like that* (inversely): *it slides forward, then comes back.*

FUT (12,0): *The carpet sinks in, then it slides; the carpet helps a bit* (= slope). *The table can't sink in and the tiddlywink can't get up.* As for the matchbox, *it's going to turn over, it's wide.* His drawing shows a five-stage rotation, but on the spot, pivoting along the width of the small side.

OLI (12,2) refers to the carpet's *bounce,* but subsequently specifies that the tiddlywink *can't go forward* (slide), *it goes off at a slant* (because of the dent). When shown the matchbox, he says, *It might turn over.* Why? (He demonstrates in slow motion.) *This side goes over backward*, thus rotation about the short back side. As for the ping-pong ball: *When you push it, it goes forward, then it comes back; the pressure you put on it when you press it makes it go forward first, then* (the inverse rotation) *it's stronger than the other and it comes back.*

All these children therefore realize that the counter *goes off at a slant* (OLI) because of the dent in the carpet. In fact, it is most interesting that the children do not grasp the significance of the slope until quite late, and there are similar findings in the catapult experiment (Chapter 10). However, in both cases, this clearly precedes their understanding of the details of the rotations, with these last children (stage III) being the first to be able to depict the rotation of the matchbox. The less advanced children, it is true, do see a close relation between this somersault and the thickness of the match-boxes, but they cannot describe it. The stage III subjects say that when you press on one side, it goes down and results in rotation of the whole object. GIL even gives an explanation that directly links this process to that of the counter's forward projection: in the latter case, *when you press* (at the back), *the front . . . goes up* and in the case of the matchbox, the same thing happens (*the box will go up*) but, as the back *sticks, it doesn't slide* and the front keeps on going up, leading to the upright position of the box (predicted before the attempt), then the fall backward. Assuredly, progress has been made, since the subjects now understand that when the object is thin it is projected forward, with the upward direction caused by the dent in the carpet, whereas when the object is thick, the pressure on the back makes this part of the object stay on the spot and raises the front.

Children generally grasp the details of the rotation at the same time as the reverse rotation and translation of the ping-pong ball, and it is interesting to compare the reactions at levels IIB and III in the two experiments.

To conclude this glimpse into the stages of conceptualization of the game of tiddlywinks, we should try to understand the reasons for them and for their slow evolution. The child's actions (getting a counter into a box, making it slide on the table, or making a box of matches do a somersault) are successfully carried out at level IA (age four) and remain exactly the same until stage III. Why are they fully understood only around eleven or twelve years of age? Furthermore, when one studies the final solutions, there is no clear impression of a radical novelty but, rather, a simple explanation of what was implicitly understood almost from the outset. To say that there is a *dent* in the carpet (level IIB) instead of simply that the carpet is *soft* or *not hard* (levels IA and B), or to show that the matchbox rotates about the short side that is pressed instead of simply saying that it *turns* backward (level IA), seems to represent only slight progress in description rather than something really new in the child's understanding.

In actuality, this evolution is more complex than is at first apparent, and the fact that the material actions involved remain the same from stage I to stage III makes it more fascinating. The most interesting findings concern the exchanges between what the subject observes regarding his own action (cognizance in the strict sense of the word) and his observations of the object (thus of the results of the action), with increasing intervention of the coordinations—the source of which has yet to be discovered.

Right from level IA, there is the problem of the cognizance of the actual action: the subject presses on the little counter with a bigger one, but describes this pressure as if there were simple contact through juxtaposition without superposition. In so doing he does not, of course, correctly observe the objects, since there is a relation between the two counters, but cognizance of the action itself nevertheless plays a part, actually a distorting or inhibiting part. The subject, although he uses different words, does not distinguish in this particular situation between the two possible actions of pushing and pressing (this does not necessarily occur in all situations despite analogies with the catapult and the ping-pong ball experiments). In point of fact, the action of pressing, studied in greater detail in a later book,[1] has many facets. You can

1. *Réussir et comprendre* (Presses Universitaires de France, Paris, 1974; forthcoming in English), which contains studies on playing-card houses, counterweights, and the like.

press on or against an object (or press one object on or against another) either to make it go forward or fall when pushed, or, by contrast, to make the object, or oneself, stay in the same place (or to hold the object pressing against the second one). So it is hardly surprising that the action in this tiddlywink situation is incorrectly analyzed at level IIA, particularly because here the child has to distinguish between pressing against and pressing on, and in this last case it is not a question of simply holding back the passive counter, but of making it jump. At level IB, however, the action of pressing is more accurately localized (the children draw the active counter as partly covering the passive one, that is, partial superposition) and better understood — corresponding progress in the house-of-cards experiment occurs with cognizance of the slopes — through an initial attempt to relate the action of pressing and its spatial conditions.

Briefly, the first level is characterized by a global (or total) act directly linking the motor action to the ultimate goal, but without the child's cognizance of this act (thus its conceptualization) being sufficiently analytical for him to realize the difference between pushing and pressing. When level IB subjects differentiate between the two actions, it might be thought that it is their more accurate observation of the object that leads them to distinguish between a partial superposition (pressing) and simple juxtaposition (pushing). Why do level IA children not see this when those at level IB do? What has changed? Clearly, while the juxtaposition or superposition of the counters is an observable feature of the object, it is also related to the subject's actions (pushing against or pressing on). Furthermore, while the latter may thus be termed an observable feature of the action, of which verification is facilitated by, if not dependent on, observation of the object, distinction between pushing and pressing requires an ability to relate one to the other. How do children become able to do this?

One can put forward the general hypothesis that cognizance of an action depends on the subject's active adjustment of it. This differs from automatic regulation in that the subject actively makes decisions about his course of action; he chooses what to do and, in so doing, must become involved in an appraisal of the pros and cons of any action, which thus leads him sooner or later consciously to relate the various factors in the situation. Because in this particular experiment the action is generally successfully accomplished by the youngest subjects, at this first level there is no question of active adjustment. But level IB sees the intervention of choices: the subjects encounter and solve the problem of where to press on the passive counter when the position of the target box (or that of the counters in relation to the box) is altered. This implies that they are beginning to relate the action to its spatial conditions. It could thus be this beginning of the spatialization of the action of pressing that explains the more acute awareness of the situation revealed by these subjects' differentiation between the actions of pushing and pressing.

While at this level the differentiation is effective with regard to the action, it is not apparent in the children's drawings, where the trajectories at ground level are still translations (as would have been the case for a push), with a final jump into the box. At level IIA, the pressure of one counter on another is conceptualized—for the carpet situation in terms of a projection with a curved trajectory, while for the table problem the trajectory remains straight. Why have these subjects now grasped the curved trajectory and the fact that the role of the carpet is important? Of course, there is a link between the form of the trajectory and the carpet: it is because of the dent in the carpet, caused by the pressure of the passive counter, that the latter starts to rise as soon as the pressure is applied by means of the active one (and not just before it gets to the box)—hence the necessity for a trajectory linking this point of departure with the box, that is, a curved trajectory. The appreciation of the role of the carpet results from the separation of the initial global action of "pressing → making the counter jump" (depending on the surface in question) into the two actions of "pressing on contact with the carpet" or "pressing the counter onto the table." While the initial action consisted in linking the manipulation directly with the target, with no analysis of how this was to be done, the same applies to the action at this level IIA despite the improved conceptualization. In other words, the "cause," instead of comprising simply "pressing" has become "pressing with the help of the carpet," but this help is reduced to a partial delegation of the power of the hand, taking account of the observable properties of the carpet as opposed to those of the table. To put it another way, the carpet becomes capable simultaneously of helping the counter to rise and of holding it so that it can jump without sliding. These subjects are no more concerned about finding out how this is possible than were those at level IA about determining whether "making the counter jump" was the same as "pushing against" or "pressing on." They simply invoke the most obvious characteristics of the carpet (*soft* or *rough*); these features are sufficient to enable the carpet to fulfill its dynamic role of assisting the counter to go forward and brake. This type of undifferentiated dynamics characterizes the reactions to the catapult at the same level IIA.

However dependent this stage may be on the observable features of the object and of the actual action, it nevertheless involves a beginning of coordination: the carpet is dented by the subject's pressure on the large counter, which presses on the small one and makes the dent in the carpet, which in turn acts on the small counter. This set of transmissions, together with the triggering of an action in return, already constitutes a general causal coordination. So through which process does the subject progress to level IIB, where he tries to find out how things happen and comes to explain the phenomenon by means of the dent and the slope? He perceives nothing more than he did at level IIA, and although he draws the dent in the form of a wide V, he sees nothing new to force him to do this, which he could have done much earlier if it had been a question of simple observation. It thus seems that it is a partly inferential geometric coordination that attracts the subject's attention to observable features that he had previously ignored.

Finally, understanding of the rotation of the boxes at stage III must, of course, stem from the same mechanisms. It is not just a subtle difference in the child's observation of the situation, but the grasp of a necessary set of operatory coordinations, that makes him progress from saying simply that the box *will turn over backward* to giving a detailed analysis of the rotation.

To return now to the problem raised at the beginning of this chapter, it is clear that each of the passages from one level to the next is characterized by the subject's attempt to answer the "how" question:

(a) How does the active counter launch the passive one? The level IB answer is that there is partial superposition of the first on the second and not a simple push with the two counters side by side.

(b) How does the counter get into the box? The level IIA answer is that on the carpet the trajectory is curved from the outset and not, as in the case of the table, parallel to the latter.

(c) How does the curve start? The level IIB response evokes the dent in the carpet and the slanting position of the passive counter at the start.

(d) How is this effect modified when "thick" objects (such as matchboxes) are used instead of thin counters? The stage III answer shows how the angle of inclination gradually becomes greater until the box turns over backward.

Furthermore, it emerges from these findings that each of these "how" questions is in fact a new "why" question, but applied to the preceding interpretation and enlarging the system of causal relationships, which at the previous level were considered sufficient to provide the complete solution.

Since no progress regarding the action itself is made between level IA and stage III, the interest of these successive "how" questions lies in their revelation of a sort of adjustment analogous to that of the actions in situations that give rise to what are termed "trial-and-error responses," that is, where the action is not successfully carried out from level IA. However, in this experiment, the adjustments bear on the observable features and the coordinations, as each observation or attempt at relating the various factors rapidly encounters difficulties or disturbances requiring compensations. The ensuing progress leads, in this particular case, to a grasp of the geometric coordinations—which are, however, attributed to the objects, just as in other experiments the active adjustment of the actions themselves results in various forms of logico-mathematical coordinations. Regardless of whether actions are progressively adjusted in order to attain a goal (whence questions of the "how do we do it?" type) or whether it is the subject who adjusts to the actions of objects (whence questions of the "how do they do it?" type), there appears to be a developmental relationship between the successive steps, in that there is an ordered sequence of regulations or progressive corrections, in other words, a constant search for equilibrium.

7 The Impact of One Ball on Another

In our earlier causality experiments involving the impact of balls, the subjects were asked to predict and explain what happens in situations that were selected and directed by the interviewer. The experiment reported here is, however, far simpler, with the child merely being given a target at which to aim. The idea behind this is to analyze his actions and, above all, to try to determine the level of his cognizance and the conceptualization on which it is based. In fact, despite a necessary final convergence, it was not at all certain that the results of the two experiments, each undertaken from a different point of view, would be identical. Conditions in the causality experiment were determined beforehand and the subject was asked to deduce their consequences, thus immediately to seek out the functions (such as impact) and the inferential coordinations (explanations). By starting off in this new experiment with the child's spontaneous actions, the

With the collaboration of Catherine Dami.

aim is to establish what he observes about his own actions (cognizance) and regarding the objects (that is, the effects of these actions on them) and to find out how the conceptualization—in other words, the product of the relationships established between these two sets of observations—results in coordinations. Should the success in actions be found to be of a higher level than that of the conceptualization, then the interesting problem would become that of the sources of the causal coordination. Does it proceed directly from specific actions, of which all in fact already contain causal links, or does it rest solely on the coordination of the actions—or is it derived from both these sources, but with results of different values in the two cases?

The technique used is very simple. There are two small balls A and B, and a small skittle (referred to as "the man"); the subject throws A at B in order to make B hit the target. All three objects are first placed on a carpet, in line with the subject, who is asked initially to make the man fall over; no conditions are laid down. The interviewer then describes task I: the child has to knock the man over using both balls (not just one) and without altering their specified starting positions (which was originally allowed). In task II, the child has to make A hit B in such a way that neither ball knocks the man over—again without altering the starting positions of the balls or the man. Finally, in task III, the man is placed to one side of B so that the line between him and B is at about 45 degrees to the line AB; the child is asked to hit the man with B, by hitting B with A. On completion of these practical tasks, regardless of his success in carrying them out, and with the child being allowed as many attempts as he wishes in order to produce his best effort, the interviewer asks him how he did it and particularly whether (but without suggestive questioning) he consciously chose a particular point of impact—and if so, why. As in the other experiments, the interviewer may ask the child to draw the situation or to tell him (the interviewer) what to do; in this case the interviewer attempts to carry out the instruction, but feigns a certain incompetence. Finally, if the child cannot succeed in tasks II or III, the interviewer can show him how it is done, then ask him to explain what happened and to try to do the same thing.

Level IA

Examples

CRI (4,6): With these balls you've got to knock over the little man (one ball only). (Misses.) *They go around all by themselves!* What should you do? *We've got to put the man nearer.* (Succeeds.) What did you do? *I threw it very gently . . . If you don't throw it gently, you can't hit it. If you throw it hard, the ball goes there* (to one side) *on the table.* Task I: Fails three times, then succeeds. *I threw it very gently and the man fell over.* Task II: he tries using only one ball, so not true success. *I did it quickly.* But how did you do it? *I threw it to the side* (of the man). Now with two balls: he takes one in each hand and throws A to one side and B to the other side: No, one ball's got to push the other. (He throws A very wide of B.) *I threw it gently.* (Both balls have to move.) (He succeeds in making A brush B.) Why does one go to one side and the other to the other side? *Because there are two of them.* But why do they go to the side? *Because you throw them to one side or the other* (he draws two parallel trajectories either side of A and fairly wide apart ↑ o ↑), *or in the middle to knock the man over.* Task III: How do you do it? He draws a short curve for ball A going around B and reaching the target, then B going off along an oblique path (in the opposite direction). He offers no other solution.

KAT (5,10): The session starts with task II. She first throws the ball very gently, so that it does not reach the man. But the ball's got to go past the man. (Throws to the side of B.) *I threw it hard and to this side.* But you have to move the second one (B). (She moves B and throws A at it, but again to one side.) *I threw it quite straight, the ball rolled to the side* (of the man). Now try again. (The inter-

viewer puts them back in their original positions.)
(She succeeds.) *The red one* (B) *goes this side.* Was
it you who made it go to the side? *No.* Was it the
balls? *Yes.* Can you throw them just any way at all?
No. You have to throw straight. Task I: succeeds.
How do you throw? *Quite straight.* Did you throw
it straight before? *Yes.* Why do they sometimes go
straight and sometimes go the side? *Because they
go all by themselves.* She fails in task III.

BER (5,6). Task I: succeeds. *With both balls and just
one hand, I made the Japanese man fall down.*
What did the balls do? *They made the Japanese
man fall down.* Both of them? *Yes.* Task II: he
throws *A* to the side, then moves both balls to the
same side. The interviewer puts them back: this
time the child succeeds. How did you do it? *I put
the second ball* (B) *a bit to the side.* But no, it was
in line. Try again. (Succeeds.) How do you do it?
(He again moves *B* to give the same explanation.)
That didn't make the Japanese man fall down.
Why does he sometimes fall down and sometimes
not? *Don't know.* Show me where the first ball has
got to touch the second for the man to fall down.
(Points to the middle.) And where so that he
doesn't fall down? (Again points to the middle.) The
same place? *Almost the same place,* and so on.
Who makes the man fall or stay standing up? *The
balls. I push them and they make him fall down or
not fall down.* Task III: fails (moves the balls so
that the three objects are again in a straight line).

STE (5,6): In task II, like BER, he moves *B* to one
side, then makes *A* hit it right in the middle. The
interviewer puts them back in line and this time
the child succeeds: How did you do it? *I hit it in
the middle and* (B) *went over there.* Was it you who
made it go over there? *No, the ball went all by itself.* Tell me how I can do it. *You've got to take* (A)
and throw it straight.

ALA (5,11). Task I: *The ball rolled and went into the man.* Which one (*B*)? And that one (*A*)? *It didn't do anything.* And what did you do? *I made it roll.* Task II: initially moves *B*, but finally succeeds. *When they get near the man, so that they don't bump into him, they turn all by themselves.* (He draws *A* hitting *B*, with both balls continuing in a straight line until they get near the man, at which point *B* curves off to one side and *A* to the other.) When you throw the ball, do you do the same thing if you want the man to fall down as if you don't want him to fall down? *I throw the same way.*

NOE (5,11) reacts in much the same way as previous subjects. The interviewer shows the child how to succeed in task II. NOE imitates him correctly and says, *I pushed over there onto one side of B,* revealing more accurate observation of someone else's actions than of his own. But immediately afterward: Where do you hit it to make the man fall down? *There* (in the middle of *A*). And where so that he doesn't fall down? *Here* (also in the middle).

JEA (6,0) also is shown what to do for task II, but his observation is not so good as NOE's: *It (B) turns; when you touch it, it goes off course.*

FRA (6,6) succeeds in task II before being shown how to do it. *It turned.* Was it you who made it turn? *It turned all by itself.* Can you tell where it's going to go before it gets there? *No.* Look. (Interviewer demonstrates.) *It's because it turns and goes to one side of the man.* How did I do it? *It's because you threw it with your fingers apart.* It was I who made it turn? *They turned all by themselves.*

The first point of interest emerging from these findings is the almost general practical success in task II, with the children able in their material actions to take account of the possible variation of the points of impact. In our earlier research on causality using similar material, stage I subjects (IB as well as IA) almost always made no mention of this in either their predictions or their explanations. Here, as early as four and a half years of age, CRI, for example, starts by making A pass to the side of B, then rolls A with one hand and B with the other one, to each side of the skittle sufficiently far away not to touch it. However, once the instruction has been repeated and these wrong solutions ruled out, he manages to make A brush against B without either of them hitting the man. KAT, BER, STE, and ALA start off in the same way, but manage to make A really hit B. NOE and JEA doubtless would have reacted this way also, but it was the beginning of the research and they were shown the correct solution rather too quickly—this did, however, enable us to see how they understood it. FRA rapidly finds the correct procedure. Generally speaking, therefore, at this level the subjects understand right away that in order not to touch the skittle, one has to throw the balls to one side, and they start off by doing this, forgetting the exact instruction but, once this has been recalled, they manage to make A hit one side of B so that B does not hit the man.

The second interesting fact is that, although he is successful in this task, the subject cannot say how he did it and it does seem that he really does not know. CRI, having made A brush against B and seen A and B then going off in different directions, simply says that *you throw them to one side or the other*, and illustrates this explanation by taking one ball in each hand and sending them off on parallel but separate paths, which is very instructive since it reveals the psychological origin of his final success. However, when one comes to consider his level of cognizance, it is clear that he only sees, on the one hand, the result of the act (each ball went off to one side) and, on the other, an illusory difference in the force of the action (in task I *I threw it very gently* and in task II *I did it quickly*). KAT thinks she threw the ball A *straight* toward B in task II as she had in task I. BER, like CRI, when describing his success, refers to his penultimate attempt and not to the last, and thinks he first moved B a bit to the side; as for the points of impact in tasks I and II, BER can go no further than saying that they are *al-*

most the same. STE and ALA are more categorical: they hit
B in the middle and *throw the same way* in task II as
in task I. NOE clearly sees that the experimenter made *A*
hit the side of *B*, but, having successfully imitated this
solution, maintains that *A* touched *B* in the middle as in
task I, which does suggest that it is easier for him to observe the action of others than his own. Neither JEA nor
FRA notices the lateral point of impact even when the interviewer carries out the action.

The third interesting finding, which provides confirmation
of this lack of cognizance (and not just of inaccuracy in the
child's description) is that, when asked to give a causal explanation of the result of their actions, these subjects only invoke two equally irrelevant factors. The first, and very
frequently unexplained, factor is the force of the actual action: for CRI the man falls down when you throw *A very
gently*, whereas if you throw it very hard it goes to the side
(cf. KAT). He then contradicts this, having the natural and very
common idea that if you throw the balls gently they won't
reach the skittle. The second factor is, however, more general
and more surprising: this is the power attributed to the balls
themselves, which are considered to change direction
(*turn*) by themselves and not according to the point of impact, or, more generally, as a direct result of the subject's actions.

For KAT, the balls *go all by themselves* and STE specifies
that he is not responsible for *B*'s deviation: *No, [it] went all
by itself.* Similarly, BER says: *I push them and they make
him fall down or not fall down.* ALA is still more explicit in
her attribution of a more or less animist power to the balls:
*When they get near the man, so that they don't bump into
him, they turn all by themselves.* JEA seems more rational:
When you touch it, it goes off course, but this deviation is
still tied up with the spontaneous rotation since *it turns*
and FRA is so convinced that *they turned all by themselves*
that he refuses to allow the interviewer to say otherwise.

Briefly, the subject's actions are not accompanied by any
adequate cognizance (except in task I, if one discounts the ref-
erences to the force), and because of the inaccurate concep-

tualization of the action, the balls themselves are attributed psychomorphic powers. There has to be greater coordination of the actions before the child can reach a higher level with regard to causality, and this lack of coordination is particularly apparent in the systematic failure to complete task III despite the fact that, in principle, it is the same as task II.

Level IB

The only difference between these two stage I levels is that at IB the subjects distinguish between their action on ball *A* and that of *A* on ball *B*, which may or may not come into contact with the man.

Examples

ELI (5,1). Task I: *I threw with this one* (A), *and this one* (B) *made the boy fall over.* Task II: immediately successful. How did you do it? *I threw this one* (A), *and that one* (B) *went over there.* Did you do the same thing as you did before? *No.* How did you do it? . . . Task III: the child moves *B. You've got to shoot straight.* How? (She quickly moves *B* so as to put it in line with *A* and the man.)

NIC (5,11). Task I: *I threw it and the other ball rolled and the man fell down.* Task II: the child starts off by throwing *very gently,* then succeeds the correct way. How? *I did it quickly and it turned a bit.* Why did it turn? *I don't know.* Look. (The interviewer carries out the action.) *Yes, because you turned the ball.* The drawing shows a straight line from *A* to *B,* another from *B* to just short of the target, then a semicircular detour around the target.

MIN (6,7). Task I: *I'm going to take this ball* (A) *against this ball* (B) *and then it's going to try and make the man fall down.* Task II: *The ball turns instead of going straight on.* Why? *Because it goes straight and then when it arrives, it turns.* Why? *Don't know . . . I put the ball* (A) *quite straight and then the ball* (B) *went farther and turned. I shot it straight and B turned a bit.* Is it you who make it turn? *It's me, because if I don't do it straight enough it goes off to the side.* What do you mean when you say do it straight? *The ball* (A) *has got to be in the middle of* (= opposite) *the man; it goes straight against that one* (B) *and it* (B) *goes straight.* Do it again and tell me what you're doing. (Again successful.) *I shot* (A) *against B and A turned and B did as well.* But why do the balls sometimes turn and sometimes go straight? *A slides onto* (B) *and makes it go off and they both turn.* The drawings show A hitting B and B going off toward the target, followed by a curved detour. The demonstration (keeping hold of both balls) provides no further extension of her explanation.

CAL (7,0). Task I: *I made the ball* (A) *roll, it rolled straight.* Why? *It can't turn.* Can't it come here (to the side)? *If you throw it to the side* (other direction), *it can sometimes turn.* Task II: *It didn't fall over because I didn't push hard enough.* (She ponders.) What are you thinking about? *I'm wondering if I can make the ball turn.* (She moves B to the side; the interviewer puts it back, and CAL again stops.) Now what are you thinking about? *How to try to make it turn.* Is there no way? *No.* Look. (The interviewer does it.) *The first turned here and the other one there.* Try. (Succeeds.) How did you do it? *Like you. They both turned.* Where did you hit B? *Here* (direct hit, that is, in the middle).

It is worth examining the responses of these subjects in detail, since their slightly higher level makes their reactions even more paradoxical than those of the level IA subjects. Although in comparison with the latter, their progress may appear insignificant, it fits in with what is already known about this substage IB, where there starts a sort of mediate

transmission in the form of a sequence of immediate transmissions. Of course, the level IA subjects already know that
they are throwing *A* against *B* and that it is *B* that either hits
or misses the skittle. However, in their conceptualization the
two balls constantly act in concert with each other: *they
turned all by themselves*, or *they made the man fall
down*, and when the interviewer asks if she means *both of
them*, BER just says *yes*. On the other hand, each of these
subjects differentiates between the function of *A*, which hits
B, and of *B*, which then acts alone.

Does this improved cognizance or conceptualization of the
action lead to more attention being paid to the necessary role
of the points of impact and above all to a more adequate
causal explanation of the balls' trajectories? It does not, and
this is what is most interesting about this level. ELI and NIC,
who quickly complete task II, do not know how they did it,
and when NIC watches the interviewer in action, neither his
understanding nor his observation is any better than at the
preceding level, since he thinks that *B*, pushed by *A*, continues in a straight line and then describes a semicircle when
it is near the skittle. In his verbal description MIN attributes
exactly the same trajectory to *B*, and when he is asked about
his own part in the proceedings, just says that he *shot it
straight and [it] turned* (adding that *if I don't do it straight
enough it goes off to the side*; but here the word *straight*
signifies that the three objects are arranged in a straight line
and has nothing to do with the points of impact). MIN's
drawing, analogous to NIC's, confirms this interpretation:
straight trajectory and detour at the last moment. Finally, CAL
is one of the rare subjects who does not know how to complete task II, but as soon as she sees it done, she correctly imitates and declares that she acted *like you*, that is to say, by
hitting *B* in the middle. To sum up, cognizance at this level is
no more advanced than that at level IA.

Level IIA

The first two examples are of subjects who fall between the
two levels IB and IIA.

Examples

PHI (6,5). Task II: Why do the balls miss the man? *It's the ball* (B) *that turned all by itself.* Try again. (Again successful.) How did you throw it? *I threw it straight.* And the ball? *It turned.* Was it you who made it turn? *No.* But when given task I (after task II), he thinks back to what happened before: Where did you touch it (B)? *Here* (middle). And before? *A bit here* (to the side). Is it the same as just now? *Not quite.* But where do you push? *Straight. No, I put it a bit to the side.* (This time he places it slightly out of line.) And if they are right in front of each other, can't you make it miss the man? *No, because the ball can't go off to the side.* And if you hit it here (to the side)? *Oh, yes. It goes over there* (to the left) *because that one* (A) *pushes it there* (on the right). Faced with task III, the child predicts remarkably: *You've only got to do as before.* But he misses and thinks that after impact the balls will not immediately go off to the side: *No, they go on straight for a bit* (before separating).

PAT (6,6). Task II: he moves *A* and *B* to the left. Can you do it without moving the balls? *Don't know.* Try. (Succeeds.) How did you do it? *This ball* (B) *went like that* (to the right). How come? *Perhaps I shot it like that* (points to the side of *B*) *and they went off, going away from each other.* But why does the man sometimes not fall down? *Because when the balls touch each other in the middle and not to the side, then he falls down.* Try again (task II)? (Some failures and then success.) Is there a knack to it? *Yes, but it's a little difficult.*

RAY (7,5). Task II: he pushes the ball straight forward and makes the man fall down: *I pushed too hard;* he moves *B* to one side, but then, reminded of the instruction, he puts it back and succeeds. *I pushed it to this side* (to the left) *and it went off this way*. And if I hit it here (impact on the right)? *I think it will go this way* (correct for B and A).

SAB (7,6). Task I, after missing: *It went over there because I didn't throw it properly; it went a bit out of line*. Task II: *I'm throwing it a bit out of line; I'm pushing it to the side* (indicates intended point of impact). She tries, fails four times, and then succeeds. *Sometimes I can do it, sometimes I can't, because it's easier to shoot straight than a bit out of line.*

OLI (7,11). Task II: *It* (B) *ought to go to the side, but it's not us who do it: it's the ball* A *that knocks it. We ought to hit it here* (impact to the side). Why? *I wanted to knock it a bit out of line.* Task III: *You have to do it as before*, but misses.

PIE (7,5). Task II: *I shoot there* (impact to the left) *and that pushes the ball* (B) *there* (to the right). Task III: *You have to hit it here* (correct), but misses and he thinks that if you hit it right on the side, B will go off at right angles to the line AB.

TOP (7,8). Task II: *I shoot there* (impact to the side); *when the ball* (A) *touches the other ball, that makes it turn*. Task III: fails despite impact to the side. *It hasn't enough go.*

RAP (8,1). Task II: *You've got to shoot a little out of line. It* (B) *goes the way that that one* (A) *pushed it.*

GIS (8,2). Task II: succeeds. *I threw it sort of slanting; it goes a bit out of line and doesn't touch the doll*. Why does the ball go to the left? *It can't go to the right because the ball touched it there* (on the right). Task III: his reasoning is the same, but he fails because he does not try to alter the point of impact. Where have you got to make this ball touch the other one if the man is here? *There* (the correct side). And if we put the man farther away? *Here* (same place). Is it like it was before? *No, because he's* (the man) *a bit higher.* So the first ball's got to hit the other one at the same place? *Yes.*

The seven- and eight-year-olds are therefore aware of the fact that they must make *A* hit the side of *B* when they want it to change direction, but they fail in task III. At an intermediate level, PHI (6,5) is still a little vague and PAT (6,6) is hesitant about modification of the impact point. However, the other subjects, all between seven and eight, have no such doubts. It is at this age that, in the causality experiments, the subjects correctly predict an oblique departure of the passive ball and consequently are able to distinguish, and also explain the difference, between the two directions resulting from the transmission of the movement — that is, the direction taken by the active ball thrown by the subject, and the direction taken by the passive ball, which varies according to the impact point (= continuation along the path started by the active ball when the impact is central and divergence from this trajectory when the impact is on the side). These children thus coordinate the movements of the two balls. (Although they still have difficulty in determining the exact direction taken by the passive ball in the case of a side impact, they are quite clear about what happens in the case of a central impact.) Clearly, the child must grasp this causal coordination before he can make an apparently simple observation regarding his own action: in fact, from four or five years a child is able to make *A* hit the side of *B*, but at this age he does not realize what he is doing, while it becomes evident as soon as the older subject sees in this side impact the cause of *B*'s deviation.

Two problems remain: that of the origin of this new coordination and that of its links with causality. Certainly, accurate observation of the object cannot in itself account for the grasp of this coordination, since it is precisely because they do not understand what they see that younger children fail to make an accurate observation. In fact, if we were to consider only the object, we would go around in circles: it is not observed correctly until it is understood, but to be understood it has to be correctly observed. However, if the actions are also considered, there is a new factor at this level: these subjects, unlike those at stage I, are quite clear about what happens in the case of a side impact. Thus the coordination of the directions taken by the balls results from coordination of the actions themselves.

This constitutes the new and explicable factor, since a succession of individual actions correcting one another through feedback sooner or later results in coordination, and this coordination is at a higher level than the succession of individual and uncoordinated actions. Coordination of actions therefore may be reduced to the following inferential link: having to throw A against B in order to transmit a movement to it, and having to make B move in a different direction from that of an imaginary line joining the subject to the skittle, the subject selects the impact point that he would choose if he himself were to move (or if he were to alter the position of B in order to reach a target other than the skittle), hitting B in the middle but away from the line between him and the skittle. In an earlier study in which by means of a marble fired by a small cannon the child had to send a box toward a target not directly in front of him, stage I subjects moved themselves so as to be opposite the target. In this study, stage I subjects (and PAT, RAY, and others at level IIA) start off by moving B before heeding the instruction. It is this coordination, explicable despite its novelty, that seems to account for the subjects' ability to differentiate between the successive directions of the two balls.

The effects of this coordination of the actions and that of the direction on the subjects' grasp of the causality are clear. As long as the children continue to think that the passive B must in principle continue in the same direction as the active A that hits it, they feel that the only possible explanation for its deviation is the ball's own power to *turn*. However, as soon as the coordination of the different directions is understood, the subject attributes the deviation to his own action in directing A onto the side of B, and this is what is immediately admitted by the subjects quoted at this level.

While progress in Task II is clear, the same cannot be said for task III, and the reason is simple. In task II, the child simply has to make *A* hit the side of *B* in order to succeed, while in task III he has to select a specific impact point, with an error resulting in *B*'s missing the target, which is situated at about 45 degrees from the extension of the line *AB*. While the subjects at this level IIA have discovered that a side impact sends *B* to the side, they do not yet know that any variation of this side impact corresponds to a variation in direction. GIS (8,2) makes this clear when he says that he thinks that moving the target does not mean that there must be a different impact point.

Level IIB and Stage III. Conclusion

Level IIB subjects succeed in task III because they are not content with a global generalization from the situation in task II, as was the case at level IIA (*you've only got to do as before*, PHI and OLI), but they understand that the various directions correspond to the different impact points.

Examples

RIS (8,9). Task II: *I threw it at the edge, so that the balls go away from each other.* How does that happen? *It's as if you threw the two balls one against the other at the same time . . . the collision makes them go apart.* Task III: *You've got to aim here.* And if the man is there (moved a little)? *No, here.*

ANC (9,3). Task III: *If you hit it more toward the edge of the ball, it goes more like that* (correct direction).

HUR (9,5). Task II: *When I hit the ball* (A) *that makes the other ball* (B) *go the right way . . . It pushes that one* (B) *the other way, and this one* (A) *changes its path.* Task III: *If you hit there* (very much to the side), *it goes like that.* And if you hit here (nearer the middle)? *It goes a little bit to this side* (= less marked deviation).

MIC (10,0). Task II: *Instead of aiming there* (middle), *I aim there* (to the side). Task III: Can you do it? *If I practice.* Is it more difficult? *Yes, because you've got to work out where to hit it.* There and there (two adjacent impact points), would it be the same for these two? *No, you've got to aim more toward the middle.*

Subjects at stage III are capable of a more general formulation of the law and are better at deducing directions from impact points, and vice versa, than are level IIA subjects.

PAN (11,2). Task II: *If you make it hit on one side, of course it goes to the other. It's as if you hit* (in the middle) *from here.* Task III: *The more you hit on one side, the more it goes to the other.*

ROS (11,6): *When you want it to go straight, you hit in the middle; but if you can aim at the balls from another angle, they go off at another angle* (the same angle).

What are the principal features of this development? The first striking finding is the precocious success of the children's actions in task II, compared with their far less advanced cognizance of them. This requires further clarification. Clearly, the practical success of the stage I children does not suddenly occur; it results from their varied attempts to complete the tasks (using only A to knock over the skittle, moving B in task II so that the three objects are in a line, and so forth). When they are reminded of the instruction, they throw A against B, but still tend (without realizing it) to aim to the side of the skittle, which leads them to send A to the side of B. In such a situation it is obvious that each of the successive actions is itself partly conscious: a deliberate intent (to avoid the skittle) and an awareness of a certain part of the accomplishment (moving B or throwing A against B). However, what is missing in this partial cognizance of each specific action is, in general, the influence that the earlier actions can exert on the subsequent ones and, in particular, the tendency to send *A* to the side of *B* when consciously aiming, as asked, at ball *B*. Once success has been achieved and it comes to observing what has happened to the objects, another factor intervenes that reinforces this difficulty of cognizance. The subject does not see that *A* hits the side of *B* because this would contradict his original idea that, in order to move, *B* must be hit in the middle. The higher level of the action compared with that of the conceptualization is thus not at all mysterious and simply results from use of the sensorimotor processes of adaptation that precede the level at which the child can picture all the aspects of a situation.

The second interesting finding concerns the transition from this initial elementary state to a state (level IIA) where the subject simultaneously makes a relatively correct (but not detailed) observation of the situation, is cognizant of the actions involved in aiming to the side of *B*, and gives a causal (if still global) interpretation of the relationships between the directions of the balls after impact. Is there a developmental link among these three areas of progress?

One fact seems certain: the improvement in the reading of the experimental situation is caused by the intervention of coordinations. It is these coordinations that change the incomplete and incorrect reading of stage I into the accurate observations of level IIA, made possible here by the attention paid to the impact point. Why do these subjects pay such attention to the impact points? It must be because they are beginning to understand the situation; if it were only a question of perception, this attention would be more precocious than it is and would appear much more erratically. Cognizance of the actions is, as usual, facilitated by correct observation of their effects on the object.

Briefly, the more accurate observation of the object leads the child to better cognizance of the action, but stems from a beginning of causal understanding. Why then is the subject beginning to comprehend, when this presupposes an inferential coordination based on correct observations, which can be made only if the child has begun to understand the situation? The only solution surely is to distinguish (and this is essential for a coherent psychogenetic theory) between cognizance of specific actions, which is to a great extent a function of the subject's observation of the object, and the coordination of the actions into an intelligible whole, from which through reflexive abstraction is born a conceptualization that is attributable to the objects and that constitutes the source of causal coordinations. This coordination of the successive actions into a whole consists simply in stringing together the relationships that were already at work in the trial-and-error solutions of stage I, but were then the subject of successive elaborations and post hoc corrections. This is therefore only a particular case of the usual evolution from regulation to operation, enabling the joining of the successive links and the formation of a simultaneous whole.

The various aspects of this development thus seem in conformity with the general dialectic of the subject and the object, whereby observation of the object throws light on the subject, in the form of cognizance of the specific actions, while the general coordination of the latter leads to the inferential coordinations, which in turn throw light on the causal coordinations linking the objects.

8 Pushing Symmetrical and Asymmetrical Objects

Hitting a ball onto a target by pushing it with a stick used like a bat may seem easy, but for young children the problems begin when the target is not situated more or less straight in front of them. Pushing a cylinder (or a similar device made up of two wheels of the same size, one at each end of an axle) makes the task even more difficult, while further complications are added when the object to be pushed is asymmetrical, such as a truncated cone (a tumbler) or a device with two different-sized wheels fixed to an axle (isomorphic to the two plane surfaces of the truncated cone). Because in this last situation the object's trajectory forms a curve, there arises the problem of the interpretation of the respective roles of the child's own actions when he gives the object a push with the stick, and of the objective, geometric properties of the object itself. This situation therefore provides an opportunity

With the collaboration of Isabelle Flückiger-Geneux.

to study a particular case of the cognizance of an action and of seeing how the child relates his observations on the object to what he notices of his own action.

A group of subjects is presented with the first situation mentioned above, that involving a stick (bat) and a ball. The child sits in front of a table with the target initially in front of him; he is allowed to wield the stick as he wishes (end or side forming the trajectory). The target is then moved to the side, so the subject has to rotate the stick and send the ball off in an oblique direction. Our goal, once the subject's level of success had been determined, was to find out to what degree, and how, he became cognizant of his own movements. A second group of children was presented with the same ball problem (with the same varied positions of the target) and with situations involving a cylinder (battery) and a cone (either a yogurt carton with the cylinder having the same diameter as the small surface of the cone, or a simple noncylindrical piece of chalk). Finally, the third (and largest) group of children was given two cylinders (one light and one heavy in order to judge possible differences), two cones (with similar characteristics), and two of the two-wheeled devices described above (subsequently referred to as "same-sized wheels" and "different-sized wheels").

Again the position of the target is varied. The table is covered with a felt cloth to prevent the objects from skidding.

Level IA

Examples

DAN (4,11) first fails to send the ball (just using his hand) onto a target that is situated to one side, and so not directly in front of him. Presented with the cylinder, he pushes it with his hand in various positions and fails to hit the target, except when the cylinder starts off at right angles to the target. Did you hit it? *Yes.* Do you know why? *No.* He then tries various positions with the chalk before putting it at right angles to the target. *It didn't touch.* Yet you threw it right? *Yes . . . no.* When he tries with the stick and the ball or the cylinder (target to one side), he fails except when the cylinder is almost in front of him and the stick at right angles to the target. Why is it better? *Because.* He predicts that the chalk will go straight like the cylinder: *It turned.* Do you know why? *No.*

MAR (4,11), with the target to one side (on the floor instead of on the table), starts off by pushing the cylinder straight ahead and fails, then she puts it at right angles to the target and succeeds. With a piece of chalk (conical) she makes numerous attempts without aiming and succeeds once or twice without knowing why. She then puts it at right angles to the target: *No, missed,* then succeeds by giving it a little push and redirecting it several times along the trajectory. When given a stick (in this case, a ruler) and asked to push a rectangular box (situated on one side of her) toward the target (on the other side), she starts by simply throwing the ruler at the target—this way she hits it, but does not manage to make the box hit it. So she puts herself opposite the target and the ruler at right angles to it: *I've got to push hard,* and succeeds. She also puts the truncated cone (tumbler) at right angles to the target and so misses it. Why? *Because I missed.* But why? *Because it was on the floor.* She thus invokes both her own action and the position of the object.

TAB (4,6) (without a stick), with the target to one side and the ball nearer him on the same side, immediately lines himself up with the ball and the target and so succeeds; however, he fails (again just pushing with his hand) with the cylinder, as he did not put it in the right place for it to roll toward the target. After much trial and error he discovers the right position, without knowing why it is right, and succeeds. He then tries to do the same with the chalk (still just using his hand) and attributes his failure to the fact that he rolled it differently from the time before, which was not the case. He does it again, this time pushing much harder, which makes the chalk start to slide in a straight line. *It was quite straight and afterward it turned right in front of the ashtray.* (He exaggerates.) And did the battery turn like that as well? *Yes, twice, and then it hit* (the target). He is then given the cylinder and the stick, which he first places parallel to the tiles on the floor, and so misses the target, then at right angles to the latter, and so succeeds. Why didn't it work the first time? *Because* (the cylinder) *it was straight* (should have been at an angle, as the target was to one side). And why did it work afterward? *Because it was straight* (this time in line with the target). Try with the chalk. (He does the same thing and is delighted to find that it turns.) Why didn't the battery (cylinder) turn? *Because it's bigger.* Can it go in zigzags as well? *Yes.* Try. (He tries without success.) *No.* And the chalk? *No.* Show me the way the ball went, the way the battery went, and the way the chalk went. (Each time, TAB indicates the same straight trajectory.)

JOS (5,6) thinks that the cylinder and the cone (tumbler) will travel along the same path, but he *doesn't know* about the two two-wheeled devices. With the target to one side, he pushes each in turn using the ruler and succeeds in hitting the target. He maintains that here again both objects travel straight to the target along the same path. Of course, this cannot be so because the same-size wheels do not start off facing the target and the different-size wheels, when pushed once, go around in circles. In both cases, JOS succeeds in hitting the target by keeping his hand on the devices and the ruler perpendicular to the desired trajectory, constantly correcting the natural deviations of the devices. He seems quite unaware of this. When he is asked to push the objects without using the ruler, he pushes the cone in a straight line and notes that it turns. Why? *Don't know.* Now where will it go if you push it again from here? *There toward the ashtray* (wrong). After several more incorrect answers to such questions, he concludes: *Sometimes it goes there and sometimes here.* He fails to distinguish between the effect of his own actions and the effect of the structure of the objects.

TAL (5,6), like JOS, thinks that the objects will travel along the same paths. After trying with the different-sized wheels: *I thought it would go straight.* If you make it go again from here, will it go the same way? *Don't know.* Will it go here (to the left of the target) or there (to the right)? *Don't know.* Having seen where the device goes after several more incorrect predictions, TAL concludes that she did not place the object correctly at the beginning: *It's because they* (different-sized wheels) *were turned a bit like that.* Then, when the interviewer gives her alternately the same-sized and different-sized wheels, she predicts each case to be the same as the one she has just observed. She thus maintains that the same-size wheels will go around in a semicircle because she has seen the different-size ones going round in a semicircle, and that the different-size wheels will roll in a straight line because that is how the same-size wheels rolled. During her second session, TAL's responses show that she is now nearer level IB. She correctly indicates three times where to place the target from a given starting position of the different-size wheels. However, when the position of the target is specified by the interviewer, she cannot indicate a correct starting position for the different-size wheels.

ZWA (5,11) immediately notices that the axle holding the two different-sized wheels *slopes* and that the *stick* (axle) for the same-size wheels *is straight.* However, this does not prevent his thinking that their trajectories will be *the same. It still rolls the same.* He then manages to make the cylinder go toward the target when the latter is directly in front of him, but not when it is moved to one side. He places the different-size wheels right opposite the target *because they will go straight.* (Tries.) *It turns, I don't know.* Why? *Because it slopes. When I push it, it turns!* He then has nine consecutive attempts, each time starting the wheels off from a different position selected at random, as if the main criterion for success were his own skill. During his second session he remembers that the different-size wheels *turn this way or that way,* again experiments, then points in the correct direction. However, when he tries to make these wheels hit the target, he uses his hand to keep them on course. He is clearly unaware of what he was doing. *It went straight!* How do you make it go straight when you told me that it turns? (Perhaps) *it did turn . . . I don't know.* He carries on, correcting the deviations, and when asked what will happen if he simply gives the wheels a push and takes the ruler away, he predicts first a straight path, then a path that curves around to a target situated opposite the starting position. However, he finally accepts that *it turns around!*

ELI (6,7), despite the fact that she is six and a half years old, still thinks that both the two-wheeled devices will go *straight.* She is astonished when she sees what actually happens. *They turned around there!* The end of the session still sees her placing the different-size wheels opposite the target, as if all that were required were a skillful action. (Of course, if the wheels start off quite near the target, it is possible to hit it.)

Thus at level IA children find it difficult to aim even a symmetrical object at a target that is not directly in front of them. In fact, DAN initially fails to make the ball hit such a target, while TAB succeeds only after first putting himself in line with both the ball and the target. This response provides a first example of these subjects' initial lack of differentiation between the requirements of the action and the properties attributed to the object.

The problem becomes more complicated when the subject has to make a cylinder hit a target (without the ruler), since it can roll in only two general directions; so again, for reasons of symmetry, it is easier to succeed when the target is in line with the subject than when it is placed to one side. A cylinder is similar to a wheel with an enlarged rim or to a succession of wheels fixed on the same axle (hence its analogy with the same-size wheels); there is therefore no reason why it should turn more on one of its halves than on the other. However, for it to start off in a perceptively symmetrical position it must be at right angles to the target at which it is to be aimed. When the cylinder starts off to the side of the subject, then in relation to the subject's own position its trajectory must be oblique. Therefore to succeed the subject must act as if he himself were in line with both the cylinder and the target. Responses to this situation are interesting on two counts, firstly because the child does (at least initially) succeed in hitting the target, and secondly because he does not know how he did it; there is thus no cognizance of his actions (cf. DAN and TAB).

The use of the ruler poses a similar problem. When the object to be pushed is not in line with both the subject and the target, the most advanced subjects in this particular experiment hold one end of the ruler and use it just like a bat to hit the object straight toward the target. However, the difficulty lies in understanding that one can start from any position of the ruler; regardless of the orientation of the object (it could be to one side but not in the right position for rolling), it is always possible to line up the ruler, the object, and the target.

At this level (IA), the children most frequently put themselves in line with both the object and the target and push the former, but not (which is significant) with the end of the ruler; instead they hold the ruler with both hands, at right angles to the intended path and so guide the object toward the target (cf. for instance, DAN, MAR, and JOS). Despite the very elementary nature of this response, it does not give rise to adequate cognizance. When asked why he was successful, DAN first says that he does not know and then just says *because*. MAR does not think she took sufficient precautions to keep the object on the right straight path and thinks it requires force: *I've got to push hard*, and so on.

Of course, if the difficulties of motor adaptation and then of cognizance remain great for symmetrical objects, then a fortiori they will be still greater for the cones or the two different-size wheels. At least with respect to the different-size wheels, one would think that the clearly visible asymmetry would lead the children to predict an irregular path, and this is indeed the case at level IB. However, at level IA the children have difficulty with even the symmetrical objects and it does not appear to enter their minds that the cones and different-size wheels may be more complicated than the symmetrical objects. They try to apply to the former those processes discovered through observation of the latter, that is, they either push them straight to the target with their hand or by means of the ruler placed at right angles to the path considered straight. How does the child then explain the curve in the trajectories? Does he attribute it to the properties of the object or to failures in his own action?

In fact, he makes no differentiation between these factors. This is interesting from the theoretical point of view, since it shows that at levels where cognizance is not yet complete, correct observation of the object's properties may accompany incorrect observation of the action on this object, when the two factors remain undifferentiated. DAN notes that the chalk has turned, but does not know either why it turned or if he pushed it correctly. MAR thinks that the cone turns not only because she did not push it properly, but also *because it's on the floor* (on the ground and not on the table), which she thinks makes the task more difficult. TAB thinks that he did not push the chalk in the same way as he pushed the cylindrical battery, but subsequently attributes the latter's straight trajectory to the fact that *it's bigger*. However, he makes so little distinction between the respective roles of the object and the action that he admits, during fresh attempts, that the chalk, the cylinder, and the ball will all be able to go in a straight line. Jos and TAL have the same reaction, with TAL applying to the asymmetrical objects what she has just observed regarding the symmetrical ones and vice versa. Despite the evidence of her own eyes, ELI continues to place the asymmetrical object in front of the target, clearly thinking that all that is needed is a more skillful action. Finally, ZWA makes use of a remarkable argument, worthy of separate analysis.

Sooner or later, all the children (at least, up to level IIA) discover an infallible way of making the asymmetrical objects hit the target: they keep either a hand or the ruler on them so that they can correct the trajectory as and when necessary right up to the target. This constitutes a regulation, since it consists in neutralizing a deviation through a compensation in the opposite direction. However, in this particular case, it is just one object that constantly reproduces the same deviation, hence the continuous correction by the subject so as to establish the desired straight trajectory. ZWA is so little aware of what he is doing that he cries out gleefully: *It went straight!* and does not know whether or not the different-size wheels describe a curve until the interviewer asks him to give them one sharp push with the ruler, whereupon he is forced to observe the curved trajectory.

To sum up, there are three main findings at level IA:

(a) Subjects find it difficult to make an object hit a target when they themselves, the object, and the target are not in a straight line.

(b) There is a fairly systematic difficulty regarding cognizance of the situation, with conceptualization remaining at a level below that of the practical results.

(c) There is a lack of differentiation between the observations of the object and those of the action (regardless of whether or not these are correct), even though each movement of the object results from interaction of its properties with the subject's own action.

It is possible that these difficulties stem from the complexity of the experimental material. Ten five- to eight-year-olds were therefore given a simpler version of the experiment involving a ball and, in some situations, a ruler. The level IA subject had the same difficulties when the ball was not in line with both himself and the target, although, of course, the solution was found more rapidly than with the cylinder.

Examples: Level IA (Simpler Situation)

COR (5,3) at first pushes the ball straight at the target (a beach ball), but uses both hands. How about with only one hand? *You push it.* And if the ball is here (on the right)? (Two misses.) Why didn't it hit it? *I can't do it.* And with this stick? *It can't be done.* (The target is brought nearer the subject, who then succeeds.) And if the big ball (target) is here (moved slightly to one side)? (COR puts the ruler perpendicular to the trajectory, with its center opposite the ball and misses the target.) *I put the stick the wrong way around,* and so on. After successfully hitting the target, COR tries to draw her solution: she draws the ball and the target, but when it comes to linking them by her action she simply draws the ruler (lengthways) joining the two.

GRE (5,10) reacts similarly to COR. After finally succeeding with the stick, her drawing also shows the positions of the ball and the target. However, she draws the ruler parallel to the edge of the table, starting from the ball, and then *the stick's road* between the free end of the ruler and its initial position and the target, as if the ruler had not turned around on the spot but had merely gone forward, subsequently making a detour to get to the target.

It is clear that success in this situation occurs after the same period of trial and error as in the main experiment. Furthermore, this simpler situation is no more likely to lead to immediate cognizance of what happens.

Level IB

At this level the children do predict that the symmetrical and asymmetrical objects will move differently. Why can they do this? Furthermore, how does this correct prediction modify the child's cognizance of the action and his awareness of the relationships between his action and the object?

> MIC (5,3), although only five years old, immediately predicts that the same-size wheels will go straight, but that the other ones made up of *a back wheel of a tractor and a front wheel*, will roll to the side. Where will they go? *Behind the tractor, there* (to the side of the big wheel). When asked to use the ruler to push objects onto the target, unlike the level IA subjects, he holds the ruler as an extension of the desired trajectory, making one end connect with the middle of the axle between the two wheels. Then, despite his predictions regarding the different-size wheels, he places them dead opposite the target and does exactly the same thing he did with the same-size wheels. Do you push the same way as you did before? *Yes, it's going there* (in a straight line). MIC then pushes the wheels and, each time he sees them go off course, he corrects the trajectory by making the axle perpendicular to the target again. What does it do? *It goes around in circles.* Do you remember your drawing (illustrating that the different-size wheels turn to the side of the big wheel)? *Yes, like that; it goes straight, then it turns* (not what he said before!). At the second session he remembers to which side the asymmetrical wheels turn (in the opposite direction to where he had first predicted). *This one turns, because here* (large diameter) *it's bigger and here* (small diameter) *it's smaller.* However, to make it hit the target he corrects its trajectory eight times because *you can't do it* (succeed) *with only one*

push. However, he corrects the tumbler's trajectory only once.

LAU (5,8) also predicts that the different-size wheels will turn sideways and even indicates the correct direction *because the big wheel makes it go round*. However, he also says that the same-size wheels *sometimes quickly go off straight and sometimes they turn to the left or the right*. To make them hit the target, *you have to roll them rather hard*. When this symmetrical object is placed a little to one side of him, LAU succeeds, but with difficulty, in directing it toward the target by rotating the stick (which is then parallel to the axle). What did you do? *I hit it from there. I turned the stick* (accurate cognizance). However, he places the different-size wheels opposite the target and then corrects the trajectory, compensating for the deviations. During the second session, he recalls the observations he had made at the first: *This one* (same-size wheels) *rolled straight and that one* (different-size) *turned: sometimes it went straight and sometimes it turned!* Despite this tendentious conceptualization, he places the different-size wheels parallel to the edge of the table, thus allowing for the correct curve, gives them one tap and makes them hit a target not in line with himself. On the other hand, even though when describing the cone (which is lying down as opposed to being upright) he notes that *on one side it's low and on the other high*, he persists in placing it exactly opposite the target as if it would travel along a straight path. When it comes to the two cylinders (identical except in weight), he pushes the light one and immediately concludes, *The light one goes straight, the heavy one turns*. (He does not try the latter.) Given the cones, he also starts off with the light one and declares, *Because the light one isn't heavy, it turns*. Which will you take to hit the target? *The heavy one because it goes straight.* After missing the target, he throws it really hard and hits it.

NAT (6,3) makes the ball hit a target (the two objects not initially in line with each other) by rotating the ruler and explains what she did. She has greater difficulty with the cylinder, but overcomes this using the same principle. Furthermore, NAT predicts that the chalk can turn: *Perhaps if I did it like that* (as with the cylinder), *it would turn.* (She does this.) The interviewer turns the chalk over and NAT is very surprised to see that it now turns the other way. She checks three times and concludes, *It's because I pushed there* (the side where it turns). This does not stop her from placing the chalk opposite the target, clearly imagining a straight trajectory.

PHI (6,0) starts off with reactions typical of level IA, maintaining that the asymmetrical objects, like the symmetrical ones, will roll in a straight line. However, he is classified at level IB because by the end of the second session he has discovered the part played by the impact point (realized at level IIA). Having noticed that the different-size wheels describe a curve and having corrected their trajectory in the manner already described (compensating for deviations), PHI discovers that by making the ruler hit the axle at a point near to the small wheel, the device goes close to the target, while when the impact point is in the middle of the axle, the device goes away from the target. Furthermore, during the second session, he not only makes the device hit the target, although not every time (he cannot yet predict the curved trajectory sufficiently accurately), but also (and as will be seen later, this is not the same thing), he predicts, like the level IIA subjects, where the target must be for specific starting positions of the different-size wheels.

ISA (6,1) immediately predicts that the different-size wheels will not go forward in the same way as the same-size wheels because of the large wheel, but this does not prevent her subsequently placing the asymmetrical device dead opposite the target and correcting the deviations. During the second session, she remembers the deviations and draws the curves to the side of the little wheel, even though when she actually tries to hit the target, she continues to compensate for the deviations. Her response in the tumbler situation is similar. What makes the tumbler turn? *How I throw it.* And if you push it with your hand? *It's my hand.* And if I'm the one who pushes it? *It turns also.* What will happen if I put it on this bit of wood, and the wood slopes? It will go straight. (Attempts.) *It turned!* Why? *It's the tumbler!*

Why do these five- and six-year-old children, unlike those at level IA, predict that the two two-wheeled devices will not follow the same trajectory? Before we attempt to answer this question, it must be stressed that this prediction remains global: MIC thinks that the large wheel will make the axle turn to its side, while LAU says it will make the axle turn the other way (which is correct, but doubtless not understood). Neither NAT nor ISA can say which way it will turn, and LAU thinks that the same-size wheels also can spontaneously describe curves. All these subjects start (and continue to do so for varying lengths of time) by putting the different-size wheels in line with the target and then correct the trajectory.

Now to return to the question of why this prediction is possible at this age. Two factors point toward an answer. Firstly, great importance is attached as early as level IA to symmetry, of both perceptive, motor, or sensorimotor mechanisms and the position of the child's own body when he is carrying out the required action (the children put themselves directly in line with the target, for instance). It therefore seems quite natural that fairly young children not only notice the symmetry of the same-size wheels and the perceptively striking lack of symmetry in the different-size wheels, but also imagine that although they are rolling simultaneously, in the case of the different-size wheels the large one will follow a different trajectory than the small one; in the case of the tumbler, the top part (large diameter) will follow a different trajectory than the bottom part (smaller diameter). How is it that observation of this global inequality leads these children to predict a difference in the trajectories of the symmetrical and asymmetrical objects?

Secondly, in an experiment (also conducted by Isabelle Flückiger-Geneux) involving the pushing and rotation of flat wooden bars, taking various points of pressure along the long side of the bar, it was found that subjects at this same level IB (five and a half to six years) immediately predict that when the bar is pushed with the pressure point situated in the middle of its long side *it will go straight,* but if the pressure point is situated nearer one of the ends of the long side it *will turn.* This constitutes only a very elementary notion of symmetry whereby "middle = equality of the two parts of the side that is pushed = translation extending the push" and "side impact = inequality of the parts of the side that is pushed = rotation." The dynamics of the resistances and the like play such a minor role that triangular bars, or bars with large holes in one of the halves, are thought to go straight forward if the pressure point is in the middle of the long side, as if all that were important were the fact that the side is pushed and the location of the pressure point (in the middle or to one side).

These earlier findings lead to another question regarding the children's prediction of different trajectories for the symmetrical and asymmetrical objects. Is this prediction based on a dynamic understanding (including the kinetics and intensity)? In that case the solution would be expected to be reached much later. Or is it based only on global equivalences of the type just described? In this case the children would simply be equating symmetry to translation and asymmetry to deviations or rotation.

Here again, two findings throw light on the matter. First, despite their prediction, the subjects systematically place the asymmetrical object in line with the target and force it to go in a straight line. Second, and more important, because of difficulties of cognizance they do not differentiate between the role of their own action and that of the properties of the object when trying to explain the latter's deviations. As has been pointed out, while predicting or even actually observing the curves described by the asymmetrical object, a child at this level does not hesitate to place such an object directly in line with the target and then say that it will go in a straight line to the target. In actuality, this inconsistency is an apparent one and would be real only if the deviations caused by the asymmetry of these objects constituted the necessary result of their objective properties. By contrast, if the child thinks that these deviations are even partly a result of the action of pushing, then he may think that the effects of the asymmetry can be corrected by a symmetrical situation. In other words, placing the device in line with the target will compensate for its lack of symmetry and so create a situation that will force it to go straight. Thereafter, when he compensates for each deviation the subject is simply furthering this aim. He is not merely correcting the object's trajectory, but regulating and correcting the action itself, from which results the object's movement.

The central problem emerging from these findings thus concerns the respective roles that the subject attributes to the object and to his own action in his conceptualization of the deviations in the movement of the asymmetrical objects. In this respect, the final dialogue with ISA is very enlightening: the tumbler rotates because *I throw it* and will also rotate if the interviewer carries out the action—for the same reason. However, she maintains that the tumbler will roll straight down a sloping piece of wood; it is only when she sees that this is not so that she comes to understand the necessary link between the rotations and the properties of the object (*It's the tumbler!*). Similarly, LAU believes that the way the same-size wheels are rolled determines whether they turn or go straight (he clearly does not even consider the point of impact). When he resumes his attempts with the asymmetrical object, saying *sometimes it went straight and sometimes it turned,* he clearly attributes a role to the action and not only to the asymmetry of the object. NAT has the same reactions. Briefly, it is because the level of cognizance of their own action is not sufficiently high that, although these subjects are aware of the interaction between the action and the object, they fail to dissociate the roles of the subject and the object—hence the apparently contradictory aspects of their behavior.

In the simpler version of the experiment involving only a ball, a ruler, and a target, the children are clearly more aware of the rotation of the ruler and then of its being in a perpendicular position when it comes into contact with the ball than is the case in the main experiment.

Example, Level 1B (Simpler Situation)

> ETA (5,10) starts off by missing the target. When asked to describe his action, he first shows how he held the ruler lengthwise reaching toward the target (it and the ball are situated to the same side of him), and then in two stages makes it slope in order to push the ball to the side, but without aiming properly. Subsequently, having hit the target, he draws the same stages, but with the final position of the ruler perpendicular to the path leading to the target.

This success in action and accurate cognizance must, however, be considered in relation to the behavior recalled above, which consists in predicting the translations or rotation of an object according to the location of the pressure point, even though here it is the ruler that is made to rotate before coming into direct contact with the ball.

Level IIA

This level sees the subjects able to make use of the rotations of the asymmetrical objects, to understand the part played by the impact points, and to predict, for a given starting position of the different-size wheels, the right place to put the target. Curiously enough, given the location of the target, these subjects still find it difficult to select the right starting position for an asymmetrical object and work out its trajectory; this is because of a failure to grasp the reversible or even the constant nature (forced regularity) of the curved trajectories.

Examples

NIC (7,3) predicts the deviations of both the asymmetrical and the symmetrical objects according to the point of impact. For example, after his initial attempts with the same-size wheels, he says, *Before I had hit there, and now there* (indicates impact points). At first he refuses to try to make the different-size wheels hit the target: *It can't go and hit* (the target) *because it's turning the whole time.* However, he eventually succeeds twice in succession from different starting positions. Then he puts the device opposite the target and shows how to neutralize the deviations by making the point of impact near the small wheel.

FEL (7,11) starts off by saying, *Those* (asymmetrical) *go around in circles and those* (symmetrical) *go straight.* He correctly predicts the paths of the different-size wheels for numerous starting positions, but initially says that it is impossible to determine whether or not they will hit the target, particularly since the curves could be sharp or wide. Then he succeeds in making them hit the target by starting them off nearer it or by compensating for the deviations. Nevertheless he does not believe that the reverse path (leading from the target) comes back to the same starting point.

ALA (8,0): For ALA, the asymmetrical object will deviate *because it's got one wheel bigger* (than the other), *it can turn*. It can or it's always got to? *It's got to*. (He correctly indicates the directions.) He thinks that the symmetrical objects will also turn according to the location of the impact point. *It depends, because if I push here* (to one side) *it can turn a bit*. To reach a target situated to one side of him, he puts the same-size wheels in line with himself, then the different-size ones a little farther away, thinking erroneously that he has allowed for a sufficient curve. How can you be sure you're going to hit it? *You can adjust it* (compensations, but this time clearly aware of the process). However, he does not think that for a given starting position, the object will always arrive at the same place. *No, because you don't know if it will arrive there or there*. What about the same-size wheels? *Yes, because they go straight*. Is there a way of making sure that they'll get there? (The interviewer removes the target.) (ALA places the asymmetrical object parallel to the edge of the table, then indicates the right place for the target.) And if I put it (the target) there? (The child places the wheels very close to the target and cannot choose another starting position farther away from it.)

BAR (8,4) can also place the target for a given starting position of the asymmetrical wheels, but succeeds the other way around only after numerous attempts.

ROT (8,2) immediately demonstrates how the asymmetrical object will turn and takes into account the point of impact for the symmetrical one. Given a target, he places the different-size wheels out of alignment with it but quite far to the side (and parallel to the edge of the table). Why did you put them there? *I thought that it would turn like that*. Since he has not predicted the right curve, he places the wheels somewhere else and pushes them, but not hard enough. He then makes the object retrace its trajectory to get back to the original starting position, whereupon he pushes it harder and it hits the target. However, this act, revealing a glimpse of reversibility, is simply to enable him to find his selected starting position and does not give him the idea of working from the target to determine various starting points. Still, this response does show that the child is acting on the hypothesis that the same initial position can lead to the same path, but the corresponding conceptualization is still lacking. When it comes to the heavy and light cones, ROT says that the latter will go farther than the former, but that their trajectories will be the same.

LAR (8,5) observes the changes in direction of the battery according to the points of impact and in answer to the interviewer's question, Can it make either bends or zigzags when you throw it? says, No. (She ponders.) What are you thinking about? *Whether it can or can't without us deliberately making it do it.* What about this tumbler (truncated cone)? *It's smaller there and bigger there, so it goes around in a circle* (turns). Despite this, LAR tries to make it go straight, but when the interviewer turns it through 180 degrees and LAR sees that if one pushes it, it goes in the opposite direction, she laughs and cries, *That's not right!*, clearly seeing that the curves described by the tumbler are completely independent of the action of pushing. She then allows for them and succeeds in hitting the target.

PAS (8,6) predicts the direction in which the asymmetrical object will turn *because the big wheel is on this side.* Given a target, he places the different-size wheels in line with it, but selects an impact point near the small wheel. *If I hit there it will go over there, it can go a bit straight. You'll see.* (Misses.) *Because I pushed a little* (too much) *there*

(= not enough to the side). He starts again, this time with the impact point nearer the edge of the axle, but again misses. He then puts it in the right position and at an oblique angle and succeeds. He thus thinks that the paths taken by the objects depend on the impact point and the force of the push, as well as on the starting point. However, when questioned regarding objects that are identical in shape but of different weight, he says that they will follow the same path, but that the light one will go farther than the heavy one.

The great difference between the subjects at level IB and those at IIA is that the latter do not just predict that the asymmetrical objects will not travel in a straight line, all the while continuing to place them in line with the target as if the deviations were partly caused by their own action and could therefore be corrected; they realize that these deviations are inevitable (*it's got to,* says ALA) and immediately say which way the object will turn (*because the big wheel is on this side,* says PAS). Most of these children soon see how to allow for the curves when placing the object and so no longer put it in line with the target. Admittedly, NIC and FEL initially refuse even to try with the different-size wheels, but this is precisely because they realize that the curves complicate the problem, before they see how to use the curves in the solution. Although some subjects still place the asymmetrical objects in line with the target and then correct any deviations, they do this for a specific reason. NIC tries to modify the point of impact in order to compensate for the deviations, whereas when the experimenter asks ALA how one can be sure of hitting the target, the child replies, *you can adjust it* (as and when necessary)—which shows that, unlike the younger subjects, he is well aware of what he is doing when he corrects the object's trajectory.

Although these subjects now clearly understand the nature and necessity of the deviations, this has not yet led them to understand that there is only one possible trajectory for a spe-

cific starting position. When reflecting on the object's movement, children at this level consider, more closely than was
the case at preceding levels, the role of their own action and
that of the properties of the object itself and discover that the
point of impact is important also. This makes them think
that if the object's path can depend on the point of impact, it
is impossible to be sure that, given identical starting positions, the trajectories will not be slightly modified. Furthermore, the constancy of a curved trajectory is obviously more
difficult to conceive as being necessary than that of a straight
one. FEL says that one does not know whether the curve will
be sharp or wide, and ALA states that *you don't know if it*
(the asymmetrical device) *will arrive there or there,* but that
the symmetrical wheels *go straight.*

If the child does not realize that there is only one possible
trajectory in one direction, he will, a fortiori, not understand
the reversible nature of the trajectory (FEL, and others). Nevertheless, ROT returns an object to its starting point by making
it roll back the way it had come, but he does it to remind
himself of where he had originally placed it and not with the
idea that on its return the object must necessarily follow the
same trajectory.

This absence of reversibility doubtless explains a curious
behavior frequently observed at this level. The subjects find it
easier to determine where to place the target for a given
starting position of the asymmetrical object than to determine a starting position for a given target. The two types of
question are logically equivalent and, since the children appear to consider that there is more than one possible trajectory for a given starting point, it would seem that the two
questions are equally difficult. However, from the psychological point of view, this is not the case: once a starting point
has been given, the child simply needs to extend forward the
predicted movement and, even if the latter is conceived as
variable, he thinks it legitimate to try to judge the most probable destination. If, on the other hand, a child is given the
target and asked to try to find an adequate starting point,
there are two possible methods. He can try to imagine a series
of possible positions and select the best one, which is not easy

at the level of concrete as opposed to hypotheticodeductive operations. Or he can start off from the target and imagine the path going backward to the starting point. The second method implies a grasp of the reversibility of the trajectory and is therefore not accessible to subjects at this level (but, as will be seen, becomes accessible later).[1]

To sum up, this level sees the subjects better able to grasp what in the resulting movements of both the symmetrical and asymmetrical objects results from their own actions and what from the properties of the object. With symmetrical objects, the subjects now pay attention to the impact points and are well aware that if you push such an object in the middle it will go straight, but if you push it at the side it will turn. Level IB subjects notice this when the interviewer asks them to change the impact point when pushing a flat wooden bar, but, with the exception of PHI (6,0), who spontaneously draws attention to this point, they do not think about it at all. As for the asymmetrical objects, the subjects now know that they must follow a curved trajectory, can understand why, and can indicate the direction of the curve. They have thus discovered the boundaries between the effects of their own actions and those that are caused by the particularities of the object itself. This progress must be a result of better cognizance of their own actions, an improved understanding of causality, and more accurate observation of the object. LAR, when she is questioned just as she accedes to level IIA, shows how closely accurate observation of the object is linked to accurate cognizance of the action. Doubtful about the possible deviations of a cylindrical box, she spontaneously wonders about the part played by her action and questions

1. This absence of reversibility, whence the child's inability to see that the object rolls back along the same path as it took on the outward journey, indicates the formation of the "half-logic" made up of one-way schemes that has already been noted in many other experiments. The first half has yet to be completed by its second half, in the sense that (in this instance) the child will realize that the action of going to the target is reversible. This functional half-logic (see "Psychologie et épistémologie de la fonction," volume 23 of the *Etudes d'épistémologie génétique*, Presses Universitaires de France, Paris, 1971) is present at level IB with respect to linear trajectories. The fact that it again becomes apparent at stage II may be explained by the greater complexity of the curved trajectories.

whether the cylinder could, of its own accord, go off course along a curve *without us deliberately making it do it*, that is, whether one can act in such a way as to modify the "natural" trajectory. ALA shows that he has already solved this problem when, correcting the deviations of the asymmetrical wheels, he says *you can adjust*. He clearly thinks of the curve described by the object's movements as "natural" and immediately understands that the compensations introduced by the action are linked to the latter and not just to the object. This level thus reveals marked progress in cognizance of the action itself, with this progress distinctly linked to more accurate observation of the object.

Level IIB and Stage III

Progress in this experiment was often found to be fairly slow; several eight- and nine-year-olds and even some ten-year-olds were classified at level IIA. The following example is of a child at an intermediate level (IIB) between IIA and the final stage III, at which the child understands and spontaneously uses his grasp of the reversibility of curved trajectories.

Example (Level IIB)

DEN (10,8) predicts that the smaller of the two asymmetrical wheels will describe a small circle and the large one a large circle around the first, in other words, *a path that follows the little one*. And do they go round the same number of times? *Yes, the same number of times*. When he tries to make this device reach the target, he does not start it off at quite the right angle (too small). When it has described an arc of a circle, he sends it back to the starting point. He does this several times without any modifications. Do you think you'll reach the target? *Yes, but we'll have to wait a long time; as the wheels turn I think it goes up a bit*. In other words, DEN has not grasped the reversible nature of the trajectory and believes that if he continues what he is doing long enough, the curve described by the object will become increasingly wide so that the wheels will eventually hit the target. Don't you think that it will come back to the same place? *No, because I think it's going up a little* (in height). However, for a trajectory in only one direction (if the child starts the object off again from the same point) *it will go along the same path, but not exactly the same* (possibility of slight variations). Given a specific starting point for these different-size wheels, DEN has no difficulty in placing the target so that they will hit it (as at level IIA). When the target is placed and he is asked to find an adequate starting point for the object, DEN has the idea of starting from the target and deducing the trajectory, which is thus a beginning of reversibility, but in fact he is probably just mentally reversing his response to the previous question. The next day he does not repeat this correct solution and has to be reminded of it. However, he then applies it to the truncated cone.

It is interesting to compare the above example with the following, which is characteristic of stage III.

Example (Stage III)

COI (10,1), having predicted the curves that will be described by the asymmetrical object, places the latter below and quite far to the left of the target and then pushes it. The object rolls near the target, but makes a wider curve than predicted. COI then takes the object, makes it touch the target, and gives it a push back toward the start. From this new starting position, he again gives it a push toward the target, hits it, and repeats the process. The interviewer next pushes the object and marks the trajectory by a line. If I come back, will it be along

the same road? *That depends on how you hit it.*
(He shows possible small deviations.) And if you
throw carefully? *It would be the same.*

At level IIA, therefore, subjects doubt the constancy of the
trajectories for a given starting position and have little idea of
reversibility. Level IIB shows progress in both respects as the
result of a greater understanding of the double rotation of the
asymmetrical wheels. In fact, DEN's explanations are interesting. He says that the small wheel describes small circles,
while the large wheel describes the same number of large concentric circles. However, this progress, which certainly leads
to a grasp of constancy, is not enough to bring clear understanding of reversibility. DEN spontaneously makes the
wheels go back and forth from the starting point he selected
but, nevertheless, by his comment that the curve will widen
so that the wheels will eventually hit the target, shows that
he in actuality thinks the trajectories are not reversible. COI,
however, realizes from the outset that they are reversible and
even uses this fact to find an adequate starting point for the
object.

So ends the slow and very gradual dissociation between the
initially unconscious actions (despite success in hitting the
target) and the causal nature of the properties of the object.
This causal nature is progressively assimilated as a result of
the operations engendered by these same initially unconscious actions, which have become increasingly conscious
with the child's improved observation of the object. As he
becomes more aware of what he actually does, the child
becomes able to see what is caused by his action and so can
deduce what must be a result of the properties of the object
itself.

9 Towing a Small Rectangular Box

The experiments featured in this book involve acts of practical intelligence and children's cognizance of them. Since the tasks were selected on the basis that they are all likely to be encountered by children in some form or other in their everyday lives (unlike the more contrived tasks used in research into instrumental behavior patterns), the problem discussed in this chapter seems eminently suitable. The child is required to pull a small rectangular box by means of a string attached to it along a long plank of wood without its falling off the plank; he has to guide it with a stick as he walks alongside the plank, rather like a man walking along the towpath towing a boat. There is nothing complicated about the task, and success is fairly consistent from age seven or eight on—but it can also occur with younger children. This situation provides an excellent opportunity for studying the various levels of cognizance (and therefore of conceptualization) that precede our stage III (at about eleven years of age),

With the collaboration of Christiane Gillieron.

where the subjects are fully aware of what happens, unlike younger children whose conceptualization of the situation is clearly inadequate.

In situation I, the child is given a small rectangular box and asked to make it move from one end of a long table to the other; two sides of the table are against the wall so that the child cannot stand directly at the opposite end of the table and pull the box in a straight line (see Figure 3). At first he may use his hand, but then he must make the box move without touching it himself, by using string and sticks that are made available to him. In situation II, a plank of wood is placed, for instance, across the back of two chairs sufficiently high that the child is not able to see the whole surface, nor to reach the plank with his hands. The box is then put on the plank (which looks rather like a shelf), and the child has to make it move along, again using the string and sticks, without its falling off. In the final situation (III), the interviewer draws on the floor a "lake" or "wide river." The child is asked to stand at one side of this lake and make the box move from one extremity to the other. The box is not to touch the "riverbank" and the child must not go into the river. ("Don't put your feet in the water.") Again, the child is not allowed to stand at the opposite end of the lake. As he completes each task, the subject is asked to describe what he did and to explain how and why he did it, both verbally and with drawings. If necessary, the interviewer carries out the actions and the child tells him what to do and how to correct the errors that the interviewer systematically introduces.

The idea behind this particular experiment was to find out how the child pictures the trajectories of his hand, of the string(s), and of the box. How does he differentiate between them in the course of his action, and what is the level of his

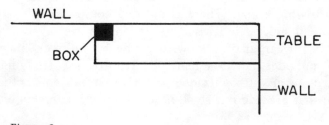

Figure 3

cognizance of this action and of the three different trajectories? (a) The trajectory of his hand (or of himself) should follow as near as possible, and parallel to, the edge of the plank. (b) The string starts off at a wide angle (\) to the straightahead direction of the box, but this angle narrows (—) as the hand moves forward (which is correctly noted by the stage III subjects. (c) If the child does not take the necessary precautions, the box simply follows the string and immediately falls off the plank. More advanced children keep it from falling off immediately, with the trajectory following a curve getting nearer and nearer the edge, but the box eventually falls off. The children who manage to prevent the box from falling off the table or plank, or from tumbling into the river (either by pushing it with the stick or pulling it with the string), follow a trajectory that starts off curved and then follows a straight line parallel to the edge of the table, or plank, or riverbank.

Stage I

Examples (Level IA)

NAT (4 years) uses the string to pull the box along the table, but prevents it from going over the edge with her hand. When she tries on the plank, she says, *It's going to fall off*, gives up the attempt with the string, and pushes it with her hand. The same thing happens in the river situation. She draws the box going straight forward, with the string represented by an oblique line coming out of the side. When she is asked how the string is when the box is about to fall off the plank, she draws it perpendicular to the plank.

CAR (5 years) first uses a stick to push the box in a straight line. When she tries to pull it with the string, the box gets near the edge and is about to fall. Why? Do you have any idea? *Because the box is shorter than the string.* (She must mean that the

string is too short for the box!) What should it be?
Bigger. I'm going to try, you tell me what to do.
(Tries.) *The string's got to be longer.* (The interviewer lengthens it). *You've got to pull straight.*
(The box gets near the edge.) *Pull it straight!* (The
box is at the edge.) Can you tell me what to do to
make it go straight? *No.* She draws a straight trajectory for the string and indicates the position of her
hand in the prolongation of this trajectory.

The only difference between the above subjects and those at
level IB is that the latter draw the box's trajectory as an
oblique straight line going toward the edge. However, they do
this only when the box falls off immediately.

Examples (Level IB)

MAT (5,11): *You can't do it . . . You've got to put
the box against the wall.* (It is there already.) However, he is finally successful. For situation I he
draws two straight trajectories for the box and for
himself (parallel to the edge). For situation II he
draws an oblique trajectory for the box and shows
two of its corners hanging slightly over the edge. In
the final situation (where the child can see the box
from start to finish) he shows the box making a
right-angle turn toward the edge.

FOL (6,1) starts off with his hand some distance
from the edge of the table, whereupon the box falls
off. He then lengthens the string and brings his
hand nearer the table. Finally, he makes the string
even longer and brings his hand still nearer the
table. The interviewer imitates this final solution,
but FOL cannot explain why the box falls off. In his
drawings, however, he marks two positions of the
box, of which one is a little nearer the edge of the
table than the other, with his hand following a path
parallel to this edge (*it goes straight*) and the string

always in a very slanting position. (He takes no account of how he modified his actual action.)

ISA (6 years): In her drawing of situation II she makes the box follow a path parallel to the edge of the plank when it does not fall and an oblique one when it is going to fall. In the latter case, she draws the box, which is still on the plank except for a tiny bit hanging over the edge, at an angle. Such a final position can only result from turning, but no sign of this appears in her drawing of its path. In situation III she draws the box's trajectory as an oblique line going toward the bank.

GEN (6 years) in situation II wisely suggests, *You pull right near the plank;* she draws two parallel trajectories for the box and for her hand and a very slightly oblique line for the string. However, when depicting the box as it falls off the plank, she first draws oblique lines for the trajectories of the box and the string and then changes her mind and draws parallel lines, which suddenly turn through a right angle and become perpendicular to the initial lines, as if the box makes an abrupt turn and falls off.

These subjects think, therefore, that if the box is pulled properly (*straight*), it will stay in the middle of the plank and travel along it in a straight line; if it is not pulled properly, it will fall off. However, their actions are more subtle than this simple conception and they sometimes correct the former by gradually moving themselves nearer the table or plank (FOL) or by lengthening the string (the link between the box and the child's hand) (CAR and FOL). Despite CAR's comments regarding the length of the string, cognizance of these actions is both very simplified and highly inadequate. If it does not fall, the box is thought to remain in the middle of the plank—none of the subjects appear to suspect that, even if it does not fall immediately, it must gradually move nearer the edge. However, such a path is drawn for situation III (river), since the box is visible the whole time (MAT and others), and with the plank (situation II) the child notices that the box always comes very close to the edge (cf. FOL). Despite this, even level IB subjects, who draw oblique lines to represent the trajectory of the box, do so only when it is going to fall; when it does not fall, they draw what they call *a straight path* (along the middle of the plank parallel to its edge). The path of the box that is going to fall, and in this case that of the string as well, is either drawn (clearly at level IB, not at all at level IA) as an oblique line or as two sides of a square, representing a straight path parallel to the edge, which suddenly makes a right turn (NAT, and GEN in her second drawing). It is interesting to compare the drawings of the paths taken by the subject's hand and by the string with those made by level IIA subjects. The latter appear to depict a lower level of conceptualization than the former. Stage I subjects either draw the paths of the hand and the string simply as an extension of that of the box's trajectory, which goes straight, or they draw the path of the hand following the edge of the plank with the string oblique. The second type of drawing is correct except that, for example, FOL, because his cognizance of the action is insufficient, takes no account of the adjustments he made during this action. However, it must be repeated that these drawings are in the main correct, whereas this is not the case at level IIA. The reason is simple: because the subject does not know why the box falls (CAR and FOL, for instance) and does not picture its path gradually nearing the edge of the plank unless it falls immediately, there is no contradiction for him between a right-angle trajectory of his hand (either on the plank or parallel to its edge) and an oblique (or a perpendicular) trajectory of the box that is going to fall: the action was not successful, and that is all there is to it. The level IIA subjects, however, try to understand what is happening and are particularly curious about the various paths. They are not satisfied with the stage I solutions. This dissatisfaction leads them to complicate the problem.

Stage I subjects therefore picture only two trajectories for the box in situation II: parallel to the edge if it stays on, and very oblique when it falls. Only in situation III, the river, do they observe and draw oblique paths that do not go over the edge, but simply bring the object nearer to it—which for them does not constitute a problem. At seven to eight years, by contrast, which is an age at which (as has been shown by all previous research) children begin to be concerned about apparent illogicalities regarding direction, the subject has the following difficulty. He knows full well that if the box is pulled straight it will stay in the middle of the plank, and that if it is pulled to the side it will fall off the plank. However, he also notices that if he pulls the string obliquely, but sufficiently near to the edge, he makes the box follow a path which, although it is not straight, does not immediately lead to the box's falling off the plank—a path that is not the same as that of the string, nor that of his hand, when he walks beside the plank. When the subject discovers this third trajectory (visible in the case of the river, but at this level immediately inferred in the case of the plank), he cannot explain it because he does not know enough about vectorial composition of forces. What is interesting is that, because he cannot explain it, he tries to introduce some coherence by (unconsciously) modifying his actual observations, either regarding the object (string) or the action itself (movement of the hand).

Examples (Level IIA)

STI (7,7) notices that on the plank the box *doesn't go straight* and concludes from that that her hands go *crooked;* her drawings, however, show the path of the box as an oblique line going straight off the plank, or as a straight line, with her hand as an extension (she tries to execute this, but is unsuccessful and pushes the box with her other hand whenever it goes off course).

BUC (7,9) describes the string's path: *Before, it went a bit like that* (oblique), *so I pulled like that* (straight). Then he tries pulling, first from one side of the plank and then from the other, so that the box proceeds in a series of zigzags. Finally, he succeeds, but in his drawing he simplifies the trajectories in such a way that the box travels in a straight line and his hand, which started off a fair distance from the plank, gradually gets nearer to it.

BUN (7,6) first thinks that when the box goes obliquely toward the edge it falls off because *it was heavier one side than the other*, and so the string does not pull each side of the box with equal force. After succeeding in the task, he explains: *I pull very slowly and after* (at the end) *I put the string over the top of the chair* (which supports the plank). He shows in detail what he did using a box of matches, but his drawing of the situation does not match his actions with the matchbox and represents the box's trajectory in two segments, one oblique and the subsequent one straight.

ARI (7,6) starts off by drawing an oblique line to represent the path of the box, then (while saying that the box goes to the edge of the plank) replaces this single line by two straight lines, one in the middle of the plank and parallel to the edge (the string) and the second skirting the edge (his hand). A second drawing shows the box having made a right-angle turn from its initial path (but in the wrong direction) and skirting the edge, with the paths of the string and his hand remaining parallel to the edge.

CLA (8,9) makes a doll carry out the action, specifying its movements and arm positions. He maintains that the box's path is governed by the position of the subject when he is pulling the string. For instance, when the doll pulls the string crookedly, the box still goes straight forward until the doll, who is moving gradually away from the edge, ends up holding the string perpendicular to the box, which then falls. If the box does not fall, he says that it is because the doll is right at the edge of the plank and able to pull it from the front.

VIC (8,6) thinks that to correct the box's oblique trajectory there must be a second string that may be pulled from the other side of the plank. He then fixes one string in the middle of the box and the other to one side (at the near edge of the plank): *I wanted to pull one* (middle), *then, when the box came to the edge, to pull with the other.* How would you pull? *As near as possible to the side of the plank.* In his drawing of the box's fall (with for the first time a long oblique line representing the box's path, which brings him near to level IIB) he nevertheless shows his hand moving progressively farther away from the plank with the string getting correspondingly longer and longer: Did your hand go along the same path as the string? *Yes.* In his drawing representing the movement without the fall, he returns, however, to the straight horizontal path for the box, with his hand still moving farther away from the edge (but less than on the other drawing). Doesn't it fall? *No, because I had two strings here.*

TAM (8,6) first of all draws a straight horizontal trajectory for the box when it does not fall, then an oblique one when it does, and arrives at a synthesis of the two—an oblique segment up to, but not over, the edge and a horizontal one from this point onward. He even takes a matchbox and makes it travel along such a path, explaining the initial oblique segment by the fact that the box turns around slightly at the beginning. Does the string stay the same at the end as it was at the beginning? *Yes, perhaps a bit longer.* However, when he draws his hand's trajectory, he makes it follow a path similar to that of the box: when the box falls, it is oblique (hand moves away from the plank); when the box stays on, it is near and parallel to the edge of the plank.

LAR (9,6) still thinks that her hand *pulls crookedly as the box comes near the edge.* Her drawing shows three parallel oblique lines for the box, the string, and her hand. Is the path your hand goes along different from the one the box goes along, or is it the same? *I think it goes along the same path. No, not exactly, if I had hooked my string there* (to the corner of the box) *it would have.*

Thus all these children notice that the box gradually nears the edge of the plank even when it does not fall off it. STI says the box *doesn't go straight;* BUC notes that *it went a bit like that* (oblique); for BUN, it goes off course because it is *heavier one side than the other*, while LAR actually says *the box comes near the edge*, and so forth. However, none of these subjects draws a completely oblique trajectory, except for VIC when the box falls off. BUN and TAM make the box start off on an oblique path, but then make it go parallel to the edge. It seems as if the subject at this level is brushing aside this disturbing factor of which he is actively aware. Still, when it comes to the movements of his hand, it is the observable feature itself that is modified to fit in with what he thinks must happen (complete interdependence of his notions of the problem). Even though he follows as closely as possible to the edge of the plank, he imagines, when it comes to reconstructing his action, that he must have pulled *crookedly* (STI and LAR) or, which comes to the same thing, that he must have moved farther away from the plank. VIC, for example, says that he pulled *as near as possible to the side of the plank* but thinks (when making his drawing) that he got progressively farther away, lengthening the string. CLA imagines an incredible situation, where the doll that he uses to symbolize what he himself has done, ends up pulling the box perpendicularly to the edge of the plank, when the box does not fall; when it falls, its path is horizontal from the outset. Briefly, these subjects either think (which is not far wrong) that they must have gradually moved farther away from the plank, with the box traveling along the same path as the string, or that they must have pulled crookedly because the box's path was not straight.

To sum up, subjects at this level become aware of the problem constituted by three trajectories, which shows that they have progressed in comparison with the stage I child, who is unaware of it. However, they cannot yet coordinate the paths (or directions) into a general system. As a result, the observable features themselves are modified — although certainly to a lesser extent when the child is observing the effects of his action, since attention is centered on attaining the desired end result (that is, the child has not yet begun to reflect on how things happen), than when he attempts to reconstruct the action. The modifications occur regardless of whether he tries to mime his action or draws or simply describes it. The gaps in his conceptualization lead the subject to subordinate the box's trajectory to the position of the string, while at level IIB, understanding of the box's oblique trajectory leads him to make his description of his own trajectory fit in with these positions of the box. It is true that it is generally when the box falls off (failure) that the interviewer questions the child about the trajectories. Nevertheless, there remains the significant difference between levels IIA and IIB that at IIB the subject correctly reconstructs the box's oblique trajectory when the fall is deferred or avoided, whereas at IIA there is not yet this differentiation between the box's trajectories and the string's positions.

Level IIB

Examples

DOU (9,9) starts off by saying that the box travels in a straight (horizontal) line *if you put a clamp to fix it* (to keep it in the middle of the plank) or *if you pull with your arm stretched*. He draws the trajectory for the box that does not fall off as a straight line down the middle of the plank, the one for the box that does fall off as an oblique line. In the latter case, the box, the string, and his hand are shown as parallel oblique lines. However, having succeeded in the task, he notices that the string *gets less and less oblique* and he draws for the box a long oblique line leading from its initial position to the edge, very near the end of the plank. The path of his hand is shown as a line near and parallel to the edge of the plank.

CAS (9,10) correctly keeps his hand parallel and very near the edge of the plank, then takes the shortest possible length of string. He draws the box's trajectory as slightly bending, while that of the string is represented by an oblique line.

SAB (9,6) starts off by drawing a straight line down the middle of the plank for the path of the box, a line parallel to the edge for that of her hand, and an oblique line for that of the string. She then differentiates among the three paths and finally draws a slightly bending trajectory for the box and a straight line for her hand.

CAL (10,6): *The string comes* (= is pulled) *to this side* (edge), *it makes the box turn and it gets near; then it goes straight behind me.* What is the most difficult thing to understand? *Mainly where my hand goes.* He draws the path of the box that turns and meets up with the edge as an oblique line, followed by a line parallel to this edge. This trajectory of his hand starts off as an oblique line (but less oblique than the line representing the string's path), which becomes horizontal near the edge. However, CAL corrects this and draws a straight line bordering the edge.

CHA (10,6) also ends up by drawing the box's path as a slightly oblique line meeting up with the edge, with oblique parallel lines for the string, and a straight line parallel to the edge for his hand. The first of these lines thus constitutes the long side of a triangle whose two other sides correspond to the string's position at the beginning and the trajectory of the child's hand.

These subjects have more or less solved the problem of the three paths, and their different directions. Firstly, they realize that the box can travel toward the edge without necessarily falling off, and they can indicate this very clearly in their drawing, unlike the children at the preceding level who did not draw such an oblique trajectory for the case when the box remained on the plank. Secondly, the level IIB subjects draw three clearly distinct trajectories with different directions—one for the box, one for the hand which (except for DOU and CAL, who at first hesitate) borders the edge of the plank, and one for the string. The latter is drawn very oblique to start with, and some children (CHA, for instance) draw all its subsequent positions parallel to this first line. However, DOU finally makes the pertinent observation that the string becomes *less and less oblique*, but he understands this as the consequence of the inclined trajectory and not as its reason.

These subjects still have not understood that the box cannot follow a straight trajectory, as it moves more quickly toward the edge at the beginning than at the end. The box's trajectory thus includes a curve, which is understood at stage III but cannot be grasped at level IIB. By contrast, when they draw the box's trajectory as an oblique line, these subjects (without setting out to do so) make it the long side of a triangle whose two other sides are the string in its initial position and the path of their hand. This complies with the diagonal of the parallelogram of forces, or more simply with vectorial addition of the two variables representing the cause (the subject's hand and the string) through a resultant corresponding to the effect (the box's trajectory). The children at this level thus are beginning to have an intuitive grasp of the problem of the directions, which tallies with earlier research findings relative to this problem.

Stage III and Conclusions

At stage III the curve in the box's trajectory and its link with the decreasing inclination of the string are understood.

> DEM (11,6) draws the box in three successive positions. He links these by curved lines, which are in

fact extensions of the long sides of the box. Does the box travel in a straight line? *No, because it has to turn there.* And what about the string? *It stays straight* (= whatever the position of the box), *but the box was following the same way as the string . . . I pull, that makes the box come toward me and the string gets more and more taut* (= less oblique). But why does your hand go parallel to the edge and not the box? *Because the string gets more and more taut and the box follows the string.*

PIT (11,6) first draws all the positions of the string parallel to one another. However, she then corrects the second position, greatly reducing the angle. She declares that *it is curved like that,* clearly confusing it with the box's trajectory, which she has not yet drawn.

GRA (12 years) draws the string's initial position more *oblique* than the final one, which is correct, and thinks that the box did not go straight forward *because it went off course.* But why? *Because the string isn't a stick.* GRA thus attributes the changing angle of the string to the fact that it is flexible. The best responses at this level are like those described above, and DEM's must be considered excellent when one takes into account the fact that in this particular experiment the interviewer was required not to dwell on the causal questions in order to put all the emphasis on the reading of the experimental data, that is, cognizance of the actual action and observation of the objects.

Considered from this point of view, the results obtained are fairly striking. Firstly, as with the tiddlywinks experiment of Chapter 6, the subjects' actions vary little at the different levels observed. The only progress occurring after seven years of age consists in trying to pull from both sides of the plank or in using two strings fixed to different points of the box, which is of no consequence with regard to our problems. Secondly, questions put to the subjects did not concern the geometry, kinetics, or dynamics of the events observed; the interviewers asked only for descriptions (except for two or three discrete "why" questions as checks at stage III). In spite of these very serious limitations on the scope of possible answers, the five levels distinguished in the experiment (as has been shown in this chapter) show quite a considerable variation in the way the subjects register the observable features of the situation. Furthermore, there is nothing fortuitous about these variations; specific variations are more or less consistent within each level.

In this respect the first finding is very simple, although it required confirmation. Registering of observations or, one may say, conceptualization of the facts (as opposed to that of the proprio- or exteroceptive perceptions, which are not translated into representations) depends on the level of the subject's inferential coordinations—in other words, on the level of his understanding. When we studied with Bärbel Inhelder the development of mental images and the relation between memory and intelligence, we were at first able to establish that imagined representation, although (or because) it derives from an interiorized imitation, does not always (in fact, frequently does not) reproduce exactly what has been perceived, as it depends on a preoperatory or operatory reconstruction of the information. Children retain in their memory only what they have understood. After six months they progress, regress, or remain stable according to the level attained or conserved by the subject during this interval, or else according to the schemes to which this understanding gives rise. Concerning the immediate registering of the observations themselves, there are, of course, similarities in the children's imagined representation and their short-term memory. However, the following finding is of particular interest: there is a remarkable convergence between the inferential coordinations which, at each level, govern the reading of these observable features and what we have discovered through our earlier research into causality.

At level IA, we know that the subject displays no understanding of the problems of direction and, in particular, be-

lieves that—whatever the impact point—an object will move
in the same direction as the force pushing it. So there is
nothing surprising in the fact that our four- and five-year-olds
adhere to ideas of *pulling straight* or falling in the case of failure (particularly if the pull is at right angles to the path the
object is thought to have followed). At level IB, certain experiments have shown the differentiation between the pushes (or
pulls) that make the object advance (translation) and those
that make it turn: it is therefore not simply by chance that
the five- and six-year-old subjects in this experiment draw an
oblique trajectory when the box falls off the plank.

As a general rule, level IIA sees the beginning of less simple
appraisal of the directional problems and of efforts to coordinate rotations and translations. However, their grasp of these
aspects is as yet insufficient to enable them to master the
explanation of the processes involved in this particular experiment. Thus there results the situation of conflict described
above. At level IIB, progress in the synthesis of the various
factors enables the child to provide more accurate descriptions of his observations. Finally, there comes stage III, characterized especially by an understanding of the interplay
between action and reaction.

To sum up, the results obtained in this research are almost
the same as if, instead of simply being asked to describe what
they saw, the subjects had been asked to predict and explain
what would happen as a result of the required action. Of
course, in situation II (the plank), the child cannot see the box
start to go off course, while he can in situation III (the river),
which explains the slight advance in this latter situation at
level IB. However, had he examined sufficiently carefully
what he could see in situation I, he would at least have noticed that the box gradually gets nearer the edge (and that is
sufficient, without great deductive effort, to conclude that it
must have moved there!). The fact that the box changes its
position on the plank is perceived only at level IIA and accepted only at level IIB, which is further evidence of the fact
that, in common with some theoreticians, the child only sees
what he thinks he knows. An African proverb, told us by one
of our black students, says in essence: "The foreigner looks at
us with wide-open eyes, but he sees only what he knew (or

thought he knew) about us." Fortunately, in the case of our subjects the inferential coordinations become increasingly developed with each stage, and conceptualization of the observable features becomes correspondingly more accurate.

However, the discovery that cognizance of the action itself and awareness of its results that are observable on the object thus correspond to levels of understanding, does not provide the solution to our two principal problems. Firstly, how does the subject gradually manage, through his actions, to reach this final high level of cognizance and awareness? Secondly, how is it that progress in understanding results from cognizance, or increasingly accurate conceptualization of these actions, and not vice versa? In addition to the consistent variations encountered at the different levels in this experiment, it seems possible to distinguish a second group of consistent findings.

(a) First of all, there appears to be an elementary type of regulation that involves the specific actions, independently of their coordination, and leads to a conception (not necessarily correct) of the situation relative only to the results of the action. This first type could be called "sensorimotor" or "automatic," in the sense that the feedbacks are determined from outisde according to the child's part-successes or part-failures in his efforts to solve the problem through progressive selection of the actions aimed at this solution. Except for the initial movement directing the object, in this case toward the end of the plank or whatever, this selection is fortuitous and not the result of deliberation. So the children start off by trying to *pull it straight* or attribute their lack of success to the fact that the box goes off course (NAT even draws the string at a right angle to the plank). There is therefore global reconstruction according to the success or lack of success in the action, without any detailed analysis of the trajectories. With FOL (IB), the regulations are visible in detail, but, because of his lack of cognizance, he cannot describe them.

(b) A second type of regulation may be called "active adjustment" of specific actions. These involve specific choices on the part of the subject and replace the sensorimotor regulations described in (a); because of the deliberate nature of these selections, they lead to cognizance and the beginning of an analysis of the methods used to solve the problem, as opposed to the earlier simple reconstruction from the results of the action. In this particular experiment, this analysis leads the child to consider his own position and that of the string; even as early as at level IA (but after she is asked why the box is about to fall off the plank), CAR tries to lengthen the string (without paying attention to the angle it makes with the plank) and, at level IB, GEN says that one must pull *right near* the plank.

(c) This active adjustment leads the child to consider two or more factors at once as he tries to work out how to solve the problem. In this experiment the level IIA subject considers simultaneously the positions of the string and the trajectory of his hand, but as he still subordinates the trajectory of the box to the position of the string he distorts the description of his own trajectory according to what he sees happen (he thinks he pulled *crookedly* if the box falls off, and so on).

(d) Finally, all the factors are coordinated when the child correctly registers all his observations. This entails differentiation and coordination of the three paths (directions); before he can relate the path of his hand and that of the string without distorting them, the child must realize that although it is linked to these two, the box's path is quite different from them both. At level IIB this path is drawn as an oblique line (and DOU gradually reduces the angle of the string), and at stage III it is finally represented by a curve. Why are the observations more accurately recorded in (d) than in (c), thus enabling the construction of effective coordinations in place of the initial distorting relationships? The child in (c) starts to look for links between distinct factors and sooner or later comes to investigate them more thoroughly. This, with the onset of the truly inferential coordinations, leads to the accurate recording of his observations in (d).

To sum up, it seems that the progress in action (from the sensorimotor or automatic regulations to active adjustment and thence to adjustments involving many dimensions or factors) leads from the simple praxeological coordination of means and ends to awareness and cognizance of the situation and to conceptualized coordinations, which finally ensure understanding of the whole process.

10 The Catapult

Take a stick or bar and place it horizontally on top of a box so that the greater part of the stick rests on the box and one end protrudes into space. Give this free end a sharp tap, and the stick does a somersault. Young children cannot picture this somersault, as we discovered in an earlier study concerning imagined representation in which their difficulties were analyzed. Since this situation (or any similar one, with an object that is only partly supported) might be familiar to the subject, it seemed appropriate in a study on practical intelligence and cognizance of actions to construct an elementary type of catapult in order to see what the subjects do with it and how they conceptualize their actions.

The metal bar in this experiment has nine holes through which another bar may be slotted at right angles to provide the axis of rotation for the first bar. The axis of rotation must, of course, be raised so that the bar has room to rotate around it. Because of the nine holes, the position of the axis of rotation may be varied. Initially it is placed in the middle of the bar (hole 5); a small object (a match, for instance) is placed on

With the collaboration of Olivier de Marcellus.

it so that the child realizes that it may be projected. He is then given a small plasticine ball. The interviewer places target boxes at various distances from the catapult. (These are numbered 5 to 10, according to their distance from the target. When the child gets the ball into a box, he scores the appropriate number of points.) It is up to the subject to find out how to use this catapult to get the ball into the boxes. Four-year-olds use it like a simple launch pad. However, for children who want to use it effectively the main question is where to put the ball. Should they put it near the end they press, since this is nearer the boxes at which they are aiming, or should it be nearer the other end, since the catapult describes a rotation? Subsequently a weight may be suspended at the end of the bar (again, its position may be varied, as the bar is provided with hooks for this purpose). In this case the child makes use of the weight instead of simply pressing with his hand. Toward the end of the questioning, the interviewer draws the subject's attention to the possibility of pulling the bar down to various levels, suggests various extreme situations, and asks him what will happen in each case.

As usual, the child is asked to describe and explain his actions and to draw the path of the plasticine ball and (when applicable) that of the weight.

The sixty subjects in this experiment were aged between (3,7) and fourteen years (most were between five and eight).

Level IA: No Effective Use of the Catapult

Examples

PIE (3,7) does not understand how to use the bar. The interviewer shoots off a match. Does that give you an idea? *Don't know.* The child is then given the plasticine ball. He puts this at the right end[1] of the bar, which he hits as he has just seen the interviewer do. How about like that? (The interviewer puts it at the left end.) *All right.* (He uses the bar

1. The "right end" is the end of the bar nearer the boxes, while the "left end" is the opposite end. Thus "to the right" means "in the direction of the end of the bar nearer the boxes" and "to the left" means "in the direction of the opposite end of the bar."

like a bat. The interviewer gives him another demonstration. He puts the ball at the right end and
misses the box.) Look. (Further demonstration.) (He
again uses the bar like a bat.) At the interviewer's
suggestion, he then hits the bar and quickly sees
that the nearer the ball is to the left end, the farther
it travels. He therefore thinks that the best place
for the ball is near the left end. The interviewer
next turns the catapult around so that the ball flies
off away from the boxes. PIE refuses to hit the bar
and wants merely to throw the ball. (He has this
reaction three times in succession, when the direction is thus altered.) The interviewer then puts the
ball at the right end and says that he is going to hit
the bar at the left end. *You do it like that.* (He
shows how it should be done.) Where will the ball
go? *Over there* (toward the boxes, which is incorrect). (The interviewer demonstrates.) What should
we do to make it go nearer the cupboard (opposite
direction from the boxes)? *You've got to put it
nearer* (toward the left). (He thus takes no account
of what he saw with the boxes.) Well then, let's
have another try at getting it in one of the boxes.
(PIE again throws the ball.)

ARI (4 years) puts the ball at the left end and pushes
it with her hand. And if you put the ball there and
you hit here, will it go into a box? *Yes.* (She again
pushes the ball with her hand, then inclines the bar
so that the ball can roll down it.) (She is given
another demonstration.) *You made it jump!* (The
interviewer puts the ball back on the bar.) *It's going
to fall, you're going too slowly;* (she hits the bar)
I'm doing it quickly. (The interviewer puts the ball
at the right end.) *It will go farther* (beyond the
boxes). If you want the ball to go there (in the opposite direction), where must you hit the bar? (She
pushes the ball with her hand.) After a few attempts, ARI sees that the ends of the bar move more
than the middle. How about there (near the

middle)? *It will go like that* (large circle around the center). Try. (Fails.) *It's got to jump quicker.*

DAN (4,9) initially has similar reactions. When she sees the experimenter hit the right half of the bar, with the ball at the left end, she thinks that one must also hit the right half if the ball itself is on the right, and that the nearer it is to the right end, the farther it will travel in the direction of the boxes. When she tries this, she finds that it goes off toward the cupboard and so she lifts the left end of the bar to make the ball roll into the boxes. What happens if you hit it? (Draws an arc with her arm in the direction of the boxes, with no regard to the preceding failure.) And if I hit like that (tap left side, with ball also on the left)? *It will go toward the boxes.* And if I hit here (right side)? *Toward the cupboard* (both predictions thus wrong). After three opportunities of seeing and correctly describing what happens, she again incorrectly predicts that the ball will go to the right if it starts on the right side of the bar and to the left if it starts at the left end.

ISA (4,6) pushes the ball with her hand, even though the interviewer has showed her how to make the match jump. Then, instead of hitting the bar, she inclines it toward the side of the desired target. Because of this, she correctly predicts that if the ball starts on the right and one taps the left end it will go toward the cupboard. Trying this out, she starts off by inclining the bar to the left to make the ball roll, then admits that if one taps the left side the ball will do the same thing. Subsequently, she muddles up the actions of using her hand to incline the bar and of actually hitting it, but having used both large and small balls, she comes to the conclusion that the *big balls* go to the right and the *little* ones to the left.

MAR (4,6), despite all her attempts, still thinks at the end of the questioning that when she hits the left side of the bar, with the ball the same side, it will go into a box.

Two points are of particular interest in these elementary reactions. The first is that, as usual, an action of the child's own body leading directly to the target is preferred to an action with a mediator when the latter does not constitute (as does a stick) an extension of his arm or hand. Hence the tendency to throw the ball into the boxes or to use the bar as just a horizontal or sloping launch pad. Although these children watch the interviewer demonstrate how to use the device as a catapult and are often amused by its novelty (for them), as soon as they try to make the ball reach a target, they appear to forget all about this possible mediator. Furthermore, the interviewer has merely to change the direction of the ball's path for the subject, even if he has already practiced hitting the bar, to revert to simply throwing the ball.

A second aspect of these reactions is even more interesting. The children appear not to be able to take account of their observations of the object, and even of their action, when these contradict what they think ought to happen. They expect that if the ball starts at the left end it will go to the left (and vice versa), and that the nearer the ball is to this end, the greater the distance it will travel in this direction. It is clear that these children do not understand the part played by the rotation of the bar, even though they may notice that the ball travels in an arc. As they think in terms of a translation and not of a rotation (this is normal, since the subject tends to throw the object with his hand or to make it roll, and not make it turn), they feel that the ball must travel in the way they predict. It would be impossible for it to travel the other way.

What happens when they see the "impossible" happen? Although PIE indicates an optimal position for the ball in the correct direction, on the correct side of the bar, he takes no account of this in his subsequent answers. There is more involved here than a straightforward learning difficulty, in that it is the actual recording of the subject's observations on both the object and the action in question. It is obviously not sufficient to make a correct observation of something for it to be accepted, if there appear to be valid reasons for refusing (or repressing) it. If such reasons do not exist, the subject at this level is phenomenist and accepts anything, like ISA when she says that the little balls will go one way and the big ones another. However, if the subject feels that what he sees happen should not have happened, then this observation is not retained and conceptualized.

These modest findings are therefore important from the theoretical point of view since they show us that, even at very elementary levels (three to four years), assimilation of data in the form of simple conceptualized observations is dependent upon earlier coordinations. In most situations, one has to assume the existence of such coordinations and admit that they modify the subject's observations. However, in this specific case, the child starts off by throwing the ball or making it roll down the inclined bar. It is thus the initial actions that lead, through inferences, to certain coordinations that are conceived as necessary—that is, that the ball tends to go off to the right if it starts off on the right side of the bar (or vice versa) and that the nearer it is to the end of the bar, the farther it will travel in this direction. In this case, the inferential coordinations channel and modify the subject's actual observations.

Level IB: Some Idea of Direction but No Understanding of Distances

As usual, the level of five and a half to seven years, which is that of functions in process of formation, reveals marked progress in the development of actions. The subject is interested by the interviewer's demonstration of the catapult with a match and practices handling the device himself. He successfully sends the ball some distance. However, despite this success in action, the subject's conception of his observations on the object and even his cognizance of the variations of the action remain incomplete. These children still think that the nearer the ball starts off to the boxes the farther it will go in this direction, even though they have discovered that for it to go off to the right it must start on the left, and vice versa! Briefly, through his action the subject discovers in which direction the ball will travel, but this does not enable him to understand the relationships of distance.

Examples

TAM (5 years) does not know what to do with the catapult, but after the demonstration with the match, she shows interest and tries to apply the process to the ball. She starts off pressing the wrong end, in fact presses the section of the bar adjacent to the ball. She then moves the ball to the other side and gets it into a box (six points). Next she tries various starting positions for the ball to see how the changes affect the distance it travels. After five attempts: How did you manage to get it so far (the six-points box)? *Don't know.* She tries again eleven times, with results varying between eight points and zero. (The ball starts off near the middle of the bar and just falls down.) What did you do? (She correctly describes her action.) And what did you do to make it go far or not so far? *I don't know.* After another attempt, guided by the interviewer: Why did it go farther this time? *Because it was far-ther on the bar* (points to the correct place for the first time). She then moves the pivoting center, but replaces it as it was before. Where must you put the ball for it to go farther? She forgets all her discoveries and puts the ball not only nearer the center, but on the right side of the bar, that is, the side nearer to the boxes! When this does not work, she puts the ball on the left side, but close to the middle so that it is as near as possible to the opposite end. Why there? *Because it's less far from there* (the end near the boxes). Even nineteen more attempts (with four misses and one success of eight points) do not elicit a general description of the law. Her final reactions, however, are interesting. When the interviewer tells her to use the weight instead of pressing on the bar herself, and in fact puts it on the right side with the ball on the left side, TAM tries to vary its position and thinks that it must be *farther* from the right end of the bar, thus falsely applying to the weight what she refused to do for the ball!

ERI (5,6) claims to know what to do with the catapult, as he has already played *with little rulers.* So the interviewer balances a ruler on a stand and ERI says, correctly, that if the ball is put on one side it will go off to the other. *It's going to go off this side* (right) *if you press there* (left). However, when asked for the best place for the ball, he says this must be *nearer the target,* and not at the end opposite that which is nearer the target. When the interviewer goes on to the standard device, he again says that the ball will go off to the right when the left side is depressed. However, when he actually tries out the catapult, he opts for a compromise solution, putting the ball *not too far and not too near* (the target). He puts the weight near the middle of the bar. *It will go farther, it's nearer that* (the axis).

ALA (5,8) is successful, placing the ball near the left end of the rod. How can you do it better? (She brings it nearer the center.) After several attempts, she notes that *it's better* when it is at the left end, but when the interviewer reverses the rotational direction, she says *we ought to put it there* (nearer the target).

CHA (6,6) tries with a ball halfway along the correct side of the bar. "Where's the best place for the ball if we want it to go very far? *There* (brings it nearer the boxes), *it goes farther.* Why? *It's nearer* (the boxes). When he sees that the opposite happens, he tries various positions but *I can't make up my mind. I'm going to try there* (moves it a little farther from the target: better result). And if you put it at the end? *I don't know.* When he tries with the weight, he immediately brings the ball nearer the boxes. He makes several attempts, but when the interviewer puts the ball farther away from the boxes, the child brings it back nearer. Show me from where it goes the farthest? *I don't know, I can't remember.*

FRA (7,3) immediately takes the weight and inclines the bar to the side of the ball so that it can go farther down the side where the weight is. *It swings more at the front.* And why will the ball go farther? *It's the spring.* Despite this, he places the ball near the center: *There it will be nearer* (the boxes), *so it can jump farther.* After various attempts, he recognizes that this is not so and adopts a compromise solution (halfway along the right side): *In the middle, because 5 + 5, that can fall into the 5* (box 5) *or into the 10!* Finally, he feels obliged to admit what he sees: *It goes farther there* (when it starts at the end). Do you know why? *No.*

The fact that the subject discovers that he has to place the ball on one side of the bar and hit the other side certainly stems from his observation that the ball jumps in the air and does not simply roll along the rod. This is a very simple observation, which is accepted as soon as the child stops throwing the ball with his hand. Why, then, is it so difficult for him to grasp the significance of the various possible starting positions? One would have thought that TAM's five, then eleven, then nineteen attempts would have been sufficient to enlighten her, and in fact at one point she does say that the ball went farther because *it was farther on the bar* (that is, nearer the opposite end). However, this does not lead her to recognize the law, and she even reverts to the contrary hypothesis. The fact that she wrongly applies the principle to the weight (which is not projected) and not to the ball, which she has handled a great deal, is fairly indicative of conflict. For these subjects there is a contradiction in the idea that the ball can go farther into the boxes, the farther away from them that it starts; and it is this that makes them resist the evidence of their own eyes. This reaction is common at five to six years, still occurs with seven- to eight-year-olds and even happens, although only temporarily, at nine and ten years. A subject aged (9,9) started off by drawing two trajectories for the ball as two similar arcs ((, one starting farther along the bar than the other, clearly illustrating her inference that a *nearer* starting point leads to the ball going *farther*. In other words, the subject cannot accept the results of a law he does not understand, which is the case at level IB, except (and then not always) when he is already aware of the phenomenon.

What these children still seem unable to understand in this situation appears to stem from their difficulty in picturing the rotation of the bar and consequently the length of the ball's trajectories. They do understand that if you press on one side of the bar, it makes the other side go up and triggers the ball's departure, but they do not yet realize that this movement of the bar constitutes the beginning of a rotation and that, consequently, a ball placed at the end of it is at the extreme end of a rotational axis and thus will describe a longer arc. They think that the ball simply leaves the bar and goes off in a straight line toward the boxes—hence the drawing of the nine-year-old referred to above. Of course, some young children at level IB (ERI, for instance) do draw two arcs of concentric circles, but these represent only the object's climb when it leaves the bar and its descent into the boxes; the children do not even think about the length of the arcs. In short, the inference common at this level (the nearer the ball starts to the target, the farther it will go) seems to stem from a lack of understanding of the rotation and from a continuing failure to differentiate between rotation and translation. The former is reduced to the object's departure from the bar and the latter represents the path that leads it to the boxes. Most of these subjects (see ERI) finally opt for a compromise between their observation and their prediction, and select a position for the ball that is neither too far from, nor too near to, the boxes.

Stage II: Understanding of Where to Put the Ball on the Bar and the Dynamic Factors Involved. Level IIA.

From about seven or eight years of age (although we encountered at this level some precocious six-year-olds who were already familiar with the game) the child can formulate the law governing the distance the ball will travel. He discovers this law because he has become capable of explaining it.

Examples (Level IIA)

JAC (7,2) starts off by using the device to launch a matchbox, then tries the ball at various places along the bar, including in the center. Where's the best place? *At the end* (left), *I think.* Right at the end? *Yes, because it's farther. If you put it at the other end, it falls right away. At this end, it goes a long way.* Why? *Don't know.* However, he draws two trajectories, one for the ball when it starts at the left end and one for when it starts three-quarters of the way along the bar, showing that he recognizes the difference. As soon as the interviewer suggests using the weights, he puts the ball at the left end: *When it's at the end it goes farther because it's got more spring.* Furthermore, he finds a suitable position for the pivoting center, understanding the drawbacks of a situation where the two sides are too unequal (the weight would not go down far enough or the ball would not be sufficiently far away).

VLA (7,5) is told that he may use what he wants and immediately takes the weights. At first, he hesitates regarding the position of the ball, then puts it at the right end: *It will go farther because it's at the end of the bar.* Then he puts the weight near the middle *because it's nearer the plasticine* (as if this would help the action). *Wait a bit. No, that's wrong* (he puts the weight farther away). *It's better at the first* (hook). *The plasticine is thrown farther away because the weight is farther from it.* Then he moves the axis a little toward the right end of the bar, so that the ball is on the longer side. *That makes it go farther.* Why? *Well, the weight falls and the thing goes off.* He draws an almost vertical bar; the weight is at the lower end, the ball at the high end, and so goes farther.

PHI (8,0) decides to hit the bar with his hand and immediately puts the ball on the other end. Will that go better? *Yes, because it's* (the end with the ball) *higher* (once the other end has been pressed down); *you've got more time to lift and it goes higher.* And there (near the center)? *No, that's no good. It makes it go farther away* (when it is at the left end) *than there. There* (at the left end) *I think that* (it goes better) *because it's farther from there* (the boxes) *and because it goes more quickly. It flies away with more force and there* (the center) *it's too near the boxes.* Can you make it work using something other than just your hand? *Yes, with the weight.* He puts this at the left end and tries various positions for the axis. He finally puts it two-thirds of the way along the bar, thereby both allowing sufficient length of the side with the weight for the catapult to work efficiently and making the side with the ball longer so that the latter goes farther. *When the weight is there* (not right at the end), *it takes only a little bit of time for it to get down; there* (at the end) *it takes a longer time,* which makes the ball go farther.

SER (8,6) immediately puts the ball at the left end. *At the end it will go farther if* (= because) *you push down hard.*

DAV (8,6) also places the ball at the left end, because otherwise *it won't go high,* and the weight at the right end is better there than in any other position *because the bar goes lower.*

LOU (9,8) asserts that the weight must be at the left end *because if you let it go the weight goes down, and if it* (the other end where the ball is) *is right up high the ball can jump properly.*

SCO (8,10) says that if the ball is at the end *it goes farther, there's more spring.*

DIN (8,5) puts the ball at the end of the bar and shows that the angle between the original and new positions of the ball end of the bar when it rises corresponds to that between the original and new positions of the weight end when it goes down: where it only moves through a small angle *there's less spring* and the ball doesn't go as far. Curiously, he adds that when the bar is vertical and the weight *hits* (the edge of the box), *it gives it spring* like a coil spring.

These subjects' actions seem to bear witness to a growing understanding of how the catapult works; the children realize that the bar rotates and intuitively compare this rotation to that of a stick, one end of which is held in the hand. While the level IB subjects do not yet think in terms of rotation, those at stage III picture it clearly. For example, VLA draws the bar in an almost vertical position and PHI immediately refers to the ball's position at the end of the bar in terms of *higher* and not *farther* (we've *got more time to lift and it goes higher*). DAV's and LOU's reactions are similar. Finally, DIN indicates the correspondence of the angles at the two ends of the rod when the latter is inclined.

While the law of distances is thus understood in terms of the subject's actions and his intuition of the rotation involved in them, cognizance of these actions and of their results raises an interesting problem. In fact, none of these subjects deduce from this rotation that the nearer the ball is to the end, the longer its trajectory will be. Of course, they all say that it *will go farther*, but we know that until level IIB evaluation of length remains ordinal, therefore relative to the points of arrival, and does not yet involve any estimation or conservation of the intervals. Above all, what is striking—and this stems precisely frcm the child's inadequate cognizance—is that while this *farther* is not linked to the action of a longer path right from the outset, it is related to the dynamics of the action. JAC, who at first says he does not know why the ball goes farther when it starts off at the left end of the bar, subsequently finds that *when it's at the end it goes farther because it's got more spring.* (FRA, at level IB, is already talking of *spring* because at (7,3) he is near to level IIA, but he does not draw the same conclusions as the more advanced subjects.) PHI specifies that at the end *you've got more time to lift* (the bar), *it goes more quickly,* and *it flies away with more force.* SER and SCO also talk about force and spring; LOU says that as a result of the action the ball can *jump properly.* Generally speaking, these children think that the ball's position at the end of the bar both facilitates the latter's rotating action and gives the ball the spring or force necessary to get *farther;* they do not consider length to be made up of a continuous succession of individual units.

It is interesting to recall that in our earlier experiment on the somersault, the effects of the rotation were also understood well before children became able to picture the somersault itself. When young children colored the two ends of the bar red and blue, they could predict their permutation at the end of the somersault before they could draw or even describe, by means of slow-motion actions, the stages and trajectory of the rotating bar or of its ends.

As for the weight, its action fits the same dynamic model: it has more effect at one end because it *falls* (better) *and the thing* (ball) *goes off* (VLA), because it takes a longer time (PHI) and when it moves through a large angle there's more spring, and DIN even adds that hitting the edge of the box gives the ball spring.

Level IIB

At level IIB, ages nine and ten, the subject is capable of contemplating the length of the trajectories, since this is the level of conservation of metrical lengths independently of ordinal considerations. Surprisingly, he does not do this, and his cognizance of the actions carried out on the bar and their generalization in the case of the weight only lead him to refine the preceding dynamic considerations. He resorts to explaining the reciprocal actions of the suspended weight and the ball through analogy with a pair of scales.

Examples

HAR (9,2): The ball has to be at the end of the bar because then, when pressure is applied to the bar, *it gives it spring.* When he comes to the weight, like many subjects at this level, he shows he almost understands the dynamic moment: the weight must be fixed to the end of the bar *because that makes more weight.* Does it weigh more? *No, the same, but there's more bar and it goes farther.* He then moves the fulcrum nearer the right end of the bar: *It goes farther because there's more weight. Where? The bar's got more weight here* (ball side, thus reinforcing his action) *than there* (weight side). So? *When there's more bar, there's more spring.* He even shows the lifted bar and the ball's departure. However, he is not thinking of the length of the paths (he draws spaced-out parabolas) and merely shows that when the bar is inclined, the ball at the end flies off from a higher point (effect of the rotation, but no drawing of the paths).

CO (9,6) thinks that when the weight is not suspended at the end *there isn't enough weight,* while when it is suspended more nearly at the end of the bar *there's more weight.* Why is it better? *If that* (the ball) *isn't so heavy* (compared with the weight) *and you put it there* (at the end), *it goes like that* (quicker movement). At the end of the session, he again insists: *There* (right end); *there's more weight, there's more force when it's at the end.*

DIM (9,7) thinks that when the ball is not at the left end *it won't go as far because it's lower* (rotation!); *there isn't enough force.* For the weight, he places the fulcrum two-thirds of the way along the bar: *The bar's longer, so it throws it farther; there* (weight), *there's more weight, but it* (ball side) *mustn't be too long, because there wouldn't be any more weight here* (weight side). The interviewer moves the ball a quarter of the way along from the end. *That's not so good because the weight doesn't throw strongly enough.* But we didn't change the weight at all? *It's got more force there* (when the ball is at the end). The interviewer suspends the weight nearer the center: *If you do that you take away a little bit of weight!* At the end *it's got more spring, the weight goes down more and that* (the ball) *goes farther.* When asked to draw the paths, he does it correctly, but does not refer to his drawing when giving a verbal explanation.

XAV (9,9) immediately puts the ball at the end. *The end* (the ball side of the fulcrum) *is longer, it sends it off better.* The interviewer suspends the weight in two different places (right end, and a short distance from the right end) and asks which position will make the ball go better. *At the first* (end), *it's heavier; at the second, it's less heavy because there's less bar; the bar weighs as well.* He then has the marvelous reaction of weighing in his hands the weight suspended in the two positions! When it comes to describing the trajectories, he merely says *I think it turns,* showing the bar's rotation and the ball's projection.

GYS (10,0) checks that the weight goes down sufficiently *because if you pull it lower it's got more time to get up speed.* On the other hand, if the lengths are shared between the ball and the weight, *there's more weight there, and there there's less. There* (= ball side = less weight) *there's more balance, and there* (weight) *less.* So? *Yes, it's strong because there there's more weight.* In other words, despite his rather clumsy way of expressing himself, GYS seems to maintain that there must be an inequality, a source of imbalance, for the weight to give strength and speed.

NIC (10,1): You've got to put the weight at the end of the bar because *that makes more weight. It gives the spring to go off.* And the ball? *At the end, because it can go higher.*

Basically, therefore, these reactions differ little from those at level IIA. The subjects think that the pressure or the weight causes the bar to rotate; the latter then lifts the ball and sends it off with spring and speed, which explains the fact that it goes farther. The only marked novelty is the comparison of this situation with a pair of scales and the concern that the weight must be sufficiently great to propel the ball. As a result, these subjects are concerned about the position of the weight, and most of them think that the weight is heavier when it is at the end of the bar than when it is nearer the center, which is in fact the beginning of intuition of the dynamic moment. In the case of HAR, there is a reversal when the fulcrum is changed; he thinks that the weight becomes greater when it is on the ball side, which gives it spring. All the others, however, are constantly concerned with making the suspended weight heavier than the ball (CO, particularly DIM, and others). XAV weighs the weights in his hand, and GYS translates the phenomenon in terms of imbalance.

The subtlety of these analyses makes it even more surprising that there is no explicit reference to the length of the trajectories. As at level IIA, these subjects think in dynamic terms of propulsion, of height, and of spring—which makes the ball go *farther*—but they do not refer to the actual length of the trajectories.

Stage III and Conclusions Regarding Cognizance

Although there are two ten-year-olds in this category, generally speaking it is not until eleven or twelve years of age that children talk about *the longest road*, the *biggest curve*, and the like.

Examples

SYL (10,0) is a good example of what Sander and German psychologists have called real-time development—that is, in less than an hour of questioning SYL passes through all the earlier stages. She starts, as at level IA, by trying to make the ball roll on the inclined bar. When the interviewer suggests that she use the box, she puts the bar on it so that it extends over the edge and hits the protruding bit. She then places the ball nearer the boxes, as at level IB, saying, *That can make it go forward!* After this, she puts the ball at the end and comes to the rotation of level IIA: *That could go better, because the bar's longer, it lifts it higher*, in other words, it projects the ball better. Then she uses the weight and reasons as at level IIB: she puts the weight at the end *because the weight's heavier when it is at the top of the bar, it makes it go farther*. Why? *It almost goes right around* (bar rotates), whereas in the other positions *instead of going around, it stops*. Why doesn't it go so high and so far? *Here* (weight at the end) *it sends it farther, it makes it go a long way*. SYL thus reaches stage III and illustrates her idea of *a long way* by drawing, for one of the ball's starting positions, an extended arc. Her second drawing shows a tight, short curve.

TIA (10,6) starts off by reasoning as at level IIB and sums up his arguments by saying that the weight and the bar *make it go up*. He fixes the fulcrum two-thirds of the way along the bar. *It's got more force*. Why does it go better? *It goes farther*. Why farther? *Because the bar* (the ball side) *is longer, it's got more force, it goes farther*.

MIC (11,1) puts the ball at the left end, *because it goes up higher*, the weight at the right end, and the fulcrum two-thirds of the way along, because *that way there's more weight, it gives more force, it goes quicker if you pull down.* Where does the spring come from? (He shows the incline on the ball side.) *The bar starts to get its spring from there, the track's going to be bigger* (draws trajectories for two positions of the ball). Why does the ball go off? *It's the weight that makes the plasticine go off and the bar as well, that makes it move: the weight pulls and the bar makes it move.*

JEA (11,9) hesitates for a long time before deciding where to put the fulcrum: if the weight side is longer *it gives it more push,* but this hinders the ball, because *the longer it is* (the ball side), *the farther it goes, the farther it has to go.* What gives it the force? *Pushing it, but there's the bar that does something too,* since if the ball does not go high enough *then there's less to go* (in the air). Finally, *We've got to make it half and half, because the two go together: the weight's no use if there's no bar.*

GIL (12,7) arrives at the same solution.

CLA (11,11) also understands the part played by the length of the bar. If the ball side is made shorter, *there's always the same force, but the plasticine doesn't go so far.* Why? *Because* (if the ball is) *at the end, it goes higher, the path* (toward the boxes) *is longer,* and if the fulcrum is moved to the right *the plasticine goes farther.*

YVO (12,0) reasons in a similar way. If the fulcrum is moved to the right *the ball's got farther to go.*

MIN (12,2) thinks that moving the fulcrum *makes a bigger angle* (she is thinking of the arc) *and the ball goes farther.*

DAL (12,6) has the same reasoning and concludes: *There's a bigger radius, it makes a bigger circle.* He then roughly measures the trajectories.

There are two novelties at this stage and it is important to determine which leads to which. These subjects consider the length of the ball's trajectories and do not simply note the order of the arrival points. They also relate this length to that of the rotating radius, that is, to the length of the ball side of the bar. All these subjects — except for the intermediate one, SYL, who starts with lower-level reactions but ends up talking about *a long way* — understand that the ball's trajectories do not depend only on the pressure or the weight acting at the other end of the bar, but also on the length of the ball side, thus of the radius that rotates. *The weight pulls and the bar makes it move*, says MIC, and DAL comments, *There's a bigger radius, it makes a bigger circle*. Of course, the stage II subjects knew this implicitly, since they placed the ball at the end of the bar, saying that it would therefore go higher and go farther. Although they think of the bar's movements in terms of rotation, for them the ball goes farther as a result of the propulsion. *The end* (the ball side) *is longer, it sends it off better*, says XAV, which provides a good summary of the level IIB conceptualizations. Stage III, however, sees for the first time a detailed spatial representation of the situation: the longer arc of the circle during rotation (*a bigger angle*, says MIN) leads to a *bigger track* (MIC). The dynamic moment of the weight must be considered together with the lengths of the radius and the distance described by the end of this radius. *The weight's no use if there's no bar*, affirms JEA.

To return to our problem: Why do such simple representations, already implicitly contained in the stage II conception of the rotation, appear so late? Is it not because the subject at last feels the need to explain the actual length of the paths (and not only the arrival points) that he looks for the reason in the length of the radius that rotates? But why does this not happen until after the dynamic considerations of stage II?

Undoubtedly, a more general factor must be invoked — the child's cognizance of his own actions. The child's actions are usually successful from level IB on, and sometimes even at level IA, but his cognizance of them is far slower, since it appears to obey necessary laws of succession. With complex actions (as regards their sensorimotor mechanism) the child's cognizance of them proceeds from the outside in, that is, from the external result to the internal conditions of its execution. For example, walking on all fours is easy for children of any age, but is actually quite complicated and at nine or ten years only two-thirds of the subjects correctly indicate the successive movements of their hands and feet. At a less advanced level, they think that they start off with their two hands (because they are in front of their feet in the direction they are going) and then move their two feet. With the catapult, the subject's motor execution is less complex, since he simply has to hit the end of a bar, or use a weight instead of his hand. The succession of physical sequences is more complicated, yet we encounter a similar law: cognizance of the action or of the object starts from the result (the external target) and moves only progressively to the increasingly internal preliminary conditions.

The aim here is to make the ball go into the boxes. As these are placed in front of the catapult, the path leading to them is initially conceptualized as a simple translation; hence the direct actions of pushing or making the ball roll (level IA). Then comes the idea that the nearer the ball is to the boxes, the farther it will go in this direction (level IB). When the child notices that the bar rotates, the most simple coordination linking this rotation to the target is based on the idea of propulsion, since the ball is "thrown" into the air and no longer rolled forward. What the subject observes regarding the action will thus be dictated by his desire to find the most efficient way of propelling the ball. This, of course, leads to cognizance of the conditions required for the propulsion of the ball in terms of dynamic factors (stage II), since consideration of the arrival at the target imposes a direct relationship between this aim and the action itself, thus the search for a "cause" in the general sense of the "why," before finally coming to the "how." The direct relation between the aim and the action, which appears to lie behind the first "cause" invoked by the subjects, arises through their discovery of what they can do to modify the result, which was previously considered unalterable, in order to get the ball nearer the target. At level IIA, the child discovers that by placing the ball at the end of the bar he helps it to go *farther*; in his eyes, this is sufficient because the ball thereby *flies off better*, this flight being ascribed dynamic powers (force, spring, and so forth). The child does not find it necessary to explain the "how" and "why" of the flight itself. The reason is that when the child tries to find out "how," he goes back deeper into the problems by seeking the "why" for the mechanism invoked as the solution of the first "why," and so on. In this particular situation, the direct relation between the action and the aim at first makes this probing back unnecessary. However, from level IIB on, this simple cause (the spring, force, or whatever) explaining the propulsion becomes differentiated. The children take account of covariations in the relations between the suspended weight and that of the ball—hence the analogy with the scales (the "why" of the propulsion leads to an analysis of the "how"). Finally, although right at the end because of this psychologically necessary order of succession leading from the aim or result to its increasingly preliminary conditions, there are the geometrical considerations. The child discovers the necessary internal conditions for the rotation and so becomes able to explain its external results.

Briefly, development takes the following course. The child's attention is first drawn to the result of the action farthest from the action—in this experiment the final position of the ball. In other words, he looks at where he wanted the ball to go and sees where it actually went. With progress, he becomes more aware of the action itself and thus of the internal mechanism of what he says happens, with the degree of causality attributed to the latter always relative to the stages of this regressive analysis. This is why what the subjects notice depends on the coordinations grasped at each level during this general retroactive movement.

The Conflict between the Dynamic and Spatial Factors

Development of the reactions has just been summarized as if, once a subject has discovered that the distance the ball travels depends on how near the opposite end of the bar it starts off (from level IIA), progress consisted only in a gradual cognizance of the course of the results of the action. However, this cognizance does not depend only on reading the observable features of the action and the object. It is tied up with a progressive understanding that implies mastering a conflict between the dynamic and spatial factors that is latent throughout stage II. With this in view, more than thirty subjects of stages II and III were requestioned during a supplementary investigation. The conflict emerges clearly when the subject is questioned concerning the relationships between the distance $L1$ (between the weight and the fulcrum), which must be sufficiently long for the weight to be efficient (beginnings of intuition of the moment at stage II) and the distance $L2$ (between the ball and the fulcrum), which must also be long enough to make the ball go far enough (again stage II). Of course, as the bar's length is constant, $L2$ cannot be increased without $L1$'s being decreased, and vice versa — hence a conflict and the need to find an intermediate *optimum*, or a compromise. How does the subject conceptualize and overcome such a situation with or without cognizance of the conflict?

As has been seen, the distance $L2$ itself causes difficulty. The subject has to understand that, in order to go a long way, the ball must start off as far as possible from the target and not as near as possible to it — something that is not realized at stage I. The increase of $L1$ causes no problem, as from stage II on, the subject understands that if this distance is greater, the weight goes down lower and is therefore more effective. However, the simultaneous increase of $L1$ and $L2$ is, of course, impossible; and this is what causes the new and interesting conflict. It may be analyzed in terms of an opposition between the dynamic and spatial factors, since the effect of an increase in $L1$ is primarily that of increasing the action of the weight (the moment), which simply goes down. This is easily understood because the subjects know that weights tend to fall vertically. On the other hand, the increase of $L2$, although naturally linked to the dynamics of the system, raises an essentially spatial problem, which is (as we have seen) that of understanding the increase in height and in length of the ball's semicircular trajectory.

In this supplementary investigation, the interviewer begins by asking the subject where the ball must start off if it is to go as far as possible. Next he asks the child where to put the weight and the fulcrum (C) so as to make the weight as effective as possible. Then there are analogous questions about the ball that the subject has to shoot off (the interviewer suggests varying the position of C). The idea behind this is to determine both whether the child is actively aware of the conflict, which very many children are not (even at the level at which this conflict is mastered, only half the subjects are cognizant of it), and how it is mastered—it can be mastered without the child's awareness of an opposition between the demands relative to L1 and L2.

Examples (Level IIA)

LIP (8,5) starts off putting by the fulcrum C in 2 (near the weight, extreme right)[2] and the ball not far from the left end. *I thought it would go farther but it didn't work as well.* (He moves it farther back.) *That will go up higher.* (He checks.) Is there something you can change to make it work even better? (He puts C in 5 near the middle of the bar) . . . *because the weight will be able to pull better.* What does that change? *That* (distance L2) *will be shorter and the ball will go farther and lower—it will go off quicker.* With C back in 2: *Here there's not so far to go down and, as the weight doesn't go down, the ball can go farther.* How must the ball and weight be if you put C here (in 9)? *The ball's got to be heavier and the weight lighter . . . that will be the same as if it were there* (C in 2 without altering the weight). In other words, LIP understands that a light weight with a long side L1 is equivalent to a heavy weight with a short side L1, which is correct. However, he applies these *moment* relationships to the ball itself, forgetting the spatial conditions of its trajectory, which at the outset were clearly grasped.

2. The positions of C hereafter are noted as 1 to 10, with 1 nearest the right end (weight side) and 10 nearest to the left end (ball side).

PIL (8,1) similarly puts the ball at the left end of the bar and *C* in 4, understanding clearly that *that way the ball jumps*. However, like LIP, as soon as he thinks about the weight, he reasons along these lines: *when the ball's far away it's lighter so it goes farther, but when it's near the weight everything is heavier so it can't go far*. Similarly, with *C* in 8 (near the ball) *it doesn't go far because the weight turns* (= it goes down too quickly) *so it doesn't go far*.

JOS (9,1) immediately puts the ball at the end. *Right at the end*, otherwise *it doesn't jump properly and slides along the bar*. As soon as he starts thinking about the weight, however: What should you do to make it go farther? *Add more weight*. And if you haven't got any more? *Put the stick in that hole* (*C* in 6) *because it's nearer* (the ball) *and it goes farther: it's got more weight here*. He subsequently puts *C* in 2 (near the weight), but tries putting the ball near *C*. *It's going to go up because it's near the weight, so* (that makes) *more weight*. Seeing that it doesn't work, he puts the ball back at the end, saying, *It weighs more at the end. At the end it weighs more and it's* (=it goes) *farther*, thus rejecting the link between the weight and the ball, as if the weight of the latter were sufficient to make it jump a long way. After this, he thinks again about the weight at the other end and puts *C* in 6 *because it's farther and it's going to jump better*. He finally comes to the rather absurd conclusion: *When it's at the end, the ball gives weight to the other weight* (to the weight that pulls the catapult). At the end of a second session, he still maintains his arguments. Does the length of the bar come into it? *Yes, it changes the weight*.

A comparison of these subjects with those of the same level, IIA in the basic catapult experiment, shows that, as long as they think only about the ball and the distance *L2*,

they understand the relation between the ball's starting position and the distance the ball travels toward the box, although
they do not have an accurate picture of its trajectory. However, as soon as they start to think about the weight and its
relations with $L1$, they are no longer at all clear about the
ball. They cannot see how what they grasped about its situation can fit in with what they feel about the moment of the
weight side. Of course, these children do understand that in
one sense the greater the distance $L1$, the better the weight
works, because it can *pull better* (LIP), but they are still a
long way from really understanding the moment: they know
only that the weight is more efficient the farther it has to go
down, or that the weight of the bar itself in $L1$ is added to that
of the suspended weight, and so forth. Nevertheless, the necessary relationship between the action of this weight and the
length $L1$ is correctly noted. All that concerns the ball and
where it should start from in order to reach the target is
assimilated to these questions concerning the weight or the
pseudomoment. The subjects appear to forget what they said
at the beginning of the session. LIP, who moves C from 2 to 5
in order to increase the effect of the suspended weight, recognizes that $L2$ must then be smaller, but from this he concludes that, since the weight has increased, the ball will go
farther . . . lower . . . quicker. He contradicts this by
putting C back in 2. He then says that if C is put in 9 the ball
becomes lighter and the suspended weight becomes heavier
(which is right as far as the moment is concerned), and he has
to compensate for these two differences in order to find an
analogous effect to that of C in 2, and so on. Briefly, the ball's
trajectory no longer is dependent only on the weights, with
the child showing no concern for spatial aspects. PIL's arguments are similar, except that he thinks that the lighter the
ball is, the farther it will go—hence his curious conclusion
that the ball does not go far because if it is put near the suspended weight where *everything is heavier* it becomes too
heavy, while if C is in 8 the suspended weight becomes
heavier but goes down too quickly to make the ball jump
well. By contrast, JOS thinks that the heavier the ball is, the
farther it will go, because of a sort of contagion between the

suspended weight and that of the ball, which leads him to say, paradoxically, that the weight of the ball at one end increases that of the weight suspended at the other end. Briefly, as soon as the children start to think about the weight, they become completely confused and they no longer attach any importance to the spatial factors, even though at the beginning they had reasoned as well as the other level IIA children.

In some aspects, the level IIB subjects react similarly to those at level IIA, but they are slightly more advanced in that they consider the length L2 or the *length of the stick*, which helps to send the ball higher and consequently sends it a greater distance. However, it was shown in the earlier experiment that the levels IIB and III differ by the fact that in IIB the subjects do not talk about the length of the ball's trajectory, whereas at stage III this is explicitly mentioned. Is this only a stage in the development of cognizance, or is it the sign of real progress in understanding and in the removal of the conflict between L1 and L2?

Examples (Level IIB)

LOU (9,4) quickly understands that the ball has to be at the end and C in 2 for there to be *enough spring* and that the ball must be *lighter* (than the weight), otherwise the movement would be reversed; then he discovers the part played by the moment, which he interprets rather individually (*it's the bar that makes the weights different* by adding the weight of L1 to the suspended weight). He explains that when C is in 7 the suspended weight is heavier (while conserving its absolute weight) and so *it pulls too abruptly to the bottom, so the ball hasn't time to get its spring* and does not go so far: therefore if C is in 2 *it weighs less, it should go better.* Then he discovers (and this is the difference between the reactions of level IIB and those of level IIA) that if L2 is too short (he put C in 7) *the ball isn't going high because of the height which is small,* (so) *it hasn't time to get its spring and it falls nearer.* Hence the conclusion: the ball goes far *because of the weight and the height. Yes, because of them both at the same time.* However, he then encounters the conflict. Since the weight depends on $L1$ and the height on $L2$ and you cannot increase them both at the same time, you would need a bar *four times as long, that would work better.* He tries to find compromise solutions (such as C in 7), but in this case *there's a lot of weight and not enough height* and so on. He then notes an optimum with C in or near 2 and, interestingly, reverts to his explanation of the failures with C in or around 7, saying, *There's too much weight on the other side, it's too energetic, it pulls too hard, and the ball hasn't got time to go off . . . If the bar were longer, it would work better.*

ERI (9,7) starts off by putting the ball at the end and C in 5. He understands that if C is in 7 *it's too short here* ($L2$), while with C in 2, *it's longer and it would throw the ball higher because the bar* ($L2$) *is longer.* However, when he recalls that the ball flies off because of the weight at the other end and that the longer $L1$ is, the heavier the weight, he comes up against a major conflict: if C is in 5 *it would be heavier* (than if it were in 2) *but it would work less well, the ball would go less far . . . I don't understand.* When C is in 7, the problem is even more difficult: *There's less weight and yet the ball still goes further; it's funny.* He does not solve his problem.

TIA (9,6) also appears to understand that the ball must start off at the end of the bar and that it will travel less far if C is in 8 than if it is in 5, because *the ball's got to swing up more than the weight.* However, when he thinks about the weight and the moment, he is at a loss: *It's strange because if you put the holes* (C) *as far as halfway* (2 to 5) *it goes off strongly, and after* (6 to 9) *it doesn't work properly,* although the weight is heavier.

LAU (9,6): *The weight goes down and the ball goes off. When it's heavy, it does it suddenly and it goes up higher.* However, there is again conflict on discovery of the moment. When *C* is in 9 *it would be far better because that's much farther,* but it doesn't work *because the other bit (L2) is too short.* He therefore thinks the ball's weight must vary. With *C* in 1, *when the ball is at the end, it weighs more and so at the end it goes off higher* because it's heavier.

YVE (10,0), with *C* in 7, reasons like LOU: *It's heavier* (because of the moment in L1) *but it goes down too quickly,* whereas with *C* in 1 or 2, the sector *L2 is longer, the ball stays longer* (on the bar), *so it goes farther.* Why? *Because the ball gets pushed better when the stick's longer.* He concludes that the weight is the critical factor: *It's all to do with weight,* while *for the length* (of L1 and L2) *you have to have half and half* (C = 5) — *not too long, not too short.*

PIE (10,3), With *C* in 5, starts off by putting the ball at the end. He then remembers the effects of the moment and moves *C* to 9. *Yes, that makes it heavier and gives it a lot of spring.* As this does not work, he moves *C* to 7, then to 2, and says, *When it's in 7, it falls too quickly because there's a lot of weight.*

HEL (10,5) reasons in a similar way to PIE. *When C is in 7 the weight is stronger, but the ball doesn't go so far because there's not much stick (L2) so it doesn't jump far.*

LIS (10,5) argues that when *C* is *in 4 it's heavier* (than in 2) *but it didn't pull very well,* while in 2 *the bar (L2) is longer and it can push the thing* (ball).

Unlike the preceding subjects at level IIA, once these children have started thinking about the weight they do not lose sight of the length $L2$, nor of its role in the projection of the ball—hence the conflict between the variations of $L2$ and $L1$. Not all of them are conscious of this conflict, and most do not resolve it. Those who think they have found a solution think that the bar should be longer (LOU) or, despite everything, opt for a half-and-half solution (YVE). However, these cases are interesting, because they reveal even more clearly than the earlier level IIA cases that the role attributed to $L2$ does not lead to an effective coordination of the dynamic and spatial factors (shape and length of the trajectories); all emphasis is put on the former. As we have seen previously, only subjects at stage III talk explicitly about the length of the ball's trajectory. The responses of the level IIB subjects demonstrate that the lack of cognizance at this level results from a lack of understanding, since the significance of $L2$ remains basically dynamic. The dominant idea (LOU, YVE, and others) is that if $L2$ is too short, the ball *hasn't time to get its spring*, particularly because the weight reinforced by $L1$ *goes down too quickly* (YVE and PIE). LOU even thinks, as at level IIA, that the ball's weight increases with that of $L2$ and the ball thereby becomes stronger. Others give up trying to understand, but it is clear that none of them can picture adequately the shape and the length of the trajectory, in order to coordinate these spatial factors with the dynamics of the rotation caused by the weight.

Two-thirds of the eleven- and twelve-year-old subjects in this supplementary investigation achieve this coordination and talk explicitly of the length of the ball's trajectory. Three out of eight of the ten-year-olds already refer to this length, and only one out of fourteen of the nine-year-olds. The following children may be classed as intermediate between levels IIB and III.

> VIC (9,6) initially seems to understand: *If the weight is at the end and the plasticine is as well, it's got more force. Why? Because there's all the bar's force, and the weight's heavier, and it goes a greater distance;* while if the weight is farther away from the end *it hasn't got a large enough circumfer-*

ence, it hasn't got any spring. However, having considered the part played by the weight and the moment, he suggests moving the ball nearer the middle: at the end of the stick *there's a bigger circumference, but there's less force* (for the weight with C in 2) *so it's when it's in the middle that it goes the farthest.* He then returns to the optimum situation, but in his explanation he falls into the following contradiction: *The plasticine goes farther because it's got a good-sized path, while the weight's got more force because it's got a smaller path.*

MIL (10,1) puts C in 5 and the ball at the end. Then, when he thinks about the moment, he puts C in 6. *Here it's a bit better because the weight is heavier.* Having said this, he puts C in 4 *because the stick* (L2) *is bigger for sending the ball.* Then with C in 3: *There there's still more weight because there's the weight* (suspended) *as well as the stick* (L2), *which goes up high, so there's still more weight . . . a little more power.* However, when he sees that it works still better when C is in 2, he says, *It's sort of funny; I get it and I don't: here the stick can send it higher . . . and maybe farther.* First of all, he thinks that this *far* depends on the speed: *Doesn't go as far when it doesn't go off very quickly.* Then he changes his mind. *It's because of the weight and the stick* (L2) *that it will come high.* Finally, he coordinates the weight and the trajectory: with C in 7, *it doesn't go as well even if the weight is heavier, the path of the bar isn't as big, so it doesn't go as far.*

VIC, who started off as if he were almost at stage III, is clearly disturbed by the question of the weight and ends up applying the relationship between the length of the ball side and the distance the ball travels to the weight. MIL, on the other hand, is immediately aware of the conflict and finally resolves it through a coordination of stage III level.

Stage III

Examples

GER (11,4) quickly sees that if *L2* is too small *it doesn't pull as far. In 5 the ball makes a bigger turn, it goes higher; the weight throws it higher.* With *C* in 4, it is still better *because the bar (L2) is longer, it projects it higher . . . it goes around more, and so it goes farther.*

HEN (11,1), when *L2* is increased: *When it turns, it runs around a longer path and goes faster. It's like on a bike: if I pedal the same with a big wheel, I'll go faster.*

NIA (10,10) immediately puts *C* in 3 and the ball at the end. *The longer the stick is here (L2), the farther away the ball will go.*

Without in any way reducing the role of the dynamic factors, these subjects finally coordinate them with the spatial conditions of the shape and length of the trajectories, thus understanding the effect of changing the length of *L2*. Clearly, therefore, the stages of the development of cognizance described at level IIB are closely allied with progress in understanding itself. In order to demonstrate this, it was necessary to study cognizance separately and to analyze the conflict between the dynamic and spatial factors. Why is it such a long time before the children begin to see the importance of the spatial factors concerning the trajectory and no longer consider only the dynamic factors of the weight and the moment (or pseudomoment)? The part played by their cognizance of the situation seems undeniable. What interests the child and what he notices first of all is simply that the ball goes farther or less far, regardless of whether it starts off high and falls a long distance away, goes around in a circle, or goes off in a straight line. Only at stage III does he pay attention to the shape and length of the trajectories. The process of understanding is, however, no less important. It is, of course, more difficult to understand that sector $L2$ of the bar turns around the center C and traces the radius of a circular trajectory than it is to pay little attention to the shape and the length of the trajectory—once it has been grasped that *going far* depends on the length of $L2$, regardless of the form of the function it traces. In fact, the development of cognizance, like that of understanding, proceeds from the "why" to the "how," with the latter always constituting the answer to the "why" of the "why," through a regressive displacement of the problems: thus cognizance and understanding seem of necessity to be interdependent.

11 The Flying Balloon

In this experiment, in order to achieve the desired result, the subject has to carry out, or explain, an action that appears to him to be aimed in quite the wrong direction. There is a game, known commercially in Switzerland as "the flying balloon," which involves moving a lever to control the air-flow (Figure 4a) and tilting a blower (down) to make the balloon rise (Figure 4b). In both cases, cognizance depends on how active these adjustments are; but, as in the research described in Chapter 10, it is also interesting to find out whether when he comes to explain the phenomenon or his mistakes, the child remembers accurately what he observed or whether his observations are distorted—and if so, why.

The device used in this experiment consists of a kind of fan, which we call the blower (B); the blades are driven by an electric motor and the speed is adjustable by means of a rheostat. The flow of air from this blower (which we shall call the gas, G) is sufficient to enable a balloon to be held up in the air

---

With the collaboration of Alex Blanchet.

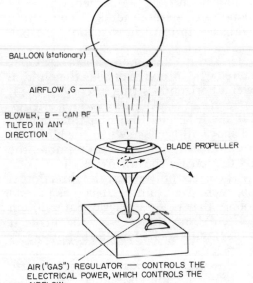

BALLOON (stationary)

AIRFLOW ,G

BLOWER, B — CAN BE
TILTED IN ANY
DIRECTION

BLADE PROPELLER

AIR ("GAS") REGULATOR — CONTROLS THE
ELECTRICAL POWER, WHICH CONTROLS THE
AIRFLOW

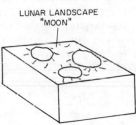

LUNAR LANDSCAPE
"MOON"

Figure 4a

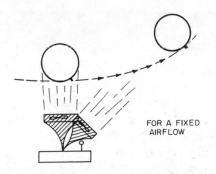

FOR A FIXED
AIRFLOW

Figure 4b

without falling. The child has a double task: he has to adjust the rate of the airflow with one hand and guide it the right way with the other. These two adjustments are difficult, because if the airflow is too great, the balloon is blown away, too little and it falls, while if the direction of the blower is altered, the balloon needs time to reach stability and one must wait for this and not try to regulate the airflow at the same time. Furthermore, all movements and adjustments must be carried out gently and smoothly, without jerks. Two preliminary tasks enable the subjects to learn how to hold the balloon at the desired height, then direct it toward a selected point. As usual, they are asked to explain any mistakes. Once this task has been mastered, the interviewer asks the child to make the balloon go over a horizontal string, then to make it go along such a string, which can be placed in various orientations. This last task is difficult because the adjustments have to be simultaneous, and above all because when the blower is tilted the balloon goes up instead of down. Furthermore, the subject tends incorrectly to increase the airflow as the balloon goes farther away — this is correct only when the direction is not altered. The problem then given to the subjects is to send the balloon "to the moon," that is, to a plastic crater 30 cm from the ground and 50 cm from the blower, and make it come back again. Of course, with such complicated problems the children cannot be expected to give an adequate explanation of the phenomena. However, by asking a subject where he made mistakes, one often obtains spontaneous explanations, which then make him change his conceptualization of his actions.

Stage I

Level IA subjects (age five) have two interesting reactions. They tend to keep on increasing the airflow (G) (often from minimum to maximum) as if the problem were analogous to that of constantly blowing on a piece of fine paper or cotton wool in order to stop it from falling. They also fail to adjust the direction of the airflow by altering the position of the blower until the interviewer's questions, or their own failures, lead them to recall that this possibility was pointed out to them when they were first shown the material.

Examples

FLO (5,3): You can touch everything. (She turns *B*.)
It's a whirligig. And what else moves? (She turns
on the gas.) They continue. I'd like you to make the
balloon go up and come as far as my hand (*B* is vertical). (She increases the airflow considerably, but
does not move *B*.) *I can't make it fly*. But you did
before. (She tips *B* a little and the balloon goes off.)
Come this way, to my hand. (She again considerably increases *G*, but does not alter the position of
B.) What else have you got to move to make it
come to my hand? (Points to rheostat for *G*.) Isn't
there anything else? *No*. What else could you
move? *That* (*B*). Similarly, in each of the subsequent tasks, when she is asked to describe her action (as is common at this age, the description is
always accompanied by motor repetition), it is only
when the interviewer has asked her And after that?
that she admits to tilting *B* as well as adjusting *G*.
Even then, FLO indicates a sort of twisting of *B* and
not the adjustment of direction that she correctly
carried out—revealing inadequate cognizance.

Why do subjects at this level spontaneously attach no significance to the direction of *B*? The explanation lies in their
conception of air. It is not movable in the same way that a
movable solid object is and thus, unlike the latter, it goes
wherever the situation demands.[1] Consequently, the children
hope that if the airflow is sufficient, it will push the balloon
to the target.

Level IB sees progress in two areas. The children make the
blower point in the direction of the various targets set for the
balloon, and they sometimes reduce the airflow instead of
each time automatically increasing it. Several children are

1. See "Les Explications causales," volume 26 of the *Etudes d'épistémologie
génétique* (Presses Universitaires de France, Paris, 1971), hereafter referred to
as the *Etudes*.

successful, although not of course systematically, which is remarkable for their age. The principal obstacle to success is that, after one adjustment, the children do not allow the balloon enough time to settle down before they make another one. The experimental situation involves progressive adjustment within this system of objects, which—naturally enough—the child does not understand. He therefore tries to govern everything himself, making compensations where he thinks necessary, but these compensations result in the opposite effect, since his variations of the airflow are too quick. On the other hand, the child obviously does not realize that tilting the blower will make the balloon rise. If, through trial and error, he manages to do this, it is without cognizance or even awareness of the link between the two.

> OLI (6,2) starts off by continuously increasing the airflow, then slows down. He makes the balloon go toward the target, but its return is far from smooth (actually a series of stop-and-go movements) and the balloon falls to the floor. Why? *Because there wasn't enough air any more.* He also succeeds in making the balloon go over the string; although in so doing he had tilted the blower, he does not attribute the balloon's rise to this action. How did you get it to the right height? *I accelerated.* But to the right height? *I accelerated and then afterward I slowed down.*

Clearly, although the child makes the balloon rise, he does not understand the part played by the direction of the blower—and even less the fact that he tilted it instead of putting it upright. He ends up thinking that he has increased the airflow, thereby distorting an observation according to what he thought should happen, as is often the case at stage I and sometimes even at more advanced levels. Conceptualizations at this level thus consist only in successions of motor recollections. There is no overall plan or reference to the goal in the actions described by the child, and he wrongly links the balloon's height to the force applied.

Level IIA

At level IIA (seven or eight years) the airflow is correctly adjusted—the subject has become capable of dissociating the regulations of his behavior from those of the object.

Examples

> YVE (7,5), after only two attempts, leaves *G* constant and, in order to change the balloon's direction, merely tilts *B* (in jerks) until he finds the right orientation. He is successful in the various tasks, except that of the *moon*. *Tell me what I should do. Pull the lever* (airflow rheostat) *to here, make that* (B) *lean against the moon, turn off the gas again, tip that* (B), *increase the gas more, lower that a little more* (B), *slow down, slow down a bit more, start it up again, and suddenly stop.* After failure: *I put too much at the beginning and it went too far. You've got to put it* (B) *lower and slow down, increase it a bit, then come back* (put *B* back upright) *quickly.* He finally sends the balloon to the moon and even gets it back again. *I tipped* B *a little more, that lifted it from the bottom, then afterward, I made it go like that* (B upright). *I slowed down a bit and once it was just above, I stopped and it fell in just the right place.*

At this level, therefore, better active adjustment clearly corresponds to better cognizance of the actions. Furthermore, the children now show evidence of an overall plan that assigns a goal to each action and are constantly concerned with quantification, which, although naturally not metrical, can be fairly precise: *A little less, less and less fast, accelerate a tiny bit, not much gas, not too much or too little, just in the middle so that the balloon stays at the same height,* and so on. In addition, in most cases, the subject has become capable of describing his mistakes and of actually correcting them. The conceptualization underlying this operatory-level cognizance thus is generally correct, insofar as it retraces the series of actions and, as with YVE, it sometimes leads to a beginning of causal explanation (tilt the blower right over to make the balloon take off on its return journey). However, there is still distortion of the paradoxical relationship (tilting the blower in order to make the balloon rise; YVE does not see this except for the takeoff, which is easier to grasp), and the children still think that the intensity of the airflow must be proportional to the distance the balloon has traveled away from them — in fact, now that they distinguish between their own actions and the machine's reactions, they are even more convinced of this incorrect relationship.

Level IIB

Level IIB (nine or ten years) reveals a far less common situation and one that presents the most interesting characteristics of this research. Although some cases are analogous to those described above, where cognizance and conceptualizations revealed distortion of the observable features because of the influence of preconceived ideas, with a majority of these subjects this process takes place in two stages. Firstly, they describe more or less correctly what they actually did, including the incomprehensible or paradoxical points that until now have always given rise to the distortions referred to at level IIA. However, during the final summaries where their more or less causal interpretations come in, they distort the facts under the influence of a first idea of explanation. This distortion is in a way retroactive, since it goes as far as reorganizing and contradicting the preceding statements and the initial conceptualization of the actions.

Examples

MAR (10,4), referring to his attempt to make the balloon follow a horizontal path alongside a string, correctly notes that he made the balloon rise to the correct height *by moving* B (lowering it). And when you moved *B*, what did the balloon do? *It went up and then it went down.* And how did you adjust it? *By doing it hard.* (More in this fashion.) When given the task again later, MAR starts off by repeating his description without distorting the facts, then starts interpreting these facts, whereupon he seems no longer to know what he is recalling and what he must have done in order to make his description match this interpretation. And when it came back? *It went lower* (correct) . . . *No, higher.* Higher or lower? *Higher.* And what did you have to do? *Put a bit more air through* (correct). Put a bit more through? *No. Um . . . put a bit less through.* Are you sure? *Yes.*

CAR (10,8) similarly, when asked for an explanation, says, *If I tip the blower, it automatically goes like that* (lower in an arc). However, she remembers enough about her actions to remark, *I did exactly the opposite, but before, I ought to have let less air through.* She maintains that in a given situation *I put through less air, but now I've thought about it; you ought to put more through,* thus her interpretation after the event takes precedence over her actual experience of a successful action.

When this subject has another attempt with the balloon and finds that what she has just said is not correct, she is troubled. She starts to think that there is a contradiction or conflict, not in her own mind but in the objects themselves, and so she looks for a compromise.

CAR (continued). She puts the blower back upright, increases the airflow, and then concludes: *Well, there's just* (only) *the air that went askew and it went down lower.* Lower? *Yes, look, I did that* (raised *B*); *I don't know how it happens, it should go higher.* Is that normal? *It isn't normal, it isn't right, because it was there and it went down . . . Perhaps when I put it (B) straight there's something that slows down the propeller, I don't know.*

Others, like OLI (10,11), think that the direction of the airflow modifies the balloon's weight, for instance. Stage III reactions differ little from the preceding ones, except that these subjects take greater stock of the facts (although this is not yet general) and are more conscious of the conflict and of the inexplicability of the phenomenon. *Yes, that's the point. I know that's what I don't understand* says CRI (12,9) about the heights, *I don't get it at all.* The great difficulty of this situation is that it stems from a circular causality analogous to that of the subject's regulations of his trial-and-error procedure, and that if the causal explanation in general consists in attributing to objects operations analogous to those of the subject, it is far more difficult for the latter to attribute to the former correction mechanisms and adjustments than simple operations. There is in fact good reason for the invention of cybernetic models to have taken place so late and to have required constant recourse to inspirations drawn from analysis of human activities or organic processes, since if—even (or mainly) for realistic minds—it seems obvious that reality obeys elementary logicomathematical operations (such as additivity or transitivity) analogous to our own, it seems far more surprising and virtually anthropomorphic to endow it with various corrections or retroactions (feedbacks).

It is doubtless this absence of linear causality that explains the particularities of the child's cognizance of this situation. We have noted in various studies that success in action precedes understanding of it and cognizance of it, the latter proceeding from the observable features of the external results to the subject's acts. Furthermore, in cases of lasting conflict between observable features of the object and certain preconceived ideas, the former are distorted, and these distortions affect the subject's cognizance. All this occurs up to level IIA. However, the situation changes at level IIB, where difficulties are usually attenuated or removed. Trying increasingly hard and unsuccessfully to understand from level IIA on, the subject manages, on the one hand, to make more accurate observations of the object and of the action—hence the improved descriptions. On the other hand, when asked to explain, he encounters such a powerful conflict between these observations and his spontaneous beliefs, proved correct in so many other simpler and more intelligible contexts, that he discounts some of the observations and retroactively modifies his ideas. This results in the exceptional and paradoxical situation of an after-the-fact correction of his cognizance of the action and his knowledge of the object, in order to comply with his earlier generalizations and not with his objective reactions.

12 The Construction of Tracks by Means of Connecting Rails

In this experiment the subjects have to build a railway track between two points A and B, fixed in advance. A and B are the ends of two straight rails that have already been placed on the table. The subjects are asked to fit together a certain number of curved and straight rails in order to make all the possible tracks between A and B. As in the other studies reported in this book, the children's progress is observed and at each level of success, which in these tasks is not very rapid, we try to find answers to the following questions. What is the content of the subject's conceptualized cognizance at each level of success in action? Furthermore, depending on whether this cognizance bears on the observable features or on the coordinations, what part is played by "empirical" abstractions and what part by "reflexive" abstractions? In effect, this problem principally concerns space, given the isomorphism between the subject's geometry and the object's space

With the collaboration of Alberto Munari.

insofar as the latter can be dissociated from its temporal, kinetic, and dynamic context: in the experiments described below, this context plays only a minor role.

Five straight and eight curved plastic rails (of which four can make a circle) are used in this experiment: (a) each rail has a male and a female end; (b) the ends are symmetrical in that each rail may be placed either side up; (c) each curve thus can make either a right-hand or a left-hand bend by turning it about the two axes of symmetry; (d) it is therefore possible to turn any track about its longitudinal axis to obtain the symmetrical track, without dismantling anything; (e) it is also possible, without disturbing the construction, to turn any track about its transverse axis to obtain the inverse track; however, this rotation inverses the male and female ends, and in order to fit the new track onto A and B, the child must also rotate each rail longitudinally; (f) finally, as each curved rail constitutes a quarter of the perimeter of a circle, it is possible to construct a track of a given length, either with n straight rails or with $2n$ curved rails.

The interviewer puts two straight rails on the table, the distance between them being equal to the length of three straight rails; these two rails (A and B) remain fixed to the table throughout the experiment. He explains to the subject how to build a track by fitting the rails together, either the right way up or upside down, then presents the following tasks. (I) The all-the-rails task: they are put in a heap, and the subject is asked to build a track between A and B. (II) The 4 + 1 task: the child is given only one straight and four curved rails and is asked to build a track between A and B. Once this has been done, he is asked to construct as many other tracks as he can with the same rails (six tracks are possible). (III) The 6 + 1 task: the child has to build a track between A and B using six curved rails and one straight one. Again, once this has been done, he is asked to build as many other tracks as he can with the same rails (again six are possible). (IV) The 8 + 1 task: the child is asked to build a track between A and B using one straight rail and eight curved ones. Again, he is asked to build as many other tracks as he can using the same rails (there are twenty in all). (V) The interviewer makes a drawing of each track as it is completed and asks the subject to think about what advice he could give a friend to help him carry out the same tasks.

This material and procedure differ from many of those already described in that the object, instead of being immediately adaptable to the subject's actions (like, for instance, the sling in Chapter 2 and the tiddlywinks in Chapter 6), initially offers resistance. This is not because of causal properties unknown to the subject but, more simply, because its constant or temporary figurative aspects (straight lines, curves, and positions) can run counter to the subject's ideas on their manipulation; in some cases they do so for some time. In this chapter three factors are under scrutiny: the figurative data, the action, and the conceptualization. This is why, in addition to the links between the action and the conceptualization, there arises the question of the abstractions, either empirical (drawn from objects) or reflexive (drawn from coordinations of actions). The difficulty of the male and female ends of the rails might be thought an unnecessary complication. However, since they are simultaneously unidirectional and symmetrical, with their reverse side identical to their right side, manipulation is easy even though the subject has to turn them over and/or rotate them. Adequate use of the material involves ways of relating and transforming the objects (rotation of a single rail or of the whole track) that are possible only through the very coordinations on which the reflexive abstractions of geometric content normally bear.

In this respect, it is interesting that the rotations applied to one straight rail constitute a two-element group. By contrast, the rotations of a curved rail or of a whole track correspond to a basic four-element group (a Klein group or an INRC group, but unlike the latter it does not bear on "a set of elements"). Furthermore, if the rails, excluding A and B, are numbered as they are laid down, it is clear that, because of the constant length of the tracks to be built (equal to three straight rails), the one straight rail for each track in tasks II to IV must be an odd number and placed lengthwise in the $4 + 1$ and $8 + 1$ tasks, and an even number and placed in transverse position in the $6 + 1$ task (otherwise the constructions would be impossible).

In the following description a "simple rotation" occurs when a straight rail is turned over and a "double rotation" occurs when a curved one is turned over. A symmetrical solution results from rotation of a track about its longitudinal axis (which is possible without its first being dismantled). An inverse solution results from a track being rotated about its transverse axis (which requires an inversion of the female and male ends).

Level IA: No Rotations or Symmetries

Examples

BER (1,6) wants to use all the curved rails like straight ones, but fails to build a track linking A to B: he starts off from A with a straight rail followed by a curved one then a straight one, making an angle of 90 degrees; then comes a right-hand curve, which could have brought the track back to B, but instead he extends it with two left-hand curves, followed by two straight rails, which takes it way off to the side, away from B. His other attempts are similar.

VAL (4,6), by contrast, selects only straight rails and so goes direct from A to B. That's too easy. Do it with these (four curved rails and three straight ones). (She builds a straight track, then separately a circle of four rails, which she does not manage to close.) *It won't go, that one* (the last curved rail). But how are you going to get there (B) with those (eight curved and three straight rails)? (Straight track followed by two circles, each made up of four curved rails of which the second does not reach B.) *You can't do it.* Are you sure? *Yes.* The interviewer gives her all the rails and varies the angles of the fixed rails A and B (obliques, and so on), but VAL continues building only straight sections and circles. And you can't go from here to there (AB)? *No, you've got to turn here* (circle).

ANI (4,6) also starts off only using straight rails, hence an initial success. How about with those (four curved rails and a straight one)? (She places three curves, the third coming back toward A.) *No, I'm going to make it come back* (=toward B). (She dismantles her attempt and starts over again, this time with two right-hand then one left-hand curve,[1] which could have led to B. However, she adds another right-hand curve, which makes the track turn through 90 degrees away from B.) *That's no good either.* What do you want? *A straight piece.* (She starts all over again, with a right-hand, then a left-hand curve, followed by two straight rails, which take the track not far from B, but she ends up with two right-hand curves, which form a loop coming back to A.) If I take away this one (second straight rail), do you think we can do it? *No* (but she nevertheless does so, puts a left-hand, then a right-hand curve, and succeeds). *It's like a fishbowl* (= wide curve)! Is there another way of doing it? *No.* (She starts off the same way, but ends up well below A, no nearer to B.) How about like that? (The interviewer places three curves, taking the track above the horizontal line AB.) *Yes, we'll make a pretty snake.* (She gets to the next bend, which is in the other direction and thus gets nearer to B, without reaching it.)

CAT (4,6) starts off with a straight rail, then two right-hand curves, and continues taking the track farther away from B. For her second attempt, she starts with a straight rail at A and another at B, but ends up with the same loop as before. *I don't know* (how to do it). She then gives up trying to place the curves and builds a straight track from A to B. With four curves and one straight, she builds the same loop, but symmetrically (without being aware of

1. Compared with a straight line between A and B, which would be parallel to the edge of the table, a right-hand curve makes the track veer below this line AB and a left-hand one takes it above.

this), and again gets near *B* without touching it. Could we put the rails a bit differently? *No.* (She dismantles the whole track and reconstructs an almost similar one, but again missing *B*, as if she could not alter the position of the final rails.) Couldn't you do it with this rail? *You can't do it.* (She takes another rail, which she puts to the left and no longer to the right, and succeeds.) Could we make another track with the same pieces, but putting them differently? *Yes, putting them differently* (but she does not get anywhere). I'd like a track that turns the other way. (She starts with a straight rail at *A*, then a curve the other way, and continues, getting farther away from *B*.) *I don't know how to do it.*

NIC (4,6) starts with a straight track. With four curves and one straight rail, he puts the straight one at *A*, then a curve and another curve at *B* in the same direction, so that the two curves are divergent. *It's not right.* (He starts off again the same way.) *It's still not right.* It's this rail. (The interviewer makes as if to rotate one of the middle rails, and the child succeeds.) What about starting from here (*B*)? *I think you can do it. You've got to turn here.* (He turns over a middle rail as was previously suggested to him.) *Now that's all right* (but his track goes farther from *A*).

PHI (4,8) succeeds when he can choose from among all the rails, but fails in the 4 + 1 task: *I can't go as far as here* (B) *because the rails go this way.* (He has the rails going away from *B*.)

NAR (5,1), like PHI, fails in the 4 + 1 task but almost succeeds in the 6 + 1 task; however, instead of turning the last rail, *We've got to take another that goes up to there.*

SON (5,2) succeeds in the 4 + 1 task by putting the straight rail in the middle of her track. Could we

make another track with the same pieces? *No*. And
if we changed those around (that is, the curve
nearest *A* exchanged with the curve nearest *B*—inverse solution)? *Yes*. Try. (She ends up with two
divergent curves.) *That makes two ends like that.*
(By switching rails she succeeds.) And like that?
(The interviewer places one straight rail and two
left-hand curves. SON fails when trying to carry on
from there.) *You've got to take away those two.*
(She replaces so many rails that she ends up with a
series of straight rails, except for one curve that she
can't fit in.) *We need another straight piece here.*

TIN (5,7) has similar reactions to SON. When her last
rail goes away from *B*, the interviewer says,
Couldn't we just turn this little bit the other way
up? *Yes*. (She again dismantles the whole track to
achieve the suggested rotation.)

BRI (6,4) starts with a straight track, then when she
tries with the curves, ends up with a loop coming
back to *A*. She changes the rails several times as if
she thought they could not be turned around and
concludes: *It's* (all) *the same, they all go the same
way.* Then after renewed but identical attempts,
They're on the wrong side. I'm going to help you,
just take those (4 + 1). (New identical attempt, in
which she then keeps trying different curved rails.)
No, it can't be done. (She is given another four
curves and a straight rail. She puts the straight rail
at *B* and the four curves at *A*, alternately left-hand
and right-hand, but her overall direction is wrong.)
That's quite straight, then it turns (from *A*). She
finally makes a correct curve, but thinks it impossible to alter the position of the straight rail because of the end. (She does not think of turning it
over.)

The most remarkable characteristic of these reactions is the
subject's submission, not only to the object, but also to the

way it appears once it has been laid down on the table. There is no anticipation of the shape of the track, except where it comprises a simple straight line from A to B. The general attitude of these subjects is summed up by PHI, when he declares, *I can't go as far as here* (B) *because the rails go this way* (away from B), as if he himself were not free to orient them in the desired direction.

This is, of course, an effect of the lack of anticipated representation of the curved trajectories. In other studies (such as the game of tiddlywinks in Chapter 6), where subjects were able to perceive the curved path described by an object in space before it landed in a box, the children at this level indicated a straight path to the base of the outside of the box, then a loop over the top and into the container. Similarly, in this experiment, the various possible horizontal curves are not predicted. Only a straight track leading from A to B can be pictured in advance — hence the initial but very limited successes of VAL, ANI, and others. Even when the subject has chanced upon the right curve (ANI's *fishbowl*), he cannot reproduce it.

However, this inability to imagine the whole track in advance is far from the only explanation of the lack of success at this level, although it does account for the subject's need to place one rail at a time. Why does the child, after placing each rail, not ask himself whether this new rail brings the track nearer to or farther away from the target? In the latter case, he would then be free to change it or to try and turn it around to make it point in the right direction (left or right) for B. Yet, remarkably, all he does is place one rail and go on to the next. Regardless of where it leads, he clearly regards this rail as the only one possible, or its position as the only one possible, as if he were noting a predetermined result and had no power to modify it. VAL, having ended up with two circles, concludes that nothing else can be done and that *you've got to turn here*, thus twice around in a circle, with no continuity. After failing, ANI manages to make a plan to *come back* toward B, that is, to place the first rails in a better direction, but this does not prevent her from ending up with a track perpendicular to the line AB, then with a loop coming back to A. (She manages to make the correct curve only after suggestions from the interviewer and does not know how to start all over again.) VAL and BRI conclude that *you can't* get from *A* to *B*, as if the lack of success stemmed from the nature of the elements and not from the manner of placing them, and CAT, while agreeing with a suggestion that you could put them differently, nevertheless fails to do so. BRI even argues that, as all the curves are *the same* (shape), *they're on the wrong side,* as if the right side were inherently inaccessible and not simply inaccessible through lack of action on the part of the subject.

When the child fails in the task, he does not try to alter the track he has just laid down, but starts all over again. For example, TIN acquiesces when asked whether one could "just turn this little bit the other way up" so that the rail in question would go toward instead of away from *B*, but instead of immediately trying to do this, she reconstructs the whole track. In order to add only *a straight piece,* ANI also starts all over again. The only spontaneous corrections consist in replacing a rail, but this also is an implicit admission that for each rail there is only one predetermined position, leading either to or away from *B*, and that this cannot be modified without making a mistake.

To sum up, these children do not consider turning over a curve (double rotation) to make a left-hand curve into a right-hand curve, or vice versa—nor, once they have succeeded in making their track reach *B* (which can happen either by chance or with help), does it occur to them to turn the whole track over to get a symmetrical solution (and a fortiori to turn each rail around to obtain the inverse solution). There is a clear developmental relationship between these two factors. In both cases, in order to succeed, the child needs to act on the objects to modify their positions and directions, that is, their figurative appearance. They need to carry out operative actions on these objects instead of limiting themselves to actions that, through a sort of submission, are in conformity with this figurative appearance and with their first attempt at laying the track, which is conceived as the only one possible. In other words, at this first level the subject's actions are conceived as subordinate to the immediate (perceptive or figurative) properties of the object, instead of the latter being subjected to the transformations that could result from the subject's action.

The fact that the subject can carry out such actions on the objects is revealed by the occasional correct solution through sensorimotor or automatic regulations. A (4,0) subject, whose performance is not cited here, turns over a straight rail to affix it to A; another at (5,0) turns over a straight rail that he wants to put crosswise; CAT arrives by chance at the symmetrical solution, and so on. However, regulation of these actions remains sensorimotor and the subject is not yet capable, through reflexive abstraction, of conceptualization – although he notices, through empirical abstraction, the various figurative properties of the rails (straight, left- or right-hand curves, the curves or loops that can result from fitting several together, and the like). This is certainly not to say that at this level there is no reflexive abstraction, but rather that it bears only on the actions that both remain very general and (except for one) all concern the topological characteristics of space: adding or taking away an element, joining them together according to an order of succession and through continuous contacts, and so forth. The only Euclidian type relationships (not present before (4,0), below our level IA) consist in conserving one-way direction (straight as opposed to nonstraight lines) or the two-way direction constituted by a circle coming back to the point of departure. Furthermore, except for the relationships of neighborhood and continuity, these actions involve a topological aspect in that they also introduce one of a purely logical nature (order and partition).

Level IB

In comparison with level IA, level IB shows progress in two areas. The subject realizes the possibility of turning a rail over to make it go the other way (rotation), and he can find the symmetrical solution to a track he has already built.

Examples (Intermediate between IA and IB)

BAD (4,6) first builds a straight track between *A* and *B*. He then succeeds in the 4 + 1 task. Could we start like that and turn to the left instead of to the right? (The interviewer shows the beginning of a symmetrical track.) *Yes.* Show me how. (She indicates the symmetrical curve.) *Like that?* Yes, do it. (Success.) And another track? (Finds nothing.) And put that here (straight rail fitting onto *A* and not *B*)? *Yes.* How can we do it without first taking it all to pieces? *Turn it around.* Do it. *You can't turn it around, you've got to take it all to pieces: it* (the straight one) *must be the other side.* (She takes it all apart, puts the straight rail at *A*, and builds a track symmetrical to the previous one.)

DEL (5,0) starts off with a loop that comes back to *A*, then modifies it to make a circle, which she links to *A* and to *B*. After some trial and error, she succeeds in the 4 + 1 task. Can you make a different track with the same pieces? *Yes, like that.* She indicates the symmetrical track, then constructs a nearly symmetrical one (six rails instead of five), spontaneously rotating a curved rail that was taking the track off course.

Examples (Level IB)

CHA (5,6) succeeds in the 4 + 1 task, rotating one curved rail. He then draws in detail (seven rails, thus two too many) the symmetrical solution when asked to make *another track*. He performs similarly in the 8 + 1 task.

CRI (6,2), after reactions typical of level IA, succeeds in the 4 + 1 task; then, for another track, she predicts the symmetrical solution: *I want to do it like that* (success). She indicates a right-hand and a left-hand curve, saying, *I think that they're the same.*

To make a different track, she therefore substitutes a right-hand for a left-hand curve (hence a curve made up of five identical rails).

BRA (6,0) immediately succeeds in the 4 + 1 task. To make a slightly different track he leaves the straight rail in its place but puts the curves in a symmetrical position, having said, *Yes, I'll put them all the other way and I'll put the long one* (straight rail) *here.* Can you do it without first taking this one all to pieces? (He puts the straight rail on the other side.) *You've only got to move that one.* How about with these (6 + 1 task)? *No, it wouldn't work . . . still, I'm going to try* (succeeds). He subsequently varies this track by adding a straight rail, then by making a track with two curves (~).

DUC (6,6) starts off with an irregular track formed by eight curved rails and one straight one. In the 4 + 1 task, he puts the straight rail first, then the four curves. The interviewer asks for another track with the same pieces. *Yes, I know another one: the straight rail can go there* (at the end), *and the curves there* (the four curved rails first) *and that will make one like that* (success), which thus constitutes an elementary form of inversion, but through simple switching of the straight and the curved rails. Asked for a different track, he makes an exact replica of his previous one. That's what you did just now. *Not quite, because I can't remember it exactly,* then he constructs the symmetrical track, but without realizing that this is what it is. *Before it was like that, we'll see . . . it will be the same.* He makes several attempts before succeeding in the 6 + 1 task. Can you make a different track? *You can do it almost the same, but the other way.* (He ends up with an approximately symmetrical solution.) *Before it was like that.* When given the 8 + 1 task, he says, *I hope we'll make it* (succeeds). Could we do it on the other side? *Yes, we should be able to do that.* (succeeds). Could we just turn it over? *I think so. Like that, if I've got a track, I'd turn it over there and there* (symmetrical solution, but he does not actually build it). Where else could we put the straight rail? *There* (in the middle).

MAU (6,6) succeeds in the 4 + 1 task. Can you make a slightly different track? *Yes, like that* (indicates the symmetrical solution). Do you have to take it all to pieces again or can you turn it over? *Of course, I'm going to take it all to pieces. I can do it like this* (symmetrical solution). *I can't do it like this* (inverse solution 4 + 1 to 1 + 4). When he is given the 6 + 1 and 8 + 1 tasks, he comments, *It's getting more and more difficult,* but he succeeds and finds the symmetrical solutions.

OLI (6,8) has similar reactions for the symmetrical tracks, but at the interviewer's suggestion he says, *I'm going to try to turn the whole thing* and spontaneously does this in the 6 + 1 task.

In other studies, level IB sees the first intimations of rotation, as, for example, when a bar of chocolate placed horizontally is pushed on one of its small sides and not in the middle of one of its long sides. In our railway-track situation, subjects now rotate both the curved and the straight rails (double or simple rotations) so as to modify their position or the direction of the curve. Similarly, when a semicircular track has been built, the subject spontaneously predicts the possibility of a symmetrical curve (or accepts the interviewer's suggestion regarding it, like the intermediate subject BAD), which also amounts to a sort of rotation in thought (*if I've got a track,* says DUC, *I'd turn it over there and there*), bearing on the whole track or on the initial rails. At this level, the child obviously subjects the objects to his own operative actions and no longer, as at level IA, subordinates each of his attempts to the figurative properties of the object as it is laid down in front of him (position of a right- or left-hand curve without any possible modification, and the like), which limited the powers of the action to simple imitative accommodations without sufficient operativity. Thus CRI says of a right-hand and left-hand curve, *I think that they're the same* without first having had to turn them; whereas at level IA, as soon as these rails were laid down on the table (or even before then) they would have been regarded as belonging to two separate categories.

This new capacity for modifying the orientation or arrangement of the rails is also demonstrated by solutions other than the symmetrical one: as when CRI substitutes a curved rail for a straight one and, in the 6 + 1 task, BRA ends up with a track composed of two curves. By contrast, no subject produces the inverse solution in the more complicated tasks, although (in the 4 + 1 task) the child may, if it is suggested to him (BAD) or even spontaneously (BRA, DUC, and others) move the straight rail from *B* to *A* or vice versa. However, this still constitutes only a simple alteration of the order involving just one rail and not, as will be seen at stage II, the total inverse solution resulting from a rotation of the whole track about the transverse axis.

At this level, therefore, progress remains limited and in addition to certain lapses of memory (DUC's *I can't remember it exactly*), there is a fairly general tendency, as at level IA, to take the track apart in order to alter it (except for BRA, who changes the position of the straight rail in the 4 + 1 task), rather than to turn the whole track over, replace individual rails, or make partial modifications.

However, generally speaking, cognizance has improved, because it results from active regulations growing out of the attempts to coordinate the various possible positions of the rails. One result is a more advanced reflexive abstraction, where the child's action has become operative and where simple imitative accommodations are subordinate to the figurative properties of the rails obtaining when the child has placed them on the table. In other words, the logicomathematical geometry, at level IA still mainly undifferentiated from the object's spatiophysical characteristics, begins at level IB to become dissociated from it with respect to the operative actions of rotation, construction of symmetrical tracks, and changing the order of the rails—which are precursors of the true operations that will be developed during stage II.

Stages II and III

The most important aspect of the progress achieved from seven to eight years is that for the more complicated tracks the children realize the possibility of the inverse solution (turning the track about the transverse axis) and no longer just change the position of the straight rail in the 4 + 1 or 6 + 1 tasks.

> *Examples (Level IIA)*
>
> FRA (6,10) builds a track from *A* to *B* in the 4 + 1 task, then says, *You can do the same, but on this side* (symmetrical solution, but only after first dismantling his original track). Is there another way of doing it? *Yes, first of all by turning, then straight, then turning* (thus the straight rail in the middle). And another way? *Yes, by taking the two sides apart* (puts the straight rail at the beginning, thus 1 + 4). (She is then given the 6 + 1 task. Partial success.) And like that (the straight one crosswise)? (Hesitation.) *Ah! yes, that will be all right* (track with two equal curves, in succession and in opposit directions). Can you make a different track with the same rails? *Yes.* (She turns it, which results in an inverse and symmetrical solution.) And like that? (The interviewer puts down the first three curves.) *Yes.* (She succeeds with a large curve followed by a small one on the same side.) Can you turn it around? *Yes.* (This time FRA makes a true inversion by changing the order of the two curves and leaving both to the left of *AB*.) *It's the same, but on*

this side (referring to the order of succession and no longer to the longitudinal axis as for a symmetrical solution).

MIC (7,6) makes a track from *A* to *B* in the 4 + 1 task. Can you make a different track with the same pieces? *I can turn it over.* (He turns each of the four curves over, thus giving a symmetrical solution.) How about another one? *No, I don't think so.* Can't you put the straight one here (near *A* instead of *B*)? (He does this.) Is there another way? *No . . . you could put it on the other side* (a different symmetrical solution achieved by turning the whole track over). Still another way? (He puts the straight rail in the middle.) He correctly builds a first track in the 6 + 1 task, then makes a symmetrical one. How about another way? *I don't know what to do.* Like that? (The interviewer lays down three curves making an arc.) *I'll go on.* (He follows with a wide curve with a straight rail crosswise.) Can you put the straight one somewhere else? (He then switches the wide curve, which he moves as a whole, and the small arc, which constitutes an inverse and no longer symmetrical solution. He puts the straight rail in the middle in the 8 + 1 task and, when asked for a different solution, he moves it to one end, hence a partial inversion.)

REN (7,4), when asked for another correct solution to the 4 + 1 task, says, *You've only got to turn them.* But instead of giving the simple symmetrical solution, he also moves the straight rail from the end to the beginning. In the 6 + 1 task, he gives the track two successive curves, the second being smaller. To make a different one, he tries to turn the whole track without taking it to pieces, but is not successful and builds a second track which, in comparison with the first, is simultaneously symmetrical in relation to the longitudinal axis and inverse with regard to the order of succession of the two curves.

ANC (8,8) correctly builds a track in the 4 + 1 task. What else could you do? *I don't know . . . I think that that one* (the straight rail) *goes there and that one there* (puts the straight rail at the beginning instead of at the end). Can you do anything else? *You can do that* (the whole thing) *on this side* (symmetry). When ANC has built one correct track in the 6 + 1 task, the interviewer places three curved rails starting at *A*, whereupon ANC makes a wide curve followed by a small one near *B*. Can you make that track on the other side as well? *Yes.* He takes the whole track to pieces and rebuilds it, inverting the two curves and not giving a symmetrical solution, although subsequently he also predicts this one. He sums up his actions saying, *You can do it on the other side, like that* (symmetrical solution) *and like that* (inverse solution).

TIA (9,8) similarly predicts a symmetrical solution (*You can do the same as that but on the other side*) and manages to build inverse solutions in the case of unequal curves on the same side.

Very marked changes are not apparent at nine to ten years, which is the usual age for level IIB, except for progress in the number of possible combinations in the 4 + 1 and 6 + 1 tasks.

RIC (9,2) builds a track in the 4 + 1 task. Is there another way? *I could have done it like that* (symmetrical solution). And another way? *The straight piece there* (toward *A*) *or on the other side* (toward *B*). That makes four different tracks. Can you find two more? (He finds the middle.) *And the other way up* (middle the other side up). In the 6 + 1 task he builds the two loops and the symmetrical tracks and changes the position of the transverse straight rail. He builds both the inverse and symmetrical solutions in the 8 + 1 task.

DOM (10,4) quickly sees the six possibilities in the 4 + 1 task. In the 6 + 1 task he is not quite so quick; he finds four possibilities (equal or unequal loops and their symmetrical or inverse solutions), but has more difficulty finding the three possible positions for the transverse straight rail. He sums up his reactions by saying, *You can do little things, you can invert and you can change the bar* (straight rail) *from one side and again from the other side and to the middle.*

ART (11,6): His response is similar: *You can put it on the other side* (symmetrical solution). *You could put this loop there and the other one there* (inverse solution) and *you've got to move the straight piece.*

PIE (13,4) notices that in the 6 + 1 task it is impossible to put *this straight piece at the beginning* as in the 4 + 1 task, *because the curves have got to go after the straight piece.* The interviewer then asks him if in the 8 + 1 task the straight rail has to be put the same way (as the track = longitudinally) or crosswise? *The same way.*

CAT (13,6): *In the first thing* (4 + 1 task) *you put the straight there and there. In the second* (6 + 1 task), *with two more rails you couldn't do any more. You had to put it there, there, and there* (crosswise three times). *Now* (8 + 1 task) *with two more, oh!—that's double* (4 + 1) *so you have to start all over again like before* (for 4 + 1).

The inverse and symmetrical solutions give rise to reflexive abstractions in that the latter bear on the operations themselves. On the other hand, in the case of this law of alternation of the position of the straight rails, the subject sees only the result of his actions, linked to the properties of the rails.

He does not understand the reason behind this result and so does not reach the operatory stage of well-formed functions.

Conclusions

In most of the other studies in this book, the problem has been simply to analyze the prerequisite conditions for the subject's cognizance of observations of the action (or of the coordinations resulting from his activity) and for his correct observation of the object (or the sufficiency of the causal coordinations attributed to the object). In this particular study, causality plays only a minor role (moving the rails and fixing them together) and spatial relationships are relatively independent of the dynamics of the situation (the only dynamic aspect being the subject's moving and fitting together of the rails). Here, then, our attention may be focused on the links between the subject's geometry and the spatial properties of the objects, thus between the logicomathematical experience of space (together with the operatory coordinations and relevant reflexive abstractions) and the physical experience of the geometrical characteristics of the objects, with an "empirical" abstraction bearing on the observable features of these objects.

A reflexive abstraction is one that derives its information from the subject's actions or, more specifically, from their coordinations (ordering them, uniting them, putting them into correspondence, and the like). This process is a prerequisite for conceptualized cognizance and occurs as early as the organic levels, in the form of what are described as convergent reconstructions that go beyond the original constructions (Jean Piaget, *Biology and Knowledge*, University of Chicago Press, Chicago, 1971). Thus at level IA, subjects turn over a rail or construct a symmetrical track, but they do so through simple sensorimotor regulations and without true cognizance, because of a lack of active adjustments. The acts of turning over a rail or of constructing a symmetrical track stem from behavior developed right from sensorimotor levels (exploring the various faces of a solid by handling it, or making symmetrical movements with hands or arms in motor gestalts, for instance), and elementary types of reflexive abstractions are already at work in these developmental links, although there is as yet no conceptualized cognizance.

At level IA, the conceptualized forms of this sort of abstraction remain very general (such as additions or ordered links) and do not yet bear on the coordinations whose development would seem essential for success in the tasks: rotation of an individual rail, or turning over the track to obtain a symmetrical one. There is thus at this level a systematic predominance of empirical or physical abstraction, as the child concerns himself solely with the temporary properties of the rails he has laid down and fitted together, without any prior overall plan to direct him. Only at level IB do we begin to see the rotations and symmetrical solutions that denote serious progress in the subject's grasp of geometry. Level IIA sees the inverse solutions, and level IIB an increasing number of combinations predicted or discovered as possible.

What then constitutes the boundary between the conceptualized reflexive abstractions that are increasingly enriched from level IB on and the empirical abstractions that are predominant at level IA, but then become proportionally less important? Their origins provide a clue: those of the latter are found in the observable features of the situation, whereas the former (conceptualized reflexive abstractions) stem from coordinations of the subject's actions.

Another question concerns actions such as the simple or double rotation of the rails. Do these constitute not coordinations, but simple operations or even preoperations, since they appear from level IB on? On the one hand, an operative action consists in a transformation leading from an initial state to a final state and so already represents a coordination between two states. On the other hand, a perception, an imitation, an image, or an isolable representation do not transform anything, but bear on just one state (regardless of whether this state is stationary or moving, as in the case of the "perceptive kinetic gestalt," and not a displacement operation—that is, when the subject moves an object from one place to another). On the other hand, this operative action tends to become an operation, and an operation is always inseparable from its inverse, and so on, and thus from a general system including multiple coordinations.

Furthermore, the question becomes more delicate when it involves observation of the actual action, and of the objects insofar as they are manipulated and modified by this action. Movements of the subject's hands (or of solid objects moved by them) constitute ordinary physical data and therefore give rise only to empirical abstractions. By contrast, their operative character (when it exists and manifests itself through the intent or the decision to impose transformations on the objects, such as a rotation or even a simple movement in a straight line) stems from endogenous coordinations and is thus open to reflexive abstractions. The distinction may appear subtle, but the perception of a movement is only an isolable recording of an incident happening at that specific time and with a specific spatiotemporal content—it does not include per se any system of general coordinations (such as a comparison of successive states), while a displacement operation (both translations and rotations and the like) is contained in a "group" structure. This is why the level IA reactions force us to distinguish between the operative actions, which are still hardly represented at this level, and the actions centered on the imitative accommodation to the present and temporary states of the elements (typified by the rails).

In the area of space it is difficult to make a detailed distinction between the two types of abstraction, because there is complete isomorphism between the spatial aspects of the subject's timeless geometry and those of the spatiotemporal geometry, or of the object's dynamogeometry. However, these are not sufficient grounds for implying the former's empirical origin or, in other words, for concluding that it derives from the latter and that the reflexive abstraction is reduced to a composition of physical abstractions. The sequence of our stages in fact shows that a subject's physical activity is increasingly necessary for the progressive structuration of the spatial relations and that there are constant links with his general logical activity (for example, the appearance of inverse solutions at age seven or eight).

Our findings therefore in no way reveal a direct developmental relationship between the operations and perceptions, or even between the operative actions and imitative actions. Instead, there is a gradual subordination of the latter to the former. In this we see a developmental law that goes far beyond the limits of this small experiment and that applies to the history of the whole of geometry. Geometry began, with the land-measuring activities of the Egyptians, as an empirical science, then for the most part remained figurative, owing to the long victorious imperialism of Euclidian theory. Since the Erlangen program it has finally become a science of transformations of space, extending as far as the current abstract conquests of algebraic topology. This constitutes a striking example of the progressive primacy of the reflexive abstraction compared with the initially predominant simple abstractions.

Finally, between our level IA and stage III, this general passage from empirical abstraction (from the beginning surrounded, although to a very limited extent, by assimilatory schemes of the second type) to reflexive abstraction is revealed by the following transformations regarding the subject's cognizance. At the elementary levels the child is, of course, aware of the information obtained from his observations of the object, as well as of the failures or partial successes of his actions. However, predictions and retroactions remain very limited and, in particular, the children have only a very incomplete recollection of the sequence of actions, since these were not ordered. By contrast, with the reflexive abstractions noted from stage II on, the coordinations become clear, because the child's awareness has broadened both with regard to anticipation (he finds, step by step, the ways of getting near the target) and with regard to retrospection (he reconstructs the sequence of his acts).

13 Rings and String

In the balloon study described in Chapter 11, cognizance of the situation is difficult because the children find it so hard to explain what they see; there is a conflict between the causal explanation and their own observations. There is no problem of causality in the study we shall describe in this chapter. Here the problem is the simple one of threading a piece of string through one or two rings: the string is fixed at one end (X) and free at the other (Y) and passes through a ring in the direction AB (see Fig. 5). The subject is asked to make it go through the ring the other way BA either by turning over the string or the ring, but always leaving the string in the ring. Of course, the solution is possible only with a system of loops (Fig. 5a and 5b), which is virtually the same thing as removing the string; but as a part of the string always stays in the ring, the instruction is respected to this limited extent. Success therefore necessitates coordination of the successive movements of the string. This is a rather special type of coordination, with the result that, through trial and error and a little luck, a child can sometimes manage to succeed or to imitate

With the collaboration of Daphne Liambey and Nadine Burdet.

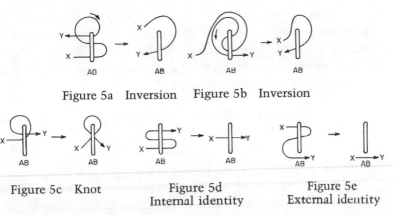

Figure 5a   Inversion   Figure 5b   Inversion

Figure 5c   Knot   Figure 5d   Figure 5e
                      Internal identity   External identity

successfully a correct solution as early as age five, but cognizance (or even simple recollection of what he has done) is particularly difficult—even for an adult. In the case of ordinary coordinations, it is generally only a question of carrying out two actions simultaneously (as with the translation and reverse spin of the ping-pong ball in Chapter 3), or linking two variables both of which are capable of + or − (as the length and height of the slopes in Chapter 5). However, in this experiment there are sections to be joined end to end like the rails in Chapter 12. The following points should be noted:

(a) The sections are constituted by the continuous parts of one string, differing one from the other only by their position and temporary direction.

(b) The positions and directions all differ from one another both in relation to the ring and to the two ends of the string.

(c) These positions and directions vary constantly according to the actions carried out on the string.

(d) The subject must always predict what will happen (position and direction) to the free end section(s) when they are pulled.

(e) The subject also has to predict the retroactive effect that pulling the end(s) will have on each and all of the preceding sections, starting from the last and working backward.

(f) Cognizance of these complex operative coordinations involves reproduction in the child's mind (representation) of all the steps, which is no easy task.

(g) When the string is pulled, this constitutes a double action, in the sense that one either has to pass an already formed loop (Fig. 5b) through the ring or else pass the end Y through it and then immediately make a loop (Fig. 5a). These subjects therefore are faced with a problem of cognizance that differs from all the preceding ones.

The first method is as follows. The material consists of one or two rings (napkin rings), or one or two flat bricks with a circular hole in each, and a long string. The ends of the string are called X and Y, and X is fixed to either a mobile or a stationary object. The interviewer passes Y through these holes in the direction AB and then asks the subject to make it go through the other way, BA; however, the string must always remain in the rings. The subject is allowed to experiment as much as he wants. The interviewer merely asks him to describe what he does, or to do it again in slow motion, or, if appropriate, to explain his mistakes. If the subject always ends up with knots or identities (Figs. 5c to 5e), he is given a demonstration (Figs 5a and 5b), then asked to imitate the interviewer's solution once or several times and to explain it. He is not given or asked to make any drawing (the figures here are for the reader only). Sometimes the interviewer suggests that the child center his attention successively on individual actions (a loop or a threading, for instance) by perhaps comparing the string to a snake (which suggests a loop), in order to see if the child will then spontaneously coordinate these actions.

In the second method (used with a second group of subjects) the subjects are asked to pass through the hole(s) first a thick, then a thin, stick, then short lengths of thick or thin rope. They observe that it is impossible to change the direction of the stick or rope, from AB to BA. The interviewer then manipulates the string (as if providing counterevidence) and asks the child to reproduce and explain the action. This exercise is particularly useful in that it allows analysis of the way in which the child understands both the contradiction between his prediction and the observed result and the fact that X comes out of the ring while Y goes back through it.

Stage I

Subjects of the preoperatory stage (five and six years) sometimes can imitate the demonstration immediately after it is given to them, but find it very difficult after a longer interval.

Examples

CAT (5,6) first of all notes that it is impossible to make the stick or rope go the other way. She expects this also to be the case with the string and is astonished by demonstration of the contrary. To imitate it, she starts off by bringing Y back into the ring and making it go over the top; pulling the string results in an external identity (Fig. 5e), which greatly astonishes her. Then she has the string make two turns of the ring and ends up with a knot (Fig. 5c), which again surprises her. Do you remember what you had to do? *Yes, make it go the other way.* She makes another knot, but with only one turn (Fig. 5c). The interviewer gives her another demonstration (Fig. 5a), which she imitates more or less correctly, except on one essential point: instead of threading Y into the ring from right to left, she threads it from left to right and makes a knot. She subsequently places it correctly and is thrilled with her success, but does not appear to know how she made this doubtless unintentional correction (automatic and not active adjustment).

FLO (5,10) starts off thinking the only solution is to switch the rings or the two ends X and Y. She is shown a Fig. 5d arrangement: Would that work? *We'll have to try.* (She pulls—hence an internal identity.) (The interviewer makes a Fig. 5a arrangement.) Will that work? *No.* (A try.) *Yes.* How do you explain that? How is it possible? (She wants to imitate it.) Well, try then. (She ends up with a Fig. 5e and pulls.) *It came out!* (Very astonished.) Why? *I did something wrong.* Show me what you did. (She thinks she is doing the same thing, but in fact ends up with a Fig. 5c, thus a knot.) Try again. (She makes another Fig. 5e.) *That's going to go back, I think.* And will the string stay inside? *Don't know, I'll have to try.* (She tries.) *It fell down.* (She starts off again the same way.) The interviewer again demonstrates (Fig. 5a) and she imitates it more or less correctly, but puts Y in the wrong way and into the loop to the right of the ring, hence a knot. *I can't do it*. What else could I do? *Like that.* (Again Fig. 5e, and an external identity; she begins again and happens upon a correct Fig. 5a.) *I got it back!* How did it get back? *Like that* (Fig. 5e—external identity). *Why did it come out?* (Starts off again, but this time puts Y into the ring, thus transforming Fig. 5e into Fig. 5a.) *But now I've done it* (just as surprised as she is delighted). How did you do it? *Look: like that* (again Fig. 5e, then she pulls a bit). *That won't work because it's pulled too much!* Subsequently, she does appear to understand when she goes on to a Fig. 5a after a Fig. 5e—but she puts Y through the ring twice, then pulls and makes a knot. *I think it's wrong.* At the end of the session, after another demonstration, FLO correctly imitates, but for a simple loop (Fig. 5e without having Y going back to the right); she says that the string *is going to come out because you just made one loop,* but she is not sure about this: *We'll have to try.*

MAR (6,1) after a few attempts (all like Fig. 5e), declares that *you can't*. The experimenter demonstrates (Fig. 5a) and the child concludes: *You took it* (the ring) *away and afterward put it back* (the other way around). The interviewer does it all again very slowly. *You did it like that* (a Fig. 5e and not a 5a). He pulls: *No, I don't know any more.* Try to remember. (He makes a Fig. 5e, then a 5c, hence a knot.) He starts again and succeeds. How did it come back? *Because I did something.* What? (He does it again, but with one loop too many; next he puts Y in from the wrong side, hence another knot; then from the right side but twice in succession, hence a third knot!) *It didn't come out!* The interviewer makes a final demonstration, which the child correctly imitates, but he thinks that arrangements like those in Figs. 5c and 5e will also be successful.

In order to find out whether the children understand when the string, if pulled, will come straight out of the ring, the interviewer makes a loop and puts half of it through the ring (Fig. 5e without the external circuit).

> CAT says that the string will not come out of the ring: *You'd have to unstick it.* Well, look. (The interviewer pulls a bit.) Did it come out or not? *No.* And like that? (Virtually no string remains in the ring.) *No.* Is it going to come out or isn't it? (The interviewer continues to pull gently.) *No . . . it's going to come out.*

> FLO, as we have seen, is astonished when she sees the string come out and attributes this to the fact that she *did something wrong.*

> MAR, similarly, does not predict that if you pull the ends the string will come out: *There are always two bits.* And like that? (The interviewer pulls.) *It's the same.* It's as if it came out? *No.*

These initial reactions are remarkable for the systematic difficulty encountered by the children in predicting the outcome of pulling Y; this tallies with the findings of Professor Inhelder and myself in our study of common knots. The subjects do not even predict in a situation like that of Fig. 5e that if you pull the string it will come out. It is therefore hardly surprising that there is no coordination between the successively observed states. The subjects make no distinction between the situations where, if the string is pulled, it goes into a knot and those where it stays in the ring (either *AB* or *BA*) but does not end up in a knot. However, their memory is sufficient to enable some of them to imitate correctly the interviewer's demonstration (Fig. 5a); when they are asked to repeat it, however, there is often confusion between Figs. 5a, 5c, and 5e (see, for instance, the end of FLO's questioning). It is therefore hardly surprising that at this level there is no cognizance whatsoever, and what is more (as will be seen), the situation does not show much improvement subsequently.

Stage II

This stage sees progress in the immediate imitation of the interviewer's demonstration and in the prediction of the outcome of pulling the string in simple situations such as one loop inside a ring or only one knot (Fig. 5c). However, there is still no combination of, or coordination between, these individual actions—and no cognizance.

LAU (7,6) predicts correctly that pulling Y on a loop inside the ring does not change the order XY, but he does not think it possible to modify it in any other way. After a demonstration he reproduces a Fig. 5b: *There, that went back,* but his description is limited to *make two turns and pull.*

OLI (7,8) also succeeds in imitating the demonstration of Fig. 5a, but finds that *it's no different* from the Fig. 5c made previously. He tries to reproduce Fig. 5a again and ends up with a Fig. 5c with two loops (double knot), then with just one. Then he recognizes that *we've turned the string,* sometimes in one direction (X) sometimes in the other (Y), but adds, *I don't see what it changes.* After numerous attempts: *You've got to try first, then you'll see that it won't work.*

REN (7,6) also successfully reproduces Fig. 5a and then repeats the whole process in slow motion. *I took the string away and put it back at the other end . . . that takes away the loop and then I put Y through there.* However, he does not imitate Fig. 5b correctly.

SYL (8,10) has several successive attempts during which she produces a Fig. 5c (knot), which she sees is wrong. Then, having made a Fig. 5d, she ends up after trial and error with Fig. 5a, but does not see that this is the solution: Isn't that right? *No, the tail (Y) is still behind the black piece (X).* She has not, in fact, tried to pull Y and cannot predict the result. She is asked to compare the 5a and 5c configurations, which the interviewer makes in front of her: *They're not the same.* You're right. Explain why. . . . If you pull here (Y in Fig. 5c), what happens? *It'll get caught there* (knot). And there (Fig. 5a)? *It'll get caught too.* She thus predicts the same knot without predicting the result of the change in direction. Up to this point only one brick has been used, but the interviewer now produces another one. SYL starts off again, instead of simply transferring to two bricks her solution with one, using combinations of Figs. 5d and 5c, then complicating them, and ending up with Fig. 5a, which is correct. Again she does not pull the string or realize that she has found the solution: *It won't work.* So when it is not just a case of imitating the interviewer's arrangement (except for the comparison of Figs. 5a and 5c), SYL either fails to find the solution or does not recognize that it is correct when she does find it.

CAT (8,5) successfully imitates the interviewer's configurations, but in explanation can say only: *It's because that* (Y) *turns.* When a little later on she tries to do it again from memory, she produces a Fig. 5c and does not understand the reason for her lack of success.

CRI (8,3) starts off with various knots (like Fig. 5c) having one or two loops going *over the top* or *underneath* the ring. When asked to recall his actions, he confesses, *I don't remember any more how I did it.* Furthermore, his initial lack of forethought is such that for one internal loop (half of Fig. 5d), he bursts out after his attempts: *Oh! I've got it; it turned around and it's coming out of the other side,* which does not stop him a moment later from being amazed about it: *How come! It's gone!* Hence during the demonstration (Fig. 5a), the incorrect prediction: *It's going to make a knot,* then

after trying it out: *It's come back! It's magic!*
. . . I'm going to try to do it again. (He produces a
Fig. 5c, then, correctly, a Fig. 5a.) *I did it like that*
(model), *I think so . . . It's magic, I'm going to see
once again.* After this, he notes that *the loop that
was outside is going back into the rings.*

PHI (9,3) is exceptionally enthusiastic. After
watching a demonstration (Fig. 5a, but on two flat
bricks), he tries to imitate it and produces various
arrangements (mixtures of Figs. 5a and 5c). He then
asks for another demonstration and finally succeeds. He is sufficiently interested to try the
problem again at home. He is questioned again after
three weeks and although he hesitates a great deal,
he remembers what must be done: *I've made a
mistake . . . oh no, that's right,* and so on.
Strangely enough, he finds it *still more difficult*
when the interviewer uses only one brick and confesses, when asked for a description of his correct
actions, *I can't remember at all!*

DAN (9,6), after a great many spontaneous combinations, says, *I tried all the loops; sometimes that
can help to find the solution.*

WAL (10,6) is amazed by the failure of the identities
of Figs. 5d and 5e (on two rings). *That should
change sides.* He then makes various knots (as in
Fig. 5c) and by chance discovers the solution (Fig.
5a); he is very surprised by this success. However,
he cannot repeat it with just one ring. He comes
back for a second session (claiming that he had
explained the thing to his parents), but only produces Fig. 5c arrangements with several loops. *I've
gone through too many times.* He nevertheless
manages to reconstitute Fig. 5a, which he describes
in terms of *reversing* (first loop), *going forward* (on
the second loop), *then reversing again.* However,
with just one flat brick, he reverts to the knots (Fig.
5c) before again finding the Fig. 5a solution.

Obviously, while there is progress in predicting simple situations (Fig. 5e) and in imitating demonstrations, mistakes occur when the subjects try to repeat their solutions (OLI and others). Furthermore, the subject does not always recognize a correct solution achieved through trial and error (SYL, for instance). It is clear, therefore, that improvement of the predictions regarding individual actions (such as a loop) or regarding the sensorimotor accommodation to the models to be imitated does not lead to any general coordination—hence the lack of progress in cognizance. Even PHI (9,3), despite his clear interest, declares that he *can't remember at all* what he did. When the interviewer makes a loop and puts half of it through the ring, the subjects at stage II generally say that the string has not left the ring, but that it will *if you pull it completely*, or that it has *almost gone out and almost not gone out*. They are thus intermediate between the stage I subjects and those at stage III who see that this is another way of unthreading the string from the ring.[1]

Stage III

At this level, and even in the case of an adult who is not an expert in geometry, the situation is scarcely different from that of stage II. Cognizance remains subordinate to the coordinations, and the latter remain difficult unless the subject is allowed to portray in a drawing the successive multiple variations. Nevertheless, stage III reactions reveal progress in that each of the subject's attempts is increasingly directed by a type of overall plan bearing on what he wants to try, without any anticipation of results.

Examples

ISA (11,2), despite her age and her general reasoning methods, which are clearly at a stage III level, reacts at a stage I level regarding the knots under consideration here. She produces only identities

1. To provide a complete record of the experiment, we must say that one (6,10) subject seemed to find the solution immediately and spontaneously. However, he gave no explanation and could not even reproduce his successful actions, quite possibly the result of a fair measure of luck.

(Figs. 5d and 5e), and after watching a demonstration (Fig. 5a), she cannot either predict the result of pulling the ends or imitate the whole process. During a second demonstration (before the ends are pulled) she says, *That makes a knot,* as if it were a Fig. 5c. Her subsequent attempts at reproducing the solution never go beyond a Fig. 5c with one or two loops and she then reverts to Fig. 5d arrangements. She successfully imitates a third demonstration, but says, *No, it's not right.* (She pulls.) *Oh!* (She is surprised at her success.) Tell me everything you do. *I go through and do as if I wanted to make a knot. Yes, if you pull like that, it makes a knot.* (Her doubts thus return.) After checking, she contests right to the end of the session that the string at Y comes out of the hole.

TOF (12,6), after producing a great many knots and loops (Figs. 5c to 5e), spontaneously discovers the solution (Fig. 5b). *That was complicated: I just had to do that* (pull Y backward) *from the beginning* (after the loop between X and the brick). But why did you do that first? *To see all the possibilities. The string comes back there, but in fact it goes around the brick. I wanted to see if that was a good way to start.* But why do you have to try? Couldn't you just work it out in your head? *I tried it out first because it takes longer to work it out in my head!* Finally, TOF is not taken in when the interviewer puts half a loop into the hole in the brick. What about that (just one loop of the two in Fig. 5d)? *It doesn't go right through.* And that (two loops in the same direction)? *It doesn't go right through. If you start this side and you stay this side, it doesn't go right through: so once or fifteen times more* (= fifteen loops in the same direction) *it's the same.*

ALF (research assistant in psychology, good interviewer, cosignatory of several of our studies) starts off with various identities (Figs. 5d and 5e), then goes on to the knots. *I suspect there's a problem of loops . . . I can't see it at all. It's completely empirical.* He again produces Fig. 5e: *This is no good, but I don't see how I could have done it any other way.* The interviewer then takes only one brick and ALF tries to combine Figs. 5c and 5e with the string in the loop of 5c and ends up with Fig. 5b (success). *I've perhaps got it: I make a loop, I put the string through the loop, I pull the whole thing, and I undo the loop, but I can't say why. I could try to understand!* He then comes back to Fig. 5e and manages to modify it into Fig. 5a. *I've understood something: a reversal cancels out the direct action, but twice the direct action, the result is different . . . But that doesn't explain why you change the side of the brick! In any case, there must be a double threading at the beginning, since the string's got to come out afterward.* When again given the two bricks, his initial hesitations return: *I should be able to use my previous experience . . . But I can't reduce that to something I've already done,* and more of the same.

TOF clearly understates the case when he says that actually trying out various solutions takes less time than working them out in his head, because even the adult does not manage to do the latter: *I can't see it at all* (ALF). However, some success occurs without help as a result of following various overall plans. For example, the subject might take the string around the brick and bring it back the opposite side to X; retaining in his mind this final action (although without being able, or even attempting, to predict the result), he can decide to modify it to see what happens and, having pulled on Y, put it back as before, this time making it come back the same side as X. Such a plan consists, as TOF says, in seeing *all the possibilities* in a given situation and, in this particular case, it leads to success without prediction or memory of anything except the very last action carried out (through retention of its scheme for a brief moment), without there being any need for representative evocation. Briefly, such attempts *to see all the possibilities* are in no way equivalent as yet to coordination of the individual actions, but represent a beginning of coordination of the subject's attempts. In other words, the subject is beginning to fit together his various efforts, but these are still not guided by an overall strategy.

One can therefore understand that practical success may be possible without either luck or cognizance. The latter must be based on a coordination of the actions themselves and not just of the attempts. However, while the individual actions remain simple, they already give rise to correct predictions. Particularly with regard to the loop through the ring (which is the key to the solution, since it is the only way the direction can be changed without taking the string right out of the ring) TOF, like the other stage III subjects, very clearly declares *it doesn't go right through* and that even if there were fifteen loops it still would not go right through.

It is not necessary to repeat in detail the reasons for this lack of coordination and representation. Briefly, it results from the difficulty of reducing the successive actions to a simultaneous picture. Such a process is not easy, because these actions and their results continuously are retroactively modified through the ensuing transformations. Of course, as soon as the whole process is represented by a drawing, as in our Figs. 5a to 5e, the problem becomes simpler; but even then interpretation is not immediate, since a small effort is required to see that in Fig. 5a the loop Y will not make a knot around the ring, since X has followed it outside the ring and no longer through it (or, if X is fixed, the string will still follow even though the end X itself does not). Translation of the successive into the simultaneous is not a simple question of memory: it also demands that the actions or operations modifying the path of the string become objects of thought, while on the material or practical level they are merely instruments of transformation. This constitutes an essential change in status, involving not only a conceptualization, but also a reflexive and even "reflected" (a "topicalized" result of the preceding) abstraction—hence the complexity of the process of cognizance.

14 The Hanoi Tower

The popular children's game known in Switzerland as "the Hanoi Tower" has often been used for research with children. However, here we are concerned only with children's cognizance of their actions and the relations between conceptualization and these actions.

Three thin sticks or posts A, B, and C are fixed vertically onto a plank (in this experiment, one post is yellow, one red, and one blue). On one (subsequently referred to as A, or the starting post) are threaded a certain number of discs (with a hole in the center) of very clearly different diameters. The largest disc (I) is at the bottom of A, then comes a smaller disc (II), and then (depending of course on the total number of discs used), in order of decreasing size, come discs III, IV, and so on. The smallest disc therefore is always at the top of the pyramid. (The order of the posts is not always the same, so A is not always yellow, and so forth.) The child is asked to move the pyramid or tower on A onto C (the finishing post) in such a way that it remains the right way up. He must move only

With the collaboration of André Cattin.

one disc at a time, never put a large disc on top of a smaller one, not rest on the table, or hold a disc in his hand while another is moved. Solution of the problem therefore demands the use of post B; for example, if A has two discs, then II must be moved to B, and I to C, so that II may then be placed on top of it on C. If A has three discs, then III must be moved first to B and then back to A, before finally being placed on top of II on C. The problem therefore involves the combination of a type of transitivity of the discs' successive positions and a type of recurrence.

Generally speaking, the minimum number of moves necessary is $2^n - 1$ where $n = $ the number of discs: three moves for two discs, seven moves for three discs, fifteen for four, and thirty-one for five. In this experiment the subject first has to move a two-disc tower from A to C, then a three-disc tower, and so on (according to his level). Each time he is asked to say what he did and why he did it. The interviewer then requests the child to repeat his solution in order to judge its stability and to see (if applicable) whether the child is able to eliminate any unnecessary moves. Subsequently, the problem is repeated but the order of the towers is changed (for instance, instead of moving the tower on yellow A to blue C the child has to move the tower on red A to yellow C). The interviewer can thus find out whether the child wrongly conserves his initial scheme without accommodating it to the new situation or whether he correctly conserves only the method, adapting it immediately to the modified conditions. After this, the interviewer asks the subject to explain to him step by step how to move the tower so that he himself can move it. This helps to determine the degree of cognizance at each level of action. Finally, another instrument of analysis is sometimes obtained by summoning a second child and asking the first to explain to the second what has to be done and how to do it.

Stage I

Subjects at this level cannot move the three-disc tower even after trial and error. They do succeed in moving the two-disc tower, but only after all sorts of attempts to get around the instructions and without being conscious of the logical links.

Examples

MAR (5,4), with I (large) and II (small), starts off by
just moving II from *A* to *C* to *B* to *A* to *C*. But I
wanted the whole tower to be here. (MAR again
moves II from *A* to *C* to *B* to *A* to *C*, and then I
from *A* to *C* to *B* to *A* to *C*, which results in the
tower's being upside down.) I wanted a tower the
right way up. (He starts off again by moving II from
A to *C* to *B* to *A* to *C*, and next to *B*, and then
makes I follow the same circuit, that is, from *A* to
C to *B* to *A* to *C*. So I ends up on *C* and II on *B*.)
What have you got to do now? (He puts II on top of
I on *C*, thus success, by chance and after a corrected
inversion.) Very good. Could you have done it more
quickly? (He takes both discs at the same time.)
No, one at a time. (He moves II from *A* to *C* and
puts I on top of it, but seeing the mistake, puts
them on the table and reestablishes the order II on
top of I.) No. How about another way? *No. I want
to take the big one first; that's better.* Try again.
(Moves II from *A* to *B* and I from *A* to *C*.) Have you
finished? *Yes. Oh, no.* (He puts II on top of I on *C*
(thus success). Good, can you do it again? (Puts II
on *B*, I on *C*, and II on top of I on *C*.) Very good.
Now (the interviewer puts back I and II on *A*),
make the tower again here (the blue post instead of
the red one—thus the original *B* becomes *C* and
vice versa). Can you do that as well? What do you
think? *Yes.* Go on, then, do it. (He puts I on top of II
on *C*.) *That's not right. That'll make a little tower
upside down.* Try anyway. (Success.) Good, now do
it again here (on original *A*, which has thus become
C)? *You've got to take the big one first. I don't
know how to do it.* There is therefore no cognizance of the sequences that led to success. Nevertheless, when the interviewer asks him if I and II
traveled the same way: *No, the little one goes farther than the big one.* Naturally, this child cannot
move the three-disc tower.

FRO (5,3) has similar reactions for the two-disc tower. When it comes to the three-disc tower, he does not comply with the instructions: he picks up two at a time, puts them on the table to reverse their order, holds one in his hand, and the like. Finally, after the interviewer's demonstration, the child maintains he can do it all himself, but soon gets in a muddle and again does not comply with the instructions. He succeeds once after seven moves, but cannot reproduce this partly fortuitous success.

PIC (6,8) also solves the problem with two discs, but uses the same methods which are hardly more rapid at six years of age than in the case of the five-year-old and also *without thinking*. She does not consider it possible to get back to the same result if C and B are interchanged. After much trial and error, PIC manages to move the three-disc tower. However, success is short-lived: Did you do the same as before? *I don't know. No. I can't remember any more.* She did note that disc I had not traveled so far because *only these two* (II and III) *were on* (B) *and not that one* (I). Why? *Because I want* (= wanted) *to do it more quickly.* And the little one (III)? *It was on* (B) *and on* (C). And the middle one (II)? *Only on* (C). Are you sure? *Don't know.* Which moves the most? *The big one* (I) *and after, these two* (II and III the same).

It is unnecessary to give further examples, as they are all alike. The striking finding at this stage is the difficulty in solving such an easy problem as that involving only two discs. The length of the trial-and-error period varies (sometimes longer and sometimes shorter than in the case of MAR). However, none of these subjects make a plan or even understand how they are going to move the tower; they only know that the two discs must be moved from A to C. At this stage it is difficult to combine inversion of the order (putting the large disc I under the small one II, while it is the small one that is grasped and moved first) with a sort of transitivity (using *B* as a necessary intermediary between *A* and *C* in order that II may be placed on top of and not underneath I on *C*). The children have no difficulty in recognizing when the tower is *upside down* (MAR). The problem arises when it comes to predicting this inversion and coordinating it with the use of a middle term, since children at this level have not yet grasped the concept of transitivity, even in simple cases where they have only to switch the contents of two glasses, *A* and *C*, using a third one, *B* (see the *Etudes*, volume 27, chapter 9). Lacking this elementary transitivity, the subject is limited to trial-and-error solutions or to disobeying the instructions: *take the big one first,* even though it is under II, as an example. Even after his repeated success, MAR has understood so little that as soon as the interviewer makes *C* the blue instead of the red post, he concludes that the same two discs, I and II, will *make a little tower upside down.* Subsequently, after succeeding in making a correct tower on the blue post purely through trial and error, he does not know what to do when the interviewer tells him to move the tower to the yellow post. Of course, under these conditions, no stable solution with three discs is possible, even if a child happens upon the correct solution.

There is thus at this level a systematic primacy of the trial-and-error procedure over any attempt at deduction, and no cognizance of any correct solution arrived at by chance. It is true that when he has moved a tower, the subject does say that the large disc has had the shortest journey, but he does not understand why, since he cannot attribute the detours of the other discs to the requirements of transitivity.

Stage II

Stage II sees immediate success with the two-disc tower. With the three-disc tower, there are still hesitations, errors, modifications, but the correct solutions become stable.

Examples

GOU (7,6), for the two-disc tower immediately moves II from *A* to *B*, I from *A* to *C* and puts II on top of I. Will it be the same or more difficult to do it with three discs? *It's all right.* She moves III from *A* to *B*, II from *A* to *C*, then puts II on top of III (a mistake that she corrects). She starts again and hesitates about moving III from *A* to *C because* (afterward) *I can't take it off to put II there.* She tries moving III from *A* to *B*, II from *A* to *C*, then III on top of II, and stops. *I'm thinking, trying to see if I can do it.* She begins again more quickly. (Puts III on *B* then on *C*, II on *B*, III on top of II on *B*, I on *C*, replaces it on *A* and then back on *C*, II on *A* then on top of I on *C*, and III on top of II.) However, she cannot describe what she has done: *I don't know any more.* Can you move it from the red post to the yellow one? (Again success in seven moves.) How about from the red to the blue? *I can do it rather the same way: the little one on the red, the middle one on the blue . . .* This time she makes thirteen moves before finding the optimum seven, which finally become very rapid when the interviewer changes the starting and finishing posts. The four-disc tower causes her much more trouble, but she finally succeeds. Are some of the moves the same with three discs as with four discs? *Yes, some are.* Which? (She again moves the four-disc tower, but with difficulty and without being able to point to the moves that are the same as in the case of the three-disc tower.)

WAL (8,8) succeeds the first time in moving the three-disc tower in seven moves, but she proceeds very slowly, with a lengthy pause after moving III from *A* to *C* and II from *A* to *B* before putting III on top of II; she ponders before each new move. When the interviewer changes the starting and finishing posts, she succeeds each time, but tends to do ex-

actly what she did before, hence adding unnecessary moves, although she thinks they are needed. *It
takes a little longer starting here; it has to go
around a bit more.* She justifies a few other moves
correctly: Why did you put III here and not there?
Because afterward you can't put II there (on III).
She eventually moves the four-disc tower in
twenty-three moves. Do you think you did it the
shortest way? *I made a lot of moves.* She then does
it in seventeen moves (instead of the optimum fifteen). Start again and stop when you are sure you're
going to get it right. (She stops after eight moves.)
There.

DAN (8,11), after several successes in seven moves
for the disc tower, says, *The big one moves less
than the others, I think.* Why? *Because you leave it
there* (A) *and at the end, no, not at the end but the
time before the end* (in fact three moves before the
end) *you move it once* (from A to C). Which moves
the most? *I think it's the small one* (III). Why? *I
don't know.* And if I add one disc (four in total),
which will move the most? *Hum, I couldn't say.*
Well, all in all, will it take longer or less time than
for the three discs? *Longer, I think.* After success:
Which moves the most? *I didn't count. It's the
little one, it moves around a lot, it was in all the
squares* (posts). Was it longer with three or with
four? *With four.* How many moves more? *I think it
was two* (in fact, fifteen as opposed to seven for the
three-disc tower).

PEL (8,1) succeeds with the three discs in thirteen
moves. The interviewer demonstrates the solution
in seven moves, which the child immediately reproduces, although he contests the idea that it is
possible to know *where to start to get there more
quickly.*

ROB (8,7) succeeds in ten moves, then in eight (he
starts off well by moving II from A to B, then from

B to *C*, although he wastes one move thereby). Does it matter where you put the little one when you start? *Yes, no, perhaps it will be better like that* (moves III from *A* to *C*: starts again). *Oh, Yes! much better.* Can you do it if you start off that other way (moving III from *A* to *B*)? *I don't know, I've never done it.* (In actuality he has done it three times.) However, several times, when the interviewer changes the starting and finishing posts, he reproduces exactly the preceding sequences, now unnecessary. Why do you do that? *It's easier if you go on the red one first.* Why? *I don't know. I've gotten used to doing it.* When he is asked how he succeeded, he simply recounts all the moves (*that one from there to there,* and so forth), repeats his actions.

One subject, FUM (7,6), has taken part in a similar experiment several months earlier. In our experiment, he is immediately successful with the three discs in several moves, then with the four discs in seventeen moves (two unnecessary ones), and even with five discs in forty moves intead of thirty-one, but very quickly and with method.

To solve the problem of the two discs one must first predict that, if II is placed directly on *C* and I placed after it, I will be on top and not underneath II. A temporary home must therefore be sought for II, before I is moved to *C*; as *B* is unoccupied, it is here that II should be placed temporarily, so that it can be transferred later to *C* on top of I. This does involve transitivity, but of a practical nature concerning the actual sequence of particular actions. There is no operatory structure of a truly verifiable nature such as $A \leqslant C$ if $A \leqslant B$ and $B \leqslant C$, which is applicable to all sorts of relationships of differing significance and content. Yet this sort of "transitivity in action" appears at the same level IIA as logicomathematical transitivity in general, which shows once again that the latter, like the other nascent operatory structures, is developmentally linked to the general coordination of practical schemes. However, the sort of transitivity in action involved in our two-disc tower cannot be considered an application of logicomathe-matical transitivity in a verifiable form. The latter seems to be a product (as does the concept of transitivity involved in causal explanations such as that of the transmission of move-ment—see volume 27 of the *Etudes*) of a sort of general transi-tive coordination of actions, resulting from progress of these actions.

In this particular case such transitive coordinations are pos-sible at stage II, because the subject no longer acts without any idea of where these actions will lead, nor is there subordi-nation of his methods to these hitherto insufficiently pre-dicted targets or results. From here on, a sufficient set of predictions and retroactions while the subject is handling the discs for the successive moves to become coordinated with one another. In other words, the basic difference in this two-disc problem between the reactions at stages I and II results from heightened differentiation between the means of solving it and the end results—hence a better subordination of the means to the ends, both being caused by progress in predic-tion. It is not yet possible to say that the action is directed by conceptualization. Conceptualization, in this particular case, is merely the product of a more or less adequate cognizance of the action, with this cognizance being more adequate the simpler the problem.

It is on this point that reactions to the three-disc problem throw more light. This level still sees continual primacy of the action, with conceptualization consisting only in in-complete descriptions with numerous omissions (*I don't know any more*, confesses GOU; *I've never done it*, says ROB about a way of starting that he has already used three times) and not in an overall plan of what must be the content of the successive actions. However, comparison of these reac-tions with those of stage I reveals clear progress. First of all, as has just been said, there is now better differentiation between the methods and the end results and a better subordination of the means to the ends. At stage I, each particular action becomes an end in itself, with the general aim more or less forgotten. (The subjects generally move all the discs to *C*, conserving the order I > II > III, without putting any discs on the table or holding any in their hands.) At stage II, every move is subordinated to this end: *I'm trying to see if I can do it*, says GOU, thinking about what she is going to do afterward. This progress, however, stems from that of the predictions. A comparison between GOU, who still makes mistakes but spontaneously corrects them, and WAL, who ponders before each move, reveals the continuous nature of this improvement in predictions throughout stage II. It is not simply a characteristic of the difference between stages I and II.

This brings us to the following question. Are these predictions a product of the actual actions, or might they not be the expression of more general operatory mechanisms outside the specific actions considered in this limited context (transport of towers from one post to another)? Repetition of any action can lead to predictions as a result of the following two factors: (*a*) trial and error with subsequent corrections, where the retroactive process leads to a proactive effect of an anticipatory nature, and (*b*) transfers arising from simple reproductive (or generalizing) assimilation. This second factor (*b*), with the automatic regulations that can accompany it, is not sufficient to provoke conscious predictions. For example, when a subject has moved a three-disc tower from yellow *A* to red *C* and is then asked to move it from yellow *A* to blue *C*, he frequently (GOU toward the end, WAL, and ROB, who even says *I've gotten used to doing it*) applies his original scheme with no alteration, instead of accommodating it to the new situation, and so makes unnecessary moves. Factor (*a*), on the other hand, because it demands more active adjustments, leads to cognizance that is manifested by thought-out predictions. It is the latter that seem to account for progress in subordination of the means to the ends.

Briefly, continuous development of the actions leads to improved predictions. This occurs without the child's actually being capable of deductions made possible by acquisition of operatory structures, because these—although they also originate in the general coordination of actions—are situated at the higher (which does not always mean later) levels involving a complex set of reflexive abstractions. Application of these operatory structures is already of an essentially deductive nature (for example, the very general conservation schemes), while the predictions emanating gradually from the actions remain primarily inductive at first, because they are merely based on earlier observations. This is the case, for example, when DAN reflects on the length of the journey of discs I (shorter), II (longer), and III (which *moves around a lot*), but cannot anticipate the number of moves for a new disc (IV) smaller than III. Stage III will see the beginnings of certain operatory deductions, already glimpsed in FUM's remarkable response. Although only seven years of age, FUM finds, four months after a first experiment, the optimum solutions with three discs and generalizes his method to the four-and even five-disc towers.

Stage III

This level, which starts at eleven to twelve years, is characterized by rapid and stable success in the problem of the three-disc tower and by an increasingly inferential anticipation in the case of towers with more discs, together with an explicit use of earlier experience.

Examples

RIB (10,0) succeeds with the three-disc tower in seven moves and adapts this solution, with no unnecessary moves, when the starting and finishing posts are changed. *You have to do the same each time, except that you have to change posts.* What do you mean by *the same? It's the principle.* With the four-disc tower: *You have to move them around more times*, but *you know the moves a bit and you repeat them.* And with eight discs? *That will be almost the same, except that there are more discs.*

ROB (11,7). Once ROB has understood the instruction, he succeeds with the three-disc tower in seven moves. *I've understood that it's all right if I put the little one on (C): I can put the middle one (on B) and then the little one on the middle one, and so I can be placed on C.* When the interviewer changes the posts around, he starts off as before, but quickly stops and accommodates his scheme: *I thought it was like before.* With the four-disc tower, he succeeds right off in fifteen moves: Was it more difficult? *A little. There's one more, you have to make more moves; otherwise it's the same system.* What system? *You always take away the smaller one (IV), then the middle one (III), then you put the small one on the middle one and you can get at the big one (II); that makes a small pyramid there, and then the way is clear and I can start all over again; it's the same story afterward* (with disc I). Subsequently, he explains the process clearly to a friend (such communications remain difficult at stage II) and their conversation ends with these words: *It's the beginning that counts, the first move at the beginning; you've got to be careful, otherwise you can't make it right, or you have to make a lot more moves.*

Clearly, instead of simply transferring his schemes with no accommodation to the new situations (different starting and finishing posts), the subject RIB generalizes the method (*principle*) that he has already used. He also does this when he moves the four-disc tower and again in his description of how he would move an eight-disc tower. ROB refers to the *same system* and describes the main points. This method, generalized *mutatis mutandis* by RIB and fairly accurately described by ROB, consists in a combination of repeated moves (two moves for disc III with three discs, and four moves for discs III and IV with four discs—hence the importance of the first move, stressed by ROB) and of the use of the transitive argument with respect to the discs' positions. This transitive argument is now justified and no longer used only in a practical way. In his explanations, ROB even announces verbally and in detail the moves to be made from each post to each of the other two in the case of a three-disc tower. This is very close to an operatory deduction. Of course, acquisition of this method is a result of earlier actions and their coordination, but from this, through reflexive abstraction, the subject elicits a sort of general model that he can then apply to relevant situations.

The change of hierarchical level required by this step marks the beginning of operatory deduction. It is only a beginning, since it stems from the subject's cognizance of actions or of coordinations not initially dictated by this deduction. In the case of more general structures (like those that intervene in conservations, quantification of inclusions, or synthesis of numbers) the necessity of the compositions is imposed through a set of reflexive abstractions retroactively modifying the actual interpretation of the actions and not simply resulting from success or failure.

15 Seriation

Success in specific actions of a causal nature generally precedes cognizance of them. The conceptualization on which the cognizance is based, which starts from the results of the act, is not only incomplete but often incorrect as well, because the child's preconceived ideas influence his reading of the situation — that is, he sees what he thinks he ought to see. By contrast, the coordinations that lead to correction of this conceptualized reading and to the child's being able to explain the situation originate in the general coordinations of the action through a reflexive abstraction. The subject may not be conscious of the sources of this reflexive abstraction, but he is aware of the reflexive reorganizations engendered by this abstraction and these coordinations.

Is such a picture valid with respect to an operatory action such as that involved in seriation? The preoperatory levels lack coordination in that subjects can put two or three elements in order at a time but cannot put all the elements in order. The operatory level sees a general (reversible and transi-

With the collaboration of Jean-Paul Bronckart and Androula Henriques-Christophides.

tive) coordination linking these specific actions into a whole. In such situations does success in action precede cognizance and conceptualization, as is the case with causal behaviors, or does the cognizance come first and direct the action? If success in action precedes cognizance, then what is the nature of the cognizance and the conceptualizations to which it leads? Are there systematic distortions in the initial stages, or is it simply that when it comes to conceptualization, the coordinations are achieved slightly later than in the case of physical action? Finally, what is the degree of consciousness of the reflexive abstractions intervening in or resulting from the construction of the coordinations themselves in order to resolve these various problems?

Various methods were used during this study. Initially, the interviewer has sets of barrels, cards, and rods, which can all be arranged in order of size: (a) six barrels (green, red, yellow, pink, blue, and orange) varying between 3.5 and 8.5 cm in diameter and 2 and 5 cm in height, fitting into each other; (b) seven white rectangular cards, all the same width, but varying in length between 11 and 15.5 cm (with differences of between 5 and 12 mm)—each card having a colored spot in one corner so that the child can identify it without reference to its size; (c) six metal rods 4 cm wide and varying in length between 11 and 16 cm, with a difference of 1 cm between each.

The three tasks are always presented in the following order: barrels, cards, and rods. The barrels are shown one inside the other and the child is asked to make "a nice line of barrels," and, if he fails, "a nicer line." As soon as the action has started, the interviewer asks the child to describe what he is doing or has to do, and sometimes how he would explain to a friend what should be done. Then the interviewer asks the child to start the "nice line" all over again and to comment as he goes along. The same procedure is followed for the cards and then for the rods.

Subsequently, three more tasks were added: (a) the interviewer hides the series and asks the child to describe it from memory; (b) the interviewer asks the child to construct the series behind a screen, helping him if this proves necessary; and (c) the interviewer asks the child to draw "what he wants to do" before he actually tries and sometimes also shows him three completed drawings and asks him to select the correct one.

Finally, a preliminary investigation was carried out with a few four- to six-year-olds using the six half-barrels and six cardboard objects (consisting of two half-moon shapes of cardboard with a slit in the middle so that one fits perpendicularly into the other), each corresponding, ("just goes in") to one of the half-barrels. The children are asked to arrange the barrels in order, then to arrange the cardboard objects like the barrels, and finally to check the two orders by fitting the cardboard objects into the barrels.

At this point, it is useful to recall the levels generally encountered in seriation tasks. At the lower stage of level IA, known as level IA(i), the child simply arranges the objects in twos (one big and one small, for instance) and cannot coordinate the pairs. At the slightly higher level IA(ii), he does the same but this time in threes or fours instead of twos. At level IB, he constructs the series but only after trial and error and subsequent correction. Finally, at level IIA, he manages the series right away by looking for the smallest (or largest) of all the elements, then the smallest (or largest) of those that remain, and so on, such that an element E is conceived as being, at the same time, bigger than D, C, B, and A and smaller than F and G. It is only at level IIA that, when he cannot see A and C at the same time, the subject grasps the concept of transitivity and understands that $A < C$ if $A < B$ and $B < C$.

Subjects Starting at and Remaining at a Preoperatory Level

The first objective is to establish the relations between the conceptualization and the action in the case where the latter remains stable.

Examples

LIL (4,11) remains at level IA(ii) (successful with three or four elements). After having ordered three rods, LIL is asked to do the same for six. She takes two rods, puts their bases at roughly the same level, and places the tallest one first. She does this with two more rods and so has 6, 3, 2, 1. She then seems to lose sight of the base line and, unable to fit in 4 and 5, ends up with 4, 6, 3, 2, 1, 5. What did you want to do? . . . Explain to me what you should put first? *The big one, the middle-size one, the little one.* How can you go down this staircase? (Points to the line of summits with a climb from 4 to 6 and then descent.) Can you do it for me again? (Lines up 6, 5, 4, 2, 1.) And that (3)? (Tries but cannot fit it in.) Tell me how they are? *The big one, the middle-size one, the little one, the big one, the middle-size one, the little one.* However, her drawing shows a range of four elements with very marked differences in height.

GUI (4,6) reaches level IB. He arranges the barrels in a line without regard to size, then rearranges them correctly. *I've put the little one, middle-size, middle-size, middle-size, big.* (The interviewer mixes up the barrels and asks GUI to do it again. Once more he starts off without regard to size, but then correctly orders them.) What's that first one like? *Big.* And the other one (and so on)? *Middle-size, middle-size as well, middle-size as well, middle-size, little.* He has the same reactions for the task with the cards, but initially describes these as *very tiny, tiny, big, big* then reverts to the usual form of trichotomy. It is the same story with the rods: practical success and trichotomy in the verbal conceptualization.

GUI is given a further session with the rods after three and a half months. The level of his action is unchanged: success through corrections and great difficulties with the screen. His conceptualization is also the same: *The little one, the middle-sized one, the other middle-size one, the big one, the other big one* . . . The drawing is intermediate between a dichotomy and a trichotomy: six little rods and four long rods, of which two are slightly shorter than the other two. Is your drawing right? *Yes.* Explain it to me. *It's big, middle-size, middle-size, middle-size, little.*

JEA (4,10) is at the same level IB, but the level of his conceptualization first corresponds to, and finally even appears higher than, that of his action. After mistakes and empirical success with the rods, *You have to put the big one, the middle-size one, there a little bit middle-size like that, there a little bit big and little, and the littlest one.* The drawing represents six elements, but it is their bases that are in order and not their tops, which are far from being in a straight line. Tell me how they are? *Big, a little bit big, middle-size, a little bit little, a bit big and little* (and the littlest). And if you start here? *The littlest, middle-size, a bit big, middle-size, and big, and the still bigger one.* Three times, JEA comes back to his *a little bit big and little.*

PIE (4,10), after similar empirical success, is asked to explain how to do it to a friend. *The smallest, the almost smallest, the middle-size one, the almost middle-size one, the tiny bit very big* (he repeats this), *the almost biggest, and the big one.*

ARC (4,6), after trial and error, correctly orders the barrels. *I put the orange one beside the blue one because it's bigger.* And this other one? *A bit bigger.* And the other one? *A bit bigger,* and the like. Next the interviewer mixes them up and asks the child to reconstruct the series. The questions are then phrased differently: Why did you put the green one here? *Because it's a little bit big.* And the red one? *Because it's a little bit big, no, a little bit littler.* The description is right for the first and last barrels, but is muddled for the ones in the middle. His response in the card task is the same. The first card is *big* and each of the following cards *a little bit big,* but then the first is *bigger* and each of the following *smaller, smaller as well,* and so on. In the rod task (again after empirical success) he justifies his selection using the relative form: *because that one is a bit smaller than that one.* However, he points to them in the wrong order and when he is given the ten rods and asked to put them in order, he succeeds only from 1 to 5 and ends up with pairs.

LEX (4,9) is also at the level of empirical success. Referring to the last four barrels, he says, *There are the middle-size ones* (getting smaller), *a little bit middle-size, really middle-size, a little bit small, small.* The first barrel (green) is removed: Where's the big one now? *It isn't there any more.* What's that one (red, now the largest) like? *Bigger than that one* (second yellow). And the yellow (second largest)? *Bigger than the orange* (third largest). (The interviewer puts the green barrel back.) What's the red one like now? *Bigger than that one* (yellow) *and smaller than that one* (green). However, this fine grasp of relativity does not last long. LEX makes several corrections to the order and ends up with 6, 5, 3, 4, 2, 1. Where should you put that one (3)? *It's the middle one, so what can you do with it!* Furthermore, when ordering the cards, he fails to place the fourth, thus reverting to level IA(ii)—or IA(iii), since five elements are in order: 1, 2, 3, 5, 6. He then alters the position of the base of card 4 (an action characteristic of the most elementary reactions) so that it looks smaller: hence the series 1, 2, 3, 5, 6, 4, with the inaccurate commentary: *big, middle-size, middle-size, a little bit middle-size, a little bit middle-size, tiny.* Apart from the final erroneous description of 4 as tiny, the regression from level IB to level IA (ii or iii) for the rods makes the conceptualization regress from an apparent grasp of the

relationship *bigger than*. He reverts to simple labeling of the objects, even incomplete labeling (four
categories out of six), which is almost a trichotomy.

These six examples are sufficient to provide the range of
possibilities for the relationships between conceptualization
and action, that is, conceptualization and action on the same
level, advance of the second over the first, or—at least apparently—an advance of the first over the second. Which is
right? It seems wise at this point to indicate immediately the
conclusions drawn from this research and leave the reader to
judge the value of the ensuing justification.

With regard to the actions, development of the concept of
seriation certainly proceeds from a level (IA) where specific
actions dominate, such as uniting a small and a large element
(pairs), to a level (IIA) where the coordinations between actions take precedence and where these coordinations dominate the actions to the extent of imposing on them a coherent
operatory form. Between these two levels, the coordinations
progressively increase from being initially minimal at level
IA(ii) (where the *middle-size ones* are added to the big and
little ones: trios) to level IB, where the subject's different attempts no longer seem so haphazard. The initial specific actions are already of a logicomathematical, as opposed to a
causal, type: uniting one large and one small according to one
of the two possible orders of position. The result is that there
is virtually no resistance from the object and little opportunity for distortion of the cognizance of these actions—hence a
close correspondence between action and conceptualization.
However, as the actions become increasingly coordinated and
the overall behavior consequently more complex, the cognizance, without really being distorted for causal reasons
(there are no dynamic resistances on the part of the object)
becomes more laborious and obeys its normal laws. Attention
thus is concentrated first on the results of the action, that is
to say, on the peripheral. Only subsequently is consideration
paid to the internal and central mechanisms, to the coordinations themselves—hence a more or less systematic delay of
conscious conceptualization over the coordinations of the ac-

tions. It remains therefore, in this interpretation, to account for the apparent exceptions. When conceptualization appears to direct action, this is either because of anticipations (as, in our view, is shown in this study) comparable to the graphic anticipations (drawing the proposed series) that remain one-way and are only semioperations, or because it is the result of a directed linguistic training, as in Hermine Sinclair's experiments, but where both coordination and verbal formulation are learned.

Three examples of the very numerous cases of correspondence of the levels of action and of conceptualization have already been quoted. No examples of the elementary level IA, where the action like the conceptualization involves only pairs, are given here; sufficient are to be found in Professor Sinclair's book and in my study with Bärbel Inhelder on memory.[1] However, levels IA(ii) and IB are interesting. The case of LIL illustrates level IA(ii), where the action is successful for three and even four elements and where the conceptualization expresses them in the form of trios: big, middle, and little. Does this verbalization direct the action, or is it the other way round? It should first be noted that with the rods the slight progress LIL makes in the action (she orders five elements) is not matched by her conceptualization. The trios, like the pairs, constitute such simple "specific" actions in comparison with the subsequent coordination of the pairs and trios (by subjects who start this way and then progress to just one series, either incomplete or complete) that such actions may be conscious from the outset. One cannot here—at least after the sensorimotor period—make a real distinction between action and conceptualization.

More complex questions are raised by the level IB reactions (such as JEA and PIE). As would be expected, this level of action, that of empirical success through a sequence of specific actions that are progressively corrected (hence a beginning of coordination, through compensation for the irregularities), corresponds to a level of conceptualization termed "label-

1. Hermine Sinclair, *Acquisition du langage et développement de la pensee,* p. 129; Jean Piaget and Bärbel Inhelder, *Memory and Intelligence,* Basic Books, New York, 1974.

ing" by Professor Sinclair. Each individual element (the specific actions) is qualified in an absolute way (right up to JEA's *a little bit middle-size* and PIE's *the tiny bit very big,* according to a process that implicitly includes relationships (the nascent coordinations). Does this conceptualization govern the actions or does it just constitute their cognizance? In this second case why is the latter adequate, and in the former where would the conceptualization preceding the action come from, if not from language? And why would this language, so different from what an adult would use in the same circumstances (see JEA and PIE), give rise to a creation (in the sense of Harris and Chomsky) before the action?

Firstly, and we shall return to this, GUI, at the same level IB of action, remains at that of the trichotomy, IA(ii), for the conceptualization. This occurs frequently, showing that conceptualization is not necessary for a child to progress in action from IA(ii) to IB. On the other hand, adequate cognizance of type IB actions is easy, since there is still little coordination of the specific actions and because the conceptualization bears on the particular individual objects without any explanation of the relationships among them.

Numerous examples of the second group of subjects were encountered in this study. GUI is the only one we have quoted. In his case, empirical success in the seriation problem is accompanied by conceptualization of the trichotomy type of solution. It is the more remarkable because even his drawing remains intermediate between the dichotomy and trichotomy types of solution, when from age five and a half (in our early statistics, obtained before the current trend of preschool education), 50 percent of the subjects can draw in advance series that they do not always know how to construct. This frequent delay of cognizance over type IB actions could, in our view, be explained by the fact that coordinations among actions are first apparent with regard to these actions. Only later is the beginning of conceptualized coordination demonstrated in the subject's labeling of the objects.

ARC and LEX are typical examples of the third group of subjects who seem to contradict our hypothesis, because in their case conceptualization apparently precedes action (about a quarter of the subjects are of this type, while three-quarters are in our first and second groups). JEA already talks on three occasions about a rod being *a little bit big and little*, which constitutes an intersection, announcing the relationship that he finally employs in terms of *still bigger*. While ARC and LEX frequently refer to this relationship, in the form A *is bigger* (or smaller) *than* B, only prerelationships are involved as long as this is not combined with the inverse relationship. At one point, LEX does maintain that the second element in the series is at the same time *bigger than* (the first) *and smaller than* (the third), which is a very exceptional formula at this age. What does this advance of verbalization over action signify? It is important to state that it has no effect on subsequent action. ARC going on from the barrels to the cards and rods conserves his type IB action, and when he is given ten instead of six rods, he ends up with pairs. LEX even regresses from type IB to type IA(ii) or (iii). In general, this conceptual or linguistic advance leaves the subsequent actions unchanged—there is no regression and no progress.

Two points are of interest regarding the nature of this reaction. The first concerns only LEX's exceptional formula: B *bigger* than A and *smaller* than C. Having first of all stated that A is the biggest and B the smallest, when A is then taken away, LEX says that B is bigger than C (not without resistance, since he starts off by saying that *the big one now* is not B but *isn't there any more*). Having successively declared that B is smaller than A and that B is bigger than C (but only after A has been taken away), he then has to conserve simultaneously his two judgments when A is put back. If the interviewer had not taken A away, he would doubtless have considered them contradictory. The second point concerns the relationship *bigger* (or smaller) in general. In what does this conceptualization consist? Is it a one-way anticipation such as that exemplified in the drawings referred to above, which are successfully completed well before operatory construction of the seriation? Or does it bear witness to a more refined analysis of the relationship? Examination of the following cases will help to throw light on this problem.

Subjects Who Change Level

It is important to determine whether progress that occurs during the session results from the action itself or whether it is helped, if not triggered, by conceptualization.

Examples

YVE (5,5) starts off at level IA, with one of his mistakes being no consistently straight base line. The interviewer again shows him the three ordered rods and the child starts over. After several attempts he succeeds. His drawing passes through the same two stages. He is then asked to explain how to put the rods in order. Are they all the same? *No, that one's big, this one's middle-size, that one's middle-size as well, then big, big, and big.* So which must I put first? *A middle-size one.* And afterward? *A big middle-size one.* And then? *Another big middle-size one, then a big one.* Do you want it the same, or smaller, or bigger? *A bigger one.* He is then asked to demonstrate what he has just described. He again begins without a base line, but after much trial and error is finally successful. How did you do it? *I put a middle-size one there, then another middle-size.* What was it like? *A bit bigger.* And afterward? *Afterward I put a bit bigger one than the one next to it.* Clearly, while YVE passes from level IA to level IB (although with relapses), similar progress seems to occur in his cognizance.

DRE (5,1), after mistakes and trial and error, reaches the level of empirical success. Explain to me what you have to do. *Place the big one.* And afterward?

The middle-size one. Then? *A little one.* And then?
Another smaller one (and so on). His drawing is
correct. When it comes to seriation behind the
screen, he says, *I can't do that, I can't see the big
one. It isn't easy.* Have a try anyway. (He finds the
big one.) And afterward? *The middle-size one.* He
continues to express himself in the same way, but
each time he puts the remaining rod upright and
systematically seeks the biggest. He makes only
one mistake.

CHA (5,3) merely lines up the barrels, without
regard to size. After several attempts he finally arranges them in the right order and describes them
as *middle-size, more middle-size, more middle-
size, . . . and tiny.* With the cards, he again starts
with a simple line and no regard to size. Just now,
what did it look like? *A staircase.* Can you try? (He
succeeds with 1, 2, 3, 5, 6, then puts 4 at one end,
takes it away, tries unsuccessfully to fit it in, puts
it at the other end, takes it away, and similarly.)
Can you tell me what you did? *You take the
biggest, then the middle-size, the middle-size, the
middle-size, the little one.* With the rods, however,
success is virtually immediate: he compares them
right away with 2, lines up 1, 2, 3, 4, compares the
two remaining ones, and puts down 5, 6. What did
you do? *You take the biggest, the middle-size, the
middle-size, the middle-size, the smallest.* And if I
take these away (1 and 6), how are they? *Bigger,
middle-size, middle-size, smaller.*

ISA (5,6), after first lining up the barrels without
regard to size, quickly sees how to put them in
order *because they get smaller and smaller.* How
did you do it, tell me? . . . Did you take one? *Yes,
the big one.* And afterward? *Smaller than the big
one.* And then? *Smaller than that one,* and so forth.
And if you were to start all over again, but from
that side there (points to it)? *It's bigger, bigger,*

bigger. But then, is the pink one smaller and bigger at the same time? *No.* Can't it be bigger and smaller at the same time? . . . Make me another nice line. (She does this faultlessly and names the barrels as she goes along.) *This one's the biggest, this one's smaller*, and so on. And if you start over there? *Smaller, bigger, bigger*, and similarly. Just now, they were smaller, now they're bigger? *Because we started at that end.* She is at the level of empirical ordering for the cards. What did you do? *I put bigger and bigger ones.* And just now? *I didn't put bigger and bigger ones.* Her ordering of the rods is almost operatory: 1, 2 and 5, 6, with 3 and 4 fitted into the gap she left between 2 and 5: *It gets smaller and smaller.* And is that one at the same time smaller and bigger? *Yes.* Can it be? *Yes.* Why? *Because the rods get smaller and smaller.*

STO (6,1) at first fails to put the cards in order of size and puts the smallest ones in the center of his line. *I've made a staircase that goes up or down.* I'd like a staircase that goes down all the time, but first tell me how you're going to make it? *I'm going to put the big one, another big one, another big one, the middle-size one, the smaller middle-size one, the smaller middle-size one, and the smaller middle-size one* (there are three *smaller middle-size ones!*). He makes just one mistake, which he corrects. Tell me what you did? (Exactly the same as before except that the six has become *the last smaller middle-size one.*) He arranges the rods in the order 1, 2, 3, 5, then immediately fits in the others, and so is almost at the operatory level. *I put the big one, the big middle-size one, the smaller middle-size one, the smaller middle-size one, the smaller middle-size one, and the last was the very small middle-size one.*

SAL (6,3) proceeds cautiously with the cards and ends up with just one uncorrected mistake. What did you try to make? *A nice staircase.* How? *A big, a little one, a little one, a little one, a little one.* However, he immediately arranges the rods in the right order. That's good. What did you place? *A big one, a little one, a little one, a little one, a little one, a little one.* The interviewer tries to get him to be more precise about the relationships, but to no avail.

In our discussion of the subjects whose level of action is not modified during the questioning, three groups were distinguished, according to whether conceptualization appears to be at the same level throughout or appears to precede or follow the action. What happens in the case of subjects whose actions progress during the experiment? Does conceptualization keep pace with this progress or even precede it, or does it lag behind? In actuality, of these three possibilities, only two were observed: progress of the conceptualized cognizance in correspondence with the action (YVE and ISA) and lagging behind it (DRE, CHA, STO, and SAL).

The latter reactions are more frequent and easier to interpret. DRE's case is particularly instructive. He starts from level IB in the action, which he conceptualizes in terms that at first appear trichotomic (for the first three elements, *big, middle-size,* and *little*), but that soon afterward become relative or prerelative (*another smaller one,* with two successive repeats for the last three elements). So DRE starts off with an apparent advance of conceptualization over the action. Subsequently, however, this advance is of no further use to him. When he has to order the rods behind the screen, his behavior is already operatory in that he finds the biggest of all, then each time the biggest of those that remain. Yet in his description (and this is probably because of a lack of an adequate cognizance, as we shall discuss in the next section) he not only makes no mention of this, but he is also content with a very basic conceptualization, distinguishing only *the big one,* then *the middle-size one,* and so on. His conceptualization does not therefore appear responsible for the progress in his action.

CHA's case is analogous, although less spectacular. He starts at level IB with his conceptualization apparently more advanced than his action (*middle-size*, repeated three times) and ends up by almost immediately arranging the rods in the right order, but describing them more or less in the trichotomy form. STO's initial action is of the IB type (just) and his conceptualization between trichotomy and labeling: his final success (with the rods) is almost operatory, but his conceptualization is almost exactly the same. Finally, SAL's progress in action is analogous (indeed even clearer) and the conceptualization remains identical and rudimentary: *a big one* and five times in succession *a little one*.

Of these four very significant cases, the last two show no conceptual progress (their level remaining very low in this respect), whereas the action progresses from IB almost to IIA. The conceptualization of the first two subjects appears to lag far behind their actions. DRE's actions become clearly operatory and CHA's almost operatory. Evidently, at this level, conceptualization is not necessary for progress in action.

Where there is correspondence between conceptualization and action, YVE progresses from level IA to IB, while his initially almost dichotomic conceptualization finally involves the relationship *bigger*, but only after a suggestive question on the part of the interviewer. ISA's case is more instructive. Her initial action is intermediate between levels IB and IIA, and her conceptualization is of the same level: *the rods get smaller and smaller*. While already capable of using in turn the relationships *smaller* and *bigger* according to the end at which she starts, she refuses to admit that an element *B* can be simultaneously *smaller* than *A* and *bigger* than *C*. By contrast, her ordering of the rods is almost operatory and she accepts this double relationship, justifying it by the fact that the rods are of decreasing size; progress in action seems here to have led to progress in conceptualization. However, there is still the problem of the various meanings of the comparative relationship and above all of the apparent advance of conceptualization over action in the cases referred to in the first section. Discussion of the latter may now be completed through a comparison with those described in this section.

The comparative relationship remains prerelative when it is

one-way, that is to say, it cannot be completed with others in the opposite direction. This is the case with the type of graphic conceptualization revealed by the anticipatory drawings to which reference has already been made. From age five and a half on, before actually constructing it, about half our subjects drew accurately a series of increasingly tall vertical rods. The fact that numerous subjects who can draw this series afterward fail to construct it is because drawing vertical strokes of increasing lengths constitutes a one-way action and encounters no resistance. By contrast, (even for empirical ordering) on the level of actions, the subject is obliged to multiply the comparisons and corrections in both directions, not yet systematically and simultaneously as at level IIA, but no less effectively, through successively relating one with another according to encounters with objects whose properties cannot be modified as simply as strokes drawn with a pencil.

Perhaps the verbal expressions, such as *get smaller and smaller* or *bigger, still bigger*, and the like, which at least at the beginning appear slightly more advanced than the actions of level IB, are simply analogous to the graphic predictions mentioned above. In both cases there is a description of the static result to be obtained or already obtained, and not of how the action is to be carried out. In fact, the subject cannot simply select smaller or bigger elements — each one must be simultaneously smaller than the preceding one and bigger than the following one (or the other way round), which is far more complex and becomes systematic and anticipatory only at stage IIA. At level IB this double relationship intervenes only in corrections after the event, that is, when the child actually sees his mistake. The comparative relationship (insofar as it is a one-way prerelationship) is not more advanced than the type IB actions. Only the double relationship accepted (but not constructed) by ISA at the end of her questioning is characteristic of type IIA actions.

Subjects Who Start at the Operatory Level IIA

What are the relations between conceptualization and action in the case of subjects who in this experiment unhesitatingly start off at level IIA, but who, judging by their age, have probably only just reached this level? These relationships can, of course, be of only two kinds, since if the action is already operatory, the conceptualization cannot be more advanced. It can only lag behind or be at the same level. If it lags behind, then it is important to determine whether insufficient verbalization (at this level, drawings are no longer very instructive) stems from language as such—that is, the child is unable to express something of which he is in fact conscious—or whether, more interestingly with respect to our hypothesis, the difficulty arises from inadequate cognizance.

Examples

SON (6,6) starts off by arranging three, and then all six, rods in order. What did you look for to do that? *I always looked for one that was getting smaller, tiny.* What did you start with? *With the biggest.* How did you look for the biggest? *I looked for it* (without seeing it immediately) *because it was last.* And afterward what did you look for? *That one* (second). How? *A middle-size one!* And then? *A middle-size one.* The same middle-size one? *No, smaller.* And afterward? *The same thing, a smaller middle one.* And afterward? *A smaller middle one and after that the tiny one.* How would you explain it to someone else? *You should place the biggest, and then afterward the middle-size one, then a smaller middle-size one.* But I have lots of middle-size ones; I don't know which to take. *The one that's a little bit smaller than the big one. After* (not the one that was after the big one but the other one), *a little bit smaller than the one that's after the big one. Then, still smaller, still smaller, and then there's the tiny one.* The drawings are naturally correct. Seriation behind the screen is entirely correct; SON presses the rods against the inside edge of the desk to judge their length at the other end. What are you looking for? *The biggest one.* (He puts it down.) How did you know it's the biggest? *It had both sides bigger than the other ones.*

BER (6,11) quickly and correctly orders the rods. *A staircase.* How do you make a staircase? *You always put a smaller one.* What do you take first? *The very big one.* And afterward? *The middle-size one.* Which middle-size one? *The middle-size, the little middle-size, the middle-size that's a bit smaller.* How would you explain it to someone else? *First you take the very big one, then the middle-size one.* What's the middle-size one like? *A little bit big, then a middle size one.* And afterward? *The tiny one, no, still a middle-size one, still a little middle-size one, a little one, and the tiny one.* Now, we'll start the other end. *The tiny one; the middle-size one; the little tiny one, oh no, it was the first one! The big middle one and the great big middle one.* A great big middle one? *A halfway middle one.* Half of what? *Half of the great big middle one* (since it is now no more than a halfway middle one). He immediately draws ten rods correctly and is successful behind the screen. *I took the biggest.* And afterward? *I put them all like that* (against his hand) *and I felt them.*

GER (6,9), in the barrel task, says, *I started with the smallest, the middle-size one, then a bit bigger, then the even bigger middle-size one, and the biggest one.* But explain to me how you did it. *By size.* What does that mean? *Higher, higher, . . . and so on.* He talks to himself while ordering the cards: *There are perhaps some smaller ones . . .* His order is correct as it is behind the screen. Explain to me as best you can what you were looking for? *The size, the biggest* (of all), *and I finished with the smallest.* The interviewer holds back the fourth element. *No, we need that one, otherwise it makes a staircase* (= a step) *too low.* (The interviewer takes away the penultimate card.)

We need that one as well because it's bigger than that one (last one).

AND (7,0) immediately arranges the barrels in the right order. Why did you put the blue (second) one here? *Because they get smaller and smaller.* So how would you describe the green one? *The biggest.* And the yellow one? *A little smaller than the red.* And the red one? *Middle-size,* and so forth.

GAN (7,0), in the barrel task, says, (You have) *to put the biggest here, then the one slightly smaller, then another smaller one, and there the tiny one.* In the card task: Why did you put the brown one there? *Because it's bigger than the yellow one.* And the yellow one there? *Because it's smaller than the brown one.* GAN puts the cards with their edges on the edge of the table to judge the lengths and each time clearly takes the largest of those remaining. He uses the same procedure for the rods (the smallest of those remaining).

MAR (7,2): In the barrel task, the interviewer asks: You hesitated for the blue one? *Because it's between the two, bigger than the orange one and smaller than the pink one.* How would you explain to a friend how to do it? *I would say that you have to place the biggest one and then you go down: small, small, then always smaller.* With the cards, he puts two side by side to find the bigger, then superposes the other cards onto the preceding ones to find their place. He uses the same process for the rods. How do you do it? *I can see if there's a space there* (too big a difference in size) *and I look to see if it's bigger . . . I've looked to see if it's a bigger space than the others.*

ANO (7,6) is the only subject of the ten in this group who alludes to the inverse order (in the cards task). Why did you put the pink one first? *Because it's the biggest.* And afterward? *The blue one.* Why?

Because it's smaller than those. (He points to the
ones that come afterward and does not say *because
it's smaller than the blue one.* How would you
explain to a friend how to do it? *The big one, then
the smaller one* (than the first), *the smaller, the
smaller,* and so on. Can't you give a general rule?
I've put them from the biggest to the smallest. In
the rod task, each time he picks up those remaining
in order to find the biggest, but gives no further
explanation.

Unless one proceeds, as at level IB, by trial and error, it is
obvious that if no mistakes are to be made in the order it is
not sufficient to look for increasingly large (or small) elements. To be successful in action the child must each time
select an element that is both smaller (or larger) than the preceding one and larger (or smaller) than all those remaining. He
can do this through two equivalent processes. He can compare the selected element to each of the others, as does GER
when, talking to himself, he says *there are perhaps some
smaller ones* (see also GAN, who places the edges of the cards
on the edge of the table so as to judge their lengths). Alterna-
tively, like MAR, before placing an element, the subject can
compare it to the last one placed to see if it is possible to put
another one in between that would comply with this double
relationship (GER also does this at the end).

It is clear from these examples that the conceptualized cognizance present at level IIA with regard to the action has a
twofold nature, depending on whether the child is simply
describing the specific actions he has successively carried out,
or whether he is explaining the relationships he has mastered
in order to coordinate these actions.

As for a description of their successive actions, the systematic inadequacy is striking. None of these subjects manages to
analyze how he went about solving the problem, and ANO is
the only one to justify the choice of the second element (in
decreasing order) by declaring, not that it is smaller than the
first (which is obvious), but that it is bigger than the next one.
However, this allusion remains so ambiguous that, when the

interviewer asks him how he would explain his method to a friend, ANO refers only to the relationship *smaller*: you have to put the big one, then a smaller one, and so on, since *I've put them from the biggest to the smallest!* Some of the other subjects go no further than labeling, and none allude to the double relationship. SON, for example, *always looked for one that was getting smaller* without saying that it had, at the same time, to be bigger than those that come after; and he describes the elements in terms of bigger or smaller middle ones. After correctly arranging the objects behind the screen, in justification of his selection of the biggest SON can only say *it had both sides bigger than the other ones.* BER, having said *always . . . a smaller one,* reverts to a virtual labeling and refers to the second relationship (bigger than the following element) only by these enigmatic words: *a little bit big, then a middle-size one.* However, BER's classification of the middle ones is more on a par with that encountered at level IB: *the little middle-size one, the big middle one, the great big middle one,* and even *a halfway middle one* —that is to say, a great big one that is thus no more than partly middle-size. AND and GAN also refer only to a one-way relationship.

In their description of their actions, these subjects talk only about the results obtained and say nothing about the method followed, because the latter presupposes a general coordination directing these actions from inside and cognizance proceeds from the periphery to the center. Though this coordination is not actually conscious, the subject's thought derives from it the new relationships involved and makes conscious and spontaneous use (and not on explicit questions like ISA) of the double relationship "smaller and bigger at the same time." Thus in answer to the question, which is in no way suggestive, "You hesitated for the blue one?" MAR says, *because it's between the two, bigger than the orange one and smaller than the pink one.* This double relationship no longer constitutes a problem for her. From such unconscious coordination emerge, through reflexive abstraction, the new conceptual instructions whose use is governed consciously.

The source of the coordination itself must be something (a

new product) not yet constructed at the earlier levels, which results from an anticipatory autoregulation uniting and systematizing in one coherent whole the partial and successive regulations at work at level IB. However, since nothing is ever absolutely new, it must draw its components from earlier and more general coordinations whose roots are found as early as the sensorimotor period (ordering and the like). This source of the coordination thus constitutes simultaneously the product of reflexive abstractions, originating in the more simple coordinations that it reorganizes in a new way, and the source of other abstractions, culminating in the double relationships described above. However, with respect to both the new point of departure and the product of earlier coordinations, they stem from the action and are not directed by the conceptualization, as is clear from these last subjects' responses.

It may be useful in this connection to introduce a distinction between not two types but two moments of the reflexive abstraction. It is, of course, an unconscious process and even constitutes one of the most deep-seated developmental factors, since it is the condition of all reequilibration. However, such a process can culminate in conscious and consequently conceptualized results, as is the case with the double relationship discussed above. One can therefore talk of reflected abstraction, the term "reflected" simply designating the possible result, in the sense of a state, of the "reflecting" process, which is a transformation leading to this state. From such a point of view, the double relationship and the constructions to which it leads may be called reflexive abstractions, while the general coordination characterizing level IIA is not and remains both the product and the source of reflexive abstractions. The whole history of mathematics is, by contrast, that of reflected abstractions, which have long remained (as with the Greeks) in the state of products of an unconscious process (reflexive abstractions). Not until about the seventeenth century was mathematics incorporated into the realm of the reflected abstractions; some concepts, such as that of mathematical group structures (raised to the level of reflected abstractions by Galois) remained reflexive even longer.

Control Experiment Using Barrels

Clearly, the structures acquired as a result of the coordinations of level IIA are not reduced to two inverse relationships $B < A$ and $B < C$. In fact, the one-way relationship $A > B > C > \ldots$, already conceptualized by some level IB subjects, differs in essentially two respects from the one-way relationships found at stage II. The first of these differences involves the method of quantification. For as long as the relationship cannot be completed by $>$ (where B is simultaneously $< C$ and $> A$) the comparison remains one-way and has an ordinal meaning that is still close to the qualitative categories of labeling. The only progress that has been achieved is that the categories have become homogeneous: *a bit bigger*, and so forth. With a grasp of reversibility, quantification becomes effective and continuous. The best indication of this transformation is revealed by the second essential difference between level IIA and the preceding ones. At level IIA these quantities lead to the formation of a law of transitivity, $A < C$ if $A < B$ and $B < C$, a law that (as has already been noted) is not grasped by level IB subjects unless they can simultaneously see A, B, and C, whereas this law appears necessary to level IIA subjects when they have been shown the two pairs AB and BC.

It therefore seemed useful to carry out a control experiment in order to determine whether this law of transitivity had been grasped. For this we devised a task different from the preceding ones, which reveals the use subjects make of their different types of conceptualization when they seek to justify their opinion (without any questioning bearing on the operational aspect of transitivity).

The interviewer gives the child first six half-barrels A, B, C, D, E, and F and asks him to put them in order of decreasing size, and then six cardboard objects 1 to 6 (made up of two half-moon shapes, each with a slit in the middle so that one fits into the other). Each cardboard object corresponds to the diameter of one of the half-barrels and therefore fits into it. The child must put the objects in order and put each one with its corresponding half-barrel, 1 for A, 2 for B, and so on, each time making sure that the object fits into the half-barrel. The interviewer then asks the child to indicate which objects can be put under barrel *B* (then *D*) in three situations: (*a*) when only *B* is in front of the child and the objects are simply in a pile; (*b*) when only *B* is in front of the child and the objects are in order; and (*c*) when both the half-barrels and objects are in order, with each object opposite the corresponding barrel.

The need for a quantification and the transitivity to which it leads is therefore plain: (*a*) barrel *B* is smaller than *A* and bigger than all the others; (*b*) object 2, which just fits into *B*, is smaller than object 1; (*c*) thus object 1 does not fit into barrel *B*, and so forth. The interest of this task is twofold: on the one hand, only level IIA subjects excluded object 1 from barrel *B*, and on the other, conception of the barrels or objects as *little* and *big*, or simple labeling, tends to hinder acceptance of the idea that the little objects fit in barrel *B* (expressed in terms of *an object that can go under this barrel*).

Examples of Preoperatory Levels

COL (4,2): Can you tell me which of these (objects) can go underneath (*B*)? *That one* (1). Any others? (2, 3, 4, 5, 6.) Can they all go? *Yes*. Why? *Because*. What's that one like (1)? *It's bigger than* (B). So, can it go underneath that (*B*)? *Yes*. And that one (6), isn't it too small? *No, it isn't too small*. And which can go under (*C*)? *Those* (3, 4, 5, 6). And those (1 and 2)? *No*. Why? *Because*. Are they too big? *Yes, that's it*. Furthermore, in her finally successful ordering, COL conceptualizes the objects' sizes as follows: *big, middle-size, bigger little, bigger middle-size, middle-size as well, and little*. The comparative thus has hardly any meaning and it is not impossible that the judgment *it's bigger than* (B) means that, like *B*, the object belongs to the *bigger ones*, thus simply to one category of size.

ZAB (4,5): Tell me all of these cardboard things (objects) that can go under this barrel (*B*)? *That one, and so on* (1, 2, and 3). And those (6, 5, and 4)? *No, it's too small, but it can go as well.* Which goes under the most, that one (1) or that one (6)? *That one* (1). Isn't it a bit too big? *No.* Are you sure? *Yes.* And that one (6), doesn't it go a little better? *Yes.* So which goes the best? *That one* (1). Yet he maintains that only 4, 5, and 6 go under D. And those that can't go? *They're bigger.*

DIN (4,8): Which of those (objects) go under this barrel (B)? *That one* (1), *that one* (2), *that one* (3), *that one* (4)? *No.* Why does that one (1) go underneath? *Because it's big.* And that one (2)? *Because it's middle-size.* And the others? *That one* (6) *can't; it's much too small.* And that one (5)? *No, because it's middle-size.* And these two (4 and 3)? *That one* (3), *it can because it's middle-size.* The objects are again put in order. Can you tell me again which go underneath this barrel (B)? *That one* (1) *and then* (2, 3). Why that one (3)? *It's big.* And which go underneath this barrel (D)? *That one* (3) *and that one* (2). No other ones? *This one* (4) *because it's big as well.* And what about these two (5 and 6)? *They're too small.*

DRI (5,6) maintains that all the objects can go under B *because they're the same size as that,* and that 3, 2, 4, 6, and 5 can go under C. Isn't this one (6) too small? *Yes, too small.* And this one (2) too big? *Yes, it's too big.* And they can go all the same? *Yes.*

BEL (5,7) says that 2, 3, and 1 will go under B *because they're the biggest.* And this one (4)? *No, because it's too small.* What about this one (5)? *No, because it's too small.* And this one (6)? *No, it's still smaller.*

FLO (6,8): *That one* (2), *that one* (3) *and . . . that one* (1) *go under* B. Why these three? *There are two middle ones and one very big one.* Are you sure? *Yes, I looked at the size.* But where was this barrel (B)? *After the biggest.* And what about the three cardboard things? *Almost the same, one's the same* (as B), *one's smaller and one's bigger.* What did I ask you? *What goes under the middle-size one. I thought that this one (1) would go because it's a bit middle-size, a little bit.* Like the other middle-size ones? *Yes.* She thinks 4, 5, and 6 will go under D, with the others being *too big. That one (4) is just right.* And this one (3)? *Perhaps.*

PAI (6,8) immediately puts the objects in order, but conceptualizes: *Bigger, smaller, again the smallest, again the smallest, again the smallest, and the tiny one.* She thinks that *that one (1) goes under* B. And the others? *Yes, those also, up to 5 they're all right.* And the last one? *It's all right too.* Which goes the most, 1 or 6? *That one (1).*

Examples of Intermediate Responses

REN (5,8) maintains that 3, 4, 5, and 6 go under B. And those (1 and 2)? *No, they're already big enough.* (He thinks he remembers that B corresponds to 3.) . . . *They're big. That one (2) is about the same size as that one (1); that one (1) won't go, so that one (2) won't either.*

SON (6,8 — see earlier) says, *That one (2) and that one (3) (go under* B) *because they're the same as that* (B). And that one (1)? *Yes* (hesitation, then tries to fit it in), *No, it's too big.* Can you only put these (2 and 3) in? *You can put those in as well* (4, 5, and 6). Do they fit as well? *Not as well, because they're too small.*

Example of a Success

BER (6,11 — see earlier). *All these (2 to 6) go under* B, *but not that one (1), no, it's too big.* And the others all go equally well underneath? *Yes, they're small, they don't take much room.*

It is clear that until level IIA, the subject does not make use of the law of transitivity or of serial correspondence when trying to determine which objects fit under B. He bases his answers only on a direct estimation of the sizes, but in semi-qualitative terms. Although the least advanced child, COL, says that object 1 is bigger than barrel B, she still thinks that it will go under it. This is not necessarily a question of verbal expression; unaware that he was being watched, the child (around the age of five) of one of our psychologist colleagues tried one day to make a big box go inside a smaller one. It could be that "bigger" simply represents a category (even its seriation) and that it is such reasoning by categories that allows COL to answer correctly for barrel C, which is middle-size and not able to contain the big objects. Similarly, DRI accepts all the objects for B but not for C. As for the other preoperatory subjects, even those who employ the comparative relationship (*bigger, smaller*) do not really compare quantitatively but judge by qualitative categories of size. In fact, as the barrels and objects have already been put in correspondence, they simply conclude that, as the barrel B is among the large ones, it must correspond to the big objects 1, 2, and 3 — thus including 1 precisely, as DIN says, *because it's big* or as BEL says, *because (1, 2, and 3) are the biggest*. FLO, at nearly seven, is particularly explicit: *I looked at the size,* she says, signifying that the objects 1, 2, and 3 are *almost the same*, with one equal to B, one *smaller*, and one *bigger*, and that since 1 was *a bit middle-size, a little bit*, thus not big enough to fall outside the category, it must be suitable for B! It is therefore clear that since *the little ones* were in another category, they would not be right for B. They can certainly fit in (*it's too small, but it can go as well,* says ZAB about 6), but the big ones are more suitable for it.

This reasoning by qualitative categories of size persists up to the two intermediate cases, but in a paradoxical way. Although he is not quite sure, REN thinks that B corresponds to object 3 and so excludes 1 and 2, but has doubts about 2, which he judges to be next to B. He therefore has a marvelous argument: *That one (2) is about the same size as that one (1); that one (1) won't go, so that one (2) won't either.* This is near to transitivity, but by categories: 1 and 2 are "big" and if 1 is not right, then none of the big ones can be. SON is already distinctly at an operatory level for ordering, but because this problem of correspondence of sizes is more complicated, he reverts in part to a reasoning by categories—first, however, excluding 1, then trying it doubtfully.

There is a clear difference in the case of BER, whose operatory solution springs from coordination of relationships that have become quantitative, with the grasp of composition and transitivity that these presuppose. The main finding of this control experiment is, in fact, our confirmation of the complete absence of effective quantification at the operatory level, even in the case of subjects who use the comparative relationship "one-way"—hence, of course, the absence of transitivity.

Conclusion

The relation between concious conceptualization and an operatory coordination, such as that involved in seriation, may be interpreted in three ways:

(a) The coordination of actions is the result of conceptualization, such that all the operations involved are conscious, including their coordinating compositions, which would then precede the effective actions.

(b) The coordination is effected at the level of the actions, with the conceptualization deriving only subsequently from it, as the child gradually (and cognizance is definitely not immediate) becomes conscious of the situation.

(c) Finally, the coordination is effected simultaneously at the levels of the action and the conceptualization, with the actions involved constantly accompanied by conscious relationships.

Admittedly, before obtaining the present results, we were vacillating between the second and third hypotheses. The first seemed to be ruled out by the fact that the operations are derived from the action, and it is not when they first appear that they can in turn direct the action, as will be the case much later on. As for the choice between the second and third hypotheses, we have, for some time, known that certain general operatory structures are inaccessible to the subject's consciousness. These express what he knows how to do (in order to solve the problem) far more than what he thinks about them — a point in favor of the second hypothesis. Yet the handling of the operations appears so conscious from about eleven or twelve years on that there may be a fair amount of truth in the third hypothesis at the onset of the operational stages, around seven to eight years, at least with regard to structures that are more complex than seriation. This point is covered in a subsequent study of ours, *Réussir et comprendre*, which is concerned with success in and understanding of, for example, questions about levers.

The findings reported in this chapter seem to show decisively that, regarding seriation, progress in action does not result from a change in conceptualization and, above all, that access to operatory composition is revealed by coordination of actions of a distinctly higher level than that of the conceptualization used. To put it more precisely, the subject has acquired some new operatory schemes that he can use in his conscious thought: reversibility (composition of a relationship $\geq$ and of its inverse), quantification, and transitivity. Yet when he is asked to explain his method, or even to describe such an apparently simple action as "always taking the smaller (or bigger) of those that remain," the child remains silent as if he were unaware that he has discovered a rational and exhaustive method.

There remains one important point. All verbalization indeed appears to imply a conceptualization and all conceptualization a certain degree of consciousness, but we have not yet taken account of the fact that the reciprocal factors are not true. On the one hand, conceptualization is possible both outside language and linked with the other forms of the semiotic function (mental image, for instance and drawing, of which only the latter was invoked). In this case, "conceptualization" is understood in the wider sense of a representative scheme, that is, of course, of its significance and regardless of the signifier. On the other hand, it seems clear, if the infant is aware of anything at all, that cognizance in relation to sensorimotor behavior occurs before the advent of the semiotic function. What can we learn about our subjects' cognizance when their verbal conceptualization is insufficient?

It might first be thought that to compensate for verbal insufficiencies the subject arrives at improved conceptualizations in the form of imagined representations. However, the study of mental images, like that of memory images,[2] has shown us that both are influenced by the subjects' level of understanding. Furthermore, the drawings of the ordered series seem to correspond to rather than be in advance of, the linguistic level, and Professor Sinclair is of the same opinion (see subsequent reference to her learning studies).

There remain the relations between cognizance and the sensorimotor functions. This is a more delicate problem, since the construction of a seriation naturally presupposes perceptions and movements and since, even without adequate verbalization, the subject would be able to know what he has done regarding the material succession of his acts. However, even without having carried out appropriate control experiments, one can still hypothesize that there exist degrees or various levels of cognizance, particularly with regard to its relations with the semiotic function. It would seem possible to distinguish an "elementary consciousness" from a "cognizance" according to the following criteria. Cognizance would constitute the passage from the action to its representation and would thus always include a reconstruction arising from the conceptualization. Elementary consciousness would be linked to an immediate extero- or proprioceptive observation. It seems clear that, arising from the semiotic function, all perception is always accompanied by an interpretation (see Jerome S. Bruner's "categorization"), which in no way means that they are one and the same, nor even that the latter necessarily acts on the former. Nevertheless, it is this interpretation (that is, any form of verbal or imagined conceptualization) that enables the perception to be integrated and that, in our view, constitutes its cognizance. Without this interpreta-

2. See Jean Piaget and Bärbel Inhelder, *L'image mentale chez l'enfant*, Presses Universitaires de France, Paris, 1966, and *Memory and Intelligence*, note 1.

tion, perception—although conscious to an "elementary" degree—remains evanescent. In fact, there are a host of perceptions forced on us by the environment that we do not record,
and cognizance of these must be fleeting. We would go so far
as to believe that "subception" or so-called unconscious perception (which doubtless plays an important part in the
child's reactions to what he observes and certainly perceives,
but does not actively notice) is only an uninterpreted perception, with an elementary consciousness that is insufficient to
penetrate into the field of conceptualization and thus to give
rise to "cognizance."

What form could a child's cognizance then take, other than
verbal conceptualization? Naturally, our first hypothesis is
that of internal language. While this certainly plays a part in
that it can accompany each specific action in order to specify
the intention (GER asking himself whether there are smaller
elements), it is very doubtful that the subject tells himself
everything he has done and intends to do and then tries to
draw from this the principle of coordination. Furthermore,
there is probably perceptive and motor awareness of each action in addition to that of its intention; still, even if the recollection of each action remains in the form of imagined representation, all this is not equivalent to cognizance of the
coordination as such. It thus seems fairly probable that, by
itself, (even if the subject's cognizance goes beyond the verbal conceptualization we are learning to recognize) the latter is sufficient to determine the limits of cognizance with
respect to the basic point of interest to us: the possibility of
achieving a sufficient coordination of actions before conceptualization, whether private or communicated, results in
the child's having an adequate image of them.

There is still one more problem. An essential fact has been
brought to light by Professor Sinclair, which could contradict
all that has been said so far. This concerns the possibility of
provoking certain limited progress in ordering (step by step,
thus from one level to the one immediately following)
through verbal training that brings about improved conceptualization—even though such effects are very clearly weaker
in the relations between verbal learning and concepts of con-

servation. However, as she herself says, the principal linguistic exercise required of her subjects, although "apparently verbal, since the subject handled nothing, in fact constitutes an operatory exercise, while nothing of this nature occurs during the conservation training sessions using the verbal method."[3]

3. Hermine Sinclair, *Acquisition du langage et développement de la pensée*, p. 120.

16 Conclusions

In general, when a psychologist speaks of a subject being conscious of a situation, he means that the subject is fully aware of it. The fact that he has become aware of it neither modifies nor adds anything to the situation—all that has changed is that light has now been thrown on a hitherto, for him, obscure situation. Freud even compares consciousness to an "organ of the internal senses," it being understood that for him a sensation can only receive and not transform an external matter. However, no one has contributed more than Freud to make us consider the "unconscious" a continually active dynamic system. The findings in this book lead us to claim analogous powers for consciousness itself. In fact, and precisely insofar as it is desired to mark and conserve the differences between the unconscious and the conscious, the passage from one to the other must require reconstructions and cannot be reduced simply to a process of illumination. Each chapter has shown that cognizance (or the act of becoming conscious) of an action scheme transforms it into a concept and therefore that cognizance consists basically in a conceptualization.

Functional Reasons for Cognizance

Although this provides a first part of the answer to the "how" question too often neglected by psychologists when they consider cognizance (even when it is justifiably linked to the psychophysiological process of alertness or "vigilance"), there remains the problem of the "why," that is, the functional reasons for its constitution. In this respect Edouard Claparède made an interesting contribution regarding consciousness of similarities and differences between objects. He showed that young children, at an age when they are prone to excessive generalizations, are more aware of differences than similarities. Cognizance would thus appear a direct consequence of a failure to adapt and would be useless as soon as the functioning (here the generalizations based on similarities) adapts itself normally. That Claparède's observation contains a great deal of truth is not in dispute, yet it seems useful to complete this notion of cognizance as a compensation for lack of adaptation by the mechanism of regulations. As has been shown in this book, cognizance is always triggered by the fact that automatic regulations (through partially negative or positive corrections by already active means) are no longer sufficient. New means must therefore be sought through a more active adjustment; this constitutes the source of thought-out choices, which presupposes consciousness. There is indeed the important factor of nonadaptation, but the actual (active or automatic) process of readaptation is of equal importance.

Moreover, the very fact that the regulations have this role shows that it would be quite wrong to think that cognizance resulted only from such lack of adaptation. Effective cognizance can occur very late as, for example, in walking on all fours or the use of a sling, without there being any lack of adaptation in these actions. Even more importantly, each time a subject wants to reach a new goal, he becomes conscious of it, regardless of whether success is immediate or achieved only after trial and error—but it is impossible to maintain that the choice (or even the acceptance, at the interviewer's suggestion) of a new goal is necessarily the sign of a lack of adaptation.

The functional reasons for cognizance may therefore be placed in a wider context than that of a lack of adaption, although the latter is included as a not negligible special case. Considered first from the point of view of the material action, before going on to that of thought (or interiorization of these actions), the general law that seems to emerge from our findings is that cognizance proceeds from the periphery to the center—these terms being defined as a function of the path of a given behavior. This behavior begins with pursuit of a goal; hence the first two observable features, which can be termed peripheral because they are linked to the triggering of the action and to the point of its application: consciousness of what this goal is—in other words, awareness of the general direction of the action needed to attain it (intention)—and cognizance of its result, either failure or success. More precisely, the periphery is not defined either by the subject, but by the subject's most immediate and external action when faced with the object: using it according to a goal (which, for the observer, amounts to assimilating this object into a previous scheme) and recording the result obtained. These two aspects of the immediate action are conscious in every deliberate activity, while the fact that the scheme that assigns a goal to the action immediately triggers off the means of effecting it (regardless of how appropriate these may be) may remain unconscious, as is shown by the multiple situations studied in this book where the child achieves his goal without knowing how he did so. Thus cognizance, starting from the periphery (goals and results) moves in the direction of the central regions of the action in order to reach its internal mechanism: recognition of the means employed, reasons for their selection or their modification en route, and the like.

While the action's result is certainly peripheral in relation to the subject, the fact of assigning a goal to this action involves more internal factors, although these are partly conditioned by the object's nature. Why, then, do we use this vocabulary of "periphery" and "center"? There are two

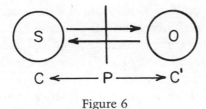

Figure 6

reasons. The first is that the internal factors at first escape the subject's consciousness. The second, completely general, reason is that, taking account only of the subject's reactions, knowledge does not proceed from the subject or from the object, but from interaction between the two, thus from point P of Figure 6, which is peripheral to both the subject (S) and the object (O). From there, cognizance proceeds toward the central mechanisms (C) of the subject's action, whereas awareness of the object moves in the direction of its intrinsic properties (in this sense also central, C'), and no longer in that of the superficial properties connected only with the subject's actions. As will be shown again later, these cognitive steps in the direction of C' and C are always correlative, and this correlation constitutes the basic law, both of the understanding of objects and of the conceptualization of actions.

At this point, however, we must continue our analysis of the functional reasons for cognizance of actual actions. As we have said, cognizance begins with the pursuit of a goal leading to the conscious noting of success or failure. In case of failure, the reason must be sought and this leads to cognizance of more central regions of the action. Starting from his observation of the object (failure to achieve the goal), the subject thus tries to find out where there was a lack of accommodation of the scheme to the object. From his observation of the action (its finality or general direction) the subject turns his attention to the means used and to how he might correct or perhaps replace them. Thus through a two-way movement between object and action, cognizance draws nearer through stages to the action's internal mechanism and thus extends from the periphery P to the center C. Such cases lend weight to Claparède's analysis of the relationships between cognizance and lack of adaptation. Why are there such relationships? We can now supply the answer. Lack of adaptation occurs at the periphery P of the action, which gives cognizance a double centripetal direction, toward C (the action itself) and toward C' (the object). However, as already shown in Chapter 1, progressive cognizance may be constituted without any lack of adaptation, in other words, even when the action's goal is achieved without any failures.

In this last case, if progress in cognizance no longer stems from the difficulties of the action, it can result only from the assimilating process itself. Assigning a goal for a specific object signifies the latter's assimilation to a practical scheme and, if the goal and the action's results are "cognizable," while remaining generalizable in actions, the scheme becomes a concept and the assimilation becomes representative, that is, capable of an increasing number of evocations. From then on, as soon as one begins to compare different situations, problems inevitably arise. Why is it easier to use one object than another? Why is one way of using it more, or less, efficient than another? In these cases, the assimilatory process, promoted to the rank of instrument of understanding (see below), will simultaneously bear on objects and actions because of its continual two-way movement between observation of each. The mechanism of cognizance of the object must therefore extend into cognizance of the action, since each is equally dependent on the other. It is not that lack of adaptation (why is a certain method not successful?) no longer plays a role, but that this role is only momentary or local. The positive problems (the reason for the success) take on primary importance with the active adjustments during the subject's attempts to find the solution. The inevitable character of the need for causal explanation cannot be limited uniquely to the objects, since the latter are known only through the actions.

Briefly, the law of the movement from the periphery (P) to the centers (C and C') is not to be limited to cognizance of the material action. This is because, while at this initial level there is already passage from consciousness of the goal (as well as of the result) to that of the means, this interiorization of the action leads, on the plane of the reflected action, to consciousness of the problems to be solved and from there to that of the cognitive (and no longer material) means used to solve them. This is what we observed on several occasions when the child was asked how he came to discover a specific process. While the young subjects merely recounted their successive actions (or at the beginning merely reproduced them with gestures and no verbalization), the older children said, for instance, *I saw that . . . so I thought . . .* or *so I had the idea . . .* and so on.

The Mechanism of Cognizance

Going on from the "why" or functional reasons for cognizance, to its "how," that is, to the effective mechanism that renders conscious the hitherto unconscious elements, it becomes clear that in no way can the process be reduced simply to throwing light on these elements without, in so doing, modifying them. On the contrary, it consists, from the outset, in a true conceptualization, or, in other words, in a passage from practical assimilation (assimilation of the object into a scheme) to an assimilation through concepts.

There has been much evidence in support of this interpretation. In particular, it has been shown that, while his reactions remain elementary, the subject is likely to distort conceptually what he observes, instead of recording it without modifications. A typical example of this is the sling: the young subjects, although they know very well how to throw the wooden ball tangentially, think, when they have done so, that they have released it opposite the target. It is clearly the observation that is distorted, since the child is asked to "do it again and have a good look." It is not, therefore, simply a case of the child's predicting what will happen—in other words, making an inference before actually seeing what happens. He really sees something, but his observation is distorted by an inference, which is something quite different.

It might, however, be objected that this inferential distortion (even if it were limited to one particular example) does not constitute a characteristic of cognizance, but results, through residual persistence, from the unconsciousness previously displayed by the subject with regard to the means employed to achieve the target: before he was asked where he had released the ball, the question had in fact never entered his mind. This possible objection raises an interesting problem about the relations between consciousness and cognitive unconsciousness during the process of acquisition of cognizance. First of all, the beginnings of cognizance are not always marked by such clear distortions as those involved here. For example, when they are asked to make a counter slide down a slope (as in Chapter 4), level IA subjects do not realize that they always imprint a downward movement on the counter, even if the latter follows an oblique or jointed path (the W task). However, when later they notice the general characteristic of this condition, initially observed only with regard to the material action, subsequent cognizance of it is not distorted because nothing appears contradictory in the idea of such a descent. It is true that the child finds it rather difficult to visualize the downward movement through a composition of the backward/forward and sideways inclinations of the cardboard, and this explains why the descent is at first noticed (and this from level IA) only when the counter goes straight down (lengthwise), but this results from a delay in conceptualization of the action and not from a basic contradiction—hence the absence of distortion. In the case of the sling, while the subject encounters an analogous difficulty (visualizing the oblique path of the ball through its preliminary rotation and subsequent straight path, there is the additional idea that it is not normal and even, in one sense, contradictory to want to send a solid object into a box without releasing it in front of the box (hence the idea of the perpendicular and not the oblique path).

From this evidence, representative of much more, a certain number of conclusions may be drawn regarding the "how" of cognizance.

(a) Cognizance must, from the start, involve conceptualization, since it even implies coordinations (between the rotation and the projection, in the case of the sling, and between the lateral and longitudinal inclines, in that of the slope).

(b) If cognizance were merely the result of throwing light on a situation, these coordinations would necessitate no new construction, since they have already been achieved at the level of the material action itself ("know-how" as opposed to "knowing"). It would therefore be sufficient for consciousness, if this were simply a mirror, to reflect objectively the hitherto unconscious movements of the action in order to obtain a "representation" (in the most direct meaning of the term) of the coordinations already being effected.

(c) The subject looks at his actions and these are assimilated, more or less adequately, by his consciousness as if they were ordinary material links situated in the objects—hence the necessity for a new conceptual construction to account for them. In fact, only a reconstruction is involved, but it is as laborious as if it corresponded to nothing already known by the subject himself. Furthermore, it presents the same risks of omissions and distortions as if the subject were required to explain to himself an external system of physical connections.

(d) Making a sheet of cardboard slope is simple, since while it involves spatial coordination between two directions (backward/forward and sideways) there is no conflict with earlier schemes: cognizance therefore progresses in line with the action.

(e) In the sling and similar experiments, there is, in addition to the problem of spatial composition (necessary for understanding the ball's tangential departure), a conflict between this construction and a (conscious) previous scheme. The latter leads the subject to think that in order to send a ball into a box he must stand opposite and aim directly at it. He cannot therefore understand the ball's oblique path to the box (released tangentially to the circle initially described by the ball) without prior correction of this earlier scheme—he must admit that while a throw from directly opposite the box is easier, it is not obligatory and an oblique path is acceptable.

(f) However, before this conscious and significant scheme is corrected, level IA subjects find a more economic solution to the problem. They simply distort their observations and seem to drive the source of the conflict back into the unconscious. A parallel occurs in the realm of affectivity, when an unconscious desire comes into contradiction with a conscious system, for example the superego and its demands, with the result that the unconscious desire, without being eliminated, does not penetrate into the conscious. In the particular case of the cognitive process, the phenomenon is analogous, although far more limited:[1] since actually projecting the ball along a tangential path contradicts the scheme of projecting it from directly opposite the target, the subject's consciousness refuses to accept or perceive such a disturbing observation and the subject honestly believes that he released the ball opposite the target.

(g) This "putting out of mind" is fairly general in conflicts of this type and also with interpretation of (physical) observations independent of the subject's own action. Having made incorrect predictions in the case of an event that is contrary to a tenacious belief (for example, that an intermediary must have moved in a molar way in order to transmit a movement while in reality it remained static), the subject also contests the unexpected evidence of his own eyes and thinks that he sees what he predicted would happen.[2] The situations discussed in this book are interesting since the contested observation is not a physical fact outside the subject, but belongs to his own action and thus is known by the subject—but unconsciously and not in his conscious conceptualization. This makes the analogy with the putting out of mind of physical data even more striking, as if the subject's cognizance proceeded in the same way as any other increase in knowledge.

(h) In the case of cognizance, the contradiction that provokes the "driving into the subconscious" cannot be localized in the unconscious action, since the latter has no problem with the motor coordination, that is, the child does not try to start off directly opposite the target (except for the youngest children's first attempts, and these are quickly corrected through automatic regulation). Furthermore, the contradiction cannot be within the subject's consciousness, since he is

1. See the report of our lecture to the U.S. Society of Psychoanalysis entitled "Affective Unconsciousness and Cognitive Unconsciousness."
2. See "La Transmission des mouvements," volume 27 of the *Etudes*, chapters 2 and 3.

not conscious of the tangential release (it is as if he hypothesized this momentarily and then rejected it because of its conflict with the earlier idea of throwing the ball from directly opposite the target). In fact, it is clear from what the subject says that he does not feel the contradiction. It must therefore be situated in the actual process of conceptualization that characterizes the process of cognizance. However, this leads to the problem of establishing the degree of consciousness displayed by the conceptualization process, as opposed to the initial unconscious action and to the final consciousness that the subject has of his action.

(i) More precisely, should one therefore admit degrees of consciousness? Three types of circumstance could make such a hypothesis plausible. The first is that, between the precociously successful action (tangential release or analogous successes) and the initial incorrect conceptions (such as the subject's idea that he released the ball opposite the target), there are intermediate stages in the form of the "compromise solutions," which Professors Inhelder, Sinclair, and Bovet observed when, during learning sessions, their subjects felt they were faced with a conflict[3]. In our experiments, the subject may say that he released the ball neither opposite the target nor at a tangent to it, but between the two, which seems to show the existence of incomplete consciousness of the action. Secondly, it is doubtful that an action that is successful after automatic regulations can be completely unconscious, even if success is extremely precocious. Thirdly, as has just been recalled, conceptualization itself constitutes a true process, since it is not immediate, and because it is a process, the degree of consciousness must vary.

(j) There appears, therefore, to be only one possible interpretation for these degrees of consciousness. They must depend on different degrees of integration. For example, what precedes conception ("subception") and is defined as an "unconscious perception" could well be accompanied by a certain consciousness at the moment it actually occurs, but

3. Bärbel Inhelder, Hermine Sinclair, and Magali Bovet, *Learning and the Development of Cognition* (Harvard University Press, Cambridge, Massachusetts, 1974), chapters 2 and 3.

this remains temporary in the sense that it does not seem to be integrated into the subsequent states[4]. In the case of actions that are precociously successful but where cognizance of them occurs only far later, it would even be difficult to conceive that the subject had knowledge only of the goals and results, without any consciousness of the means used of their regulation. However, as this conquest and the successive corrections of the means are effected step by step, the temporary states (of which the subject is only fleetingly conscious and which would have been able to characterize them) give rise to no conceptual or representative integration, since the system obtained remains sensorimotor. Similarly, in the case of the compromise solutions recalled in (i), it is more a question of the degree of integration than one of the sudden passage from the unconscious to the conscious.

(k) In sum, the mechanism of cognizance appears in all these aspects as a process of conceptualization — reconstructing, then going beyond, on the semiotic and representational planes, what was acquired on that of the action schemes. From such a viewpoint, there is therefore no intrinsic difference between cognizance of the action itself and awareness of what is happening outside the subject. Both involve a gradual elaboration of concepts, starting from a piece of information — regardless of whether this consists in material aspects of the action carried out by the subject or in the interactions between the objects.

Observable Features and Inferential Coordinations

If cognizance proceeds from the periphery to the central regions C of the action and if its mechanism is similar to that

4. Thus the author who has a far better auditory than visual memory can never remember the time he sees on his watch unless this visual perception is accompanied by a sufficient verbal formulation. If it is not, he has to take out his watch again a moment later and, seeing virtually the same time, recognizes that he has already perceived it a moment before, but without any recollection. In this case, it is very probable that the first perception was already conscious (since there was subsequently a clear, and in no way vague, recognition) but that immediately afterward there was complete evanescence of this very brief consciousness, because of lack of integration into the subsequent states (and, in this particular case, into a formulation capable of producing an auditory memory).

resulting in knowledge of the objects, then this knowledge of reality must start from the phenomenon (that is, from the peripheral appearances that it presents to the subject) before proceeding in the direction of the intrinsic nature of the things and of their causal connections—both going beyond the scope of the observable features in the direction of the central regions C', which correspond to the C regions of the subject's action. Trying to separate the psychogenetic processes that these trivial considerations overlay, one encounters complex relationships that concern both the problem of cognizance of the action itself and that of the general construction of knowledge. Having started from the periphery P of the action (see Figure 6), which thus also constitutes the phenomenal periphery of the objects, knowledge simultaneously takes the direction of the central regions C of the action and C' of the objects, and constant exchanges are observed, in the dynamics of the steps of the quest for (or of the construction of) concepts, between progress in the two directions $P \rightarrow C$ and $P \rightarrow C'$. There is thus a functional process to be examined from the point of view of the equilibration, imbalances, and reequilibration that generally characterize the gradual growth of knowledge. However, it could be that there is more in this than simply a functional synergy and that there is an epistemic solidarity between the movement of interiorization, which leads not only to cognizance of the action but also to conceptualization of logicomathematical operations, and the movement of externalization, which reciprocally and simultaneously leads to experimental knowledge and causal explanations.

(a) The findings detailed in this book throw some light on the functional process. From the very beginning of cognizance to the final stages of its acquisition, each level has been analyzed separately. At each level we encountered an exchange between data drawn from observation of the action itself and from that of the object, and then between coordinations relative to the action and those relative to the object or objects.

We should first recall the bipolarity of the only two elements conscious at the start: the goal pursued by the action and the result obtained. Clearly, both depend simultaneously

on the assimilatory scheme into which the object is incorporated and the latter's characteristics. What is more interesting, however, is that the means used at first remain unper-
ceived, particularly if they are automatically triggered by the
scheme that determines the goal, and cognizance of them
starts from the subject's observations of the object, thus from
an analysis of the results. Reciprocally, analysis of the means,
thus of the subject's observations of the action, provide the
basis of his information on the object and, gradually, the
causal explanation of its behavior.

These findings bring to light two general processes. Firstly,
there is a reciprocal but alternating action (with an interval of
varying length between the two phases of the exchange) of the
subjects' observations of the object on those of the action and
vice versa. Then, with the establishment of a relationship
between them, inferential coordinations follow. These both
go beyond the scope of the observable features, allowing the
subject to understand causally the observed effects, and
simultaneously lead to a subsequent more subtle analysis of
these features, thus maintaining and reviewing the preceding
two-way movement. The speed of this dialectic of the observable features varies with the situation. For instance, in the
case of the ping-pong ball, it is particularly slow, with the al-
ternations fairly far apart from one level to the next. At level
IA, despite some episodic successes, the subject does not see
that he presses his fingers on the back of the ball and sometimes does not even notice that he puts them on top of, and
not underneath, the ball. With the successes and particularly
the gradual partial successes of level IB—thus as a function of
the result on the object—the subject discovers that he presses
on the back of the ball and (at level IIA) that with his hand he
imparts a backward movement to it. This progress in cognizance of the action, owing to observation of its effects on
the object, does not immediately lead to corresponding
progress in the recording of observations of the object, because the subject still thinks the ball rotates in the direction
it is traveling on the outward, as well as the return, journey. It
is only at levels IIB (after much trial and error regarding the
reading of observations of the object) and III (immediately)

that this exchange between observation of the object and of the action results in the subject's understanding that pressing backward on the back of the ball makes it spin backward and thereby explains its return.

(b) This continual exchange of information between cognizance of the action and increasing knowledge of the object is accompanied by two types of interdependent asymmetries. The first results from the fact that, while each type of cognizance provides observable features able to throw light on the other (they are thus transmitted in the direction object → action, and vice versa), there are also inferential coordinations linking these observable features and able to act only in the direction action → object. In our definition of the term, an observable feature is anything that can be recorded through a simple factual (or empirical) observation—that is, a particular event, a repeatable relationship, a temporary or even regular covariation, such that one can speak of functional dependence or law. In this wide sense, regular relationships or functions between two observable features are themselves also observable features, as is the case when the ping-pong ball goes spinning off backward and once it has reached the end of its slide forward comes back toward its point of departure. By contrast, we reserve the term "inferential coordinations" for connections that are not observed but deduced through operatory composition (and not through simple extension of a generalization) and thus go beyond the scope of the observable features, particularly because they introduce necessary links—for example, coordinations based on transitivity (or on conservation of movements and of their direction—which then allow one to confer a necessary causal link to the ball's return, going beyond the simple observation of a law). It therefore seems clear that observable features of any degree can be provided both by the objects and by the actions, whereas inferential coordinations, even applied or (finally) attributed to the objects, must originate in the subject's logic—the logic that derives more or less directly from the general coordinations of his own actions.

This leads us to the second asymmetry, concerning the type of abstraction used, starting either from factual information or observable features (empirical abstraction) or from coordinations of the actions. While it is clear that any abstraction from objects is thus "empirical," the action's pole gives rise to both types: empirical with regard to observable features of the action, that is, concerning a material process (a movement, a position of the hand, and so forth), and "reflexive" with regard to inferences drawn from the coordinations themselves. However, we still have to distinguish two levels for this reflexive abstraction. It can remain unconscious, thus unknown by the subject, particularly when it is at the source of inferential coordinations themselves, or conscious, insofar as it involves reasoning—although the subject does not know where he has drawn the intrinsic necessity. By contrast, the reflexive abstraction can become conscious, particularly when the subject compares two steps that he has carried out and tries to discern the common factors (for example, the reactions of levels IIB and III for the Hanoi tower). In this second case, we shall refer to "reflected abstraction," the past participle denoting the result of the "reflexive" process.

While the two asymmetries complicate but little the functional process of the exchanges of information under discussion, when it comes to the complementary directions toward the central regions C and C', starting from the periphery P, they impose more stringent conditions on the mutual epistemic dependence of these movements of interiorization and externalization. Because of this, consideration must first be given to the evolution of the actions themselves.

Evolution of the Actions and the
Three Levels of Knowledge

In addition to enabling us to analyze how a child gains cognizance as such, this research has shown us that action in itself constitutes autonomous and already powerful knowledge. Even if this knowledge (just knowing how to do something) is not conscious in the sense of a conceptualized understanding, it nevertheless constitutes the latter's source, since on almost every point the cognizance lags, and often markedly so, behind this initial knowledge, which is thus of remarkable efficacy despite the lack of understanding.

How then does the action evolve in its links with the conceptualization that characterizes cognizance? If the latter proceeds from the periphery to the center, development of the action must represent a sequence of transformations of the center itself, and there are two possible answers to our question. Development of the action could occur through successive constructions and one-way coordinations, simply obeying laws of differentiations and integrations, without further reference to the central or peripheral regions. The latter would then concern only the cognizance and conceptualizations that superpose themselves on the actions on another level. However, there exists a second possibility, both more attractive and more in conformity with what is already known about the successive embeddings and step-by-step reconstructions that are characteristic of most organic growth. Right from the level of the action, the constructions and coordinations would succeed one another according to both a progressive and regressive, or retrospective, order. This second aspect would thus be analogous, but in new terms that require definition, to the steps leading from the periphery toward the center at the higher level, which is that of the conceptualizations.

This problem has theoretical importance, since it concerns the interpretation of the construction of knowledge. As this topic cannot be dealt with in depth here, we shall explore it in another book about success and understanding, for which the basic research bears on actions in which success is progressive and not precocious as in this study. Nevertheless, a few comments will be useful, since at the end of this book (Chapters 14 and 15) we have analyzed two cases of elementary operatory actions in order to compare them to other, basically practical, situations.

Clearly, at the action level, initial reactions consist in proceeding through isolated assimilation schemes; there is an attempt to link these to their object, but the reactions remain at the stage of temporary accommodations (see stage I of the Hanoi tower experiment). Progress consists in coordinations that first involve reciprocal assimilations of the schemes in use and then become increasingly general and independent of the specific content—the characteristics of general operatory structures with their laws of composition (transitivity and the like). Certainly, this is also a process leading from the periphery to the center, although in appearance rather different from the one relevant to the conceptualization characteristic of cognizance. The distinct common element is the peripheral point of departure where the subject's activity, in its most external or accommodating form, encounters the surface of the object. Another common element is that, from this point, the activity proceeds toward the coordinating mechanisms. However, divergencies begin with the nature of the latter. In the case of conceptualization, these mechanisms already exist (at least in part) within the action and it seems that cognizance has only to take possession of them. In the case of the action itself, coordinations appear to evolve, step by step, through entirely new and productive constructions. What we see here is in fact a double illusion. Conceptualization is far from constituting a simple reading: it is a reconstruction, which introduces new characteristics in the form of logical links, providing a connection with understanding and extensions, and so on. As for the level of the action, the coordinations that it constructs are hardly radically new, but they are derived through reflexive abstraction from earlier mechanisms, such as the processes involved in all regulation. Although the action itself cannot be called a true cognizance since it is not yet conscious, in relation to its neurological substrate, it constitutes a progressive conquest, with reconstructions and enrichments, analogous to conceptualization in relation to action.

It is therefore not exaggerated to talk of a gradual passage, even at the level of the action alone, from the periphery to the center, with the periphery situated in the initial zone of interaction of action and objects and the central regions situated in the organic sources of behavior and the operatory structures themselves.[5] In both cases, the action as well as its conceptualization, the forming mechanism is simultaneously re-

---

5. For discussion of the fundamental role of the organic sources, see Jean Piaget, *Biology and Knowledge*, University of Chicago Press, Chicago, 1971.

trospective, in that it extracts its elements from earlier sources, and constructive, in that it creates new links.

To sum up, we encounter analogous mechanisms that repeat themselves, but with great chronological differences, on two or even three successive clearly hierarchical levels. The first level is that of the material action without conceptualization, but whose system of schemes already constitutes an elaborate know-how. This level, with constructions that result in the most fundamental operatory structures (in their capacity of coordination, even though the subject remains unconscious of them) may well appear to the psychologist as a sort of absolute beginning, but this is an illusion. The first level is linked by all the intermediaries to the organic sources from which it derives its material. The second level is that of conceptualization. It derives its elements from the action as a result of cognizance, but adds to it all the aspects of the concept that are now in comparison with the scheme. The third level, contemporaneous with the formal operations at around eleven or twelve years, is that of "reflected abstractions" in the sense defined above. Its productive mechanism, which consists in second-power operations (operations new but carried out on earlier operations) shows fairly clearly that it is once more a question of abstractions from the previous level, which are formed and enriched through hitherto nonexistent combinations.

Thus a series of coordinations is progressively constituted at each of the three levels through reciprocal assimilation of the schemes, initially practical or motor (level I) and then conceptual (levels II and III). However, in addition to these "transverse" assimilations, there must also exist longitudinal reciprocal assimilations with a sort of rebound action on the preceding level of what has been constructed at the next. Thus the level II conceptualization derives its elements from the level I actions, but (at a given level) acts retroactively on these actions and partly directs them as a result of the introduction of general plans and sometimes even of new methods, which are then adapted by the action according to its own regulations. The same is true, a fortiori, for the retroactive effects of level III acquisitions on the constructions of levels II and I.

How can we know when and under which conditions these reciprocal assimilations, with influence of the superior structures on the inferior ones, begin? The answers must be sought in situations where the action does not result in complete precocious successes, but where its coordinations are constructed in stages and at the same age levels as the conceptualizations. Of course, this type of rebound action is possible only on developed actions that are contemporaneous with the conceptualizations that can act on them. It is in our book concerning success and understanding (*Réussir et comprendre*), which follows this one, that these questions will be treated.

Processes of Interiorization and Externalization

It is now possible to conclude by specifying the epistemic significance of the processes that are interdependent despite the fact that they go opposite ways, one leading from the periphery P to the central regions of the action, C, and the other to the objects, C' — in other words, the process of interiorization $(P \rightarrow C)$ and that of externalization $(P \rightarrow C')$. Briefly, the former finally results in construction of logico-mathematical structures and the latter in development of physical explanations, thus of causality. Generally speaking, any progress of one leads to progress of the other. However, after detailed study it becomes clear that it is more accurate to speak of a succession of reciprocities than of an exact symmetry, because of the asymmetric factors constituted by the differential dualities of factual knowledge and inference and because of the forms of empirical and reflexive abstraction.

As has been seen at the level of the material action, the interiorization process leads from the boundaries between the subject and object to reciprocal assimilations of schemes and to increasingly central coordinations (C) akin to the originally organic general coordinations. These latter coordinations result in the construction of a sort of logic of schemes prior to language and thought. At the heart of these schemes are already found the main types of connections — relationships of order, embedding of a subscheme into a total scheme, establishment of correspondences and intersections, a form of transitivity and associativity of monoides — in short, the main ingredients of future operatory structures. Right from the sensorimotor levels, the externalization process is marked by increasingly advanced accommodations of assimilatory schemes to objects, followed finally by the construction of instrumental behaviors, of spatio-temporal physical structures (the action group of displacements), and of an objectified and spatialized causality (after the purely phenomenist forms of the origins in P). Progress in both the directions C and C' are solidary in the following two senses. Firstly, the accommodating power of the schemes is not indefinite. For each of them there is an "accommodation norm" in a sense analogous to that used by biologists when they determine for a given genotype its "reaction norms," which give us the range and distribution of the possible phenotypical variations. This accommodation norm seems to be a function of the coordinations between schemes. The greater the links between a given scheme and other schemes, the more flexible the former becomes in its applications to objects. Inversely, the greater the number of accommodations, the more these variations favor reciprocal assimilations. Secondly, spatiotemporal group structures, object permanence, spatialization of causality and the like are made possible by coordinations of the logic of schemes which in these cases is attributed to the objects, just as the kinetic and dynamic problems imposed on the subject through experience of the objects, constitute powerful incitements to the construction of this logic of actions.

At the conceptualization level, the interiorization movement is initially marked by a general growth in cognizance of the action, thus of the interiorization of the material actions into meaning-bearing representations (such as language and mental imagery). However, from the outset, and with progress of the action itself, this cognizance becomes polarized toward the two possible types of abstractions. The empirical abstraction then provides a conceptualization which, in a way, is descriptive of the observable features of the action's material characteristics. The reflexive abstraction derives sufficient data from the coordinations of the action to construct the inferential coordinations. At the concept level, the latter enable these observable features (which are, as seen above, constantly in interaction with those of the object) to be both linked and interpreted. The conceptualization thus becomes operatory and so capable of engendering reasoning and structurations (such as operatory seriations, classifications, or numbers), yet both the underlying structures, which make this possible, and the actual mechanism of the reflexive abstraction remain unconscious.

The movement of externalization gives rise to two analogous processes. On the one hand, the empirical abstraction of information from objects allows the child to represent all their observable features starting from isolated facts or events and heading toward functions, repeatable relationships and general laws). On the other hand, the reflexive abstraction (in the direction C) is responsible for the operatory types of structurations and therefore allows a deductive interpretation of the events in the direction of the objects (C')—hence the formation of the causal explanations through attribution of operations to the objects themselves, thereby promoted to the rank of efficient operators. Both these attributions, from the subject's point of view, and the actual operatory structures in his logicomathematical inferences remain unconscious, which again points to the solidarity of these movements of interiorization and externalization.

Finally, at the third level (from eleven to twelve years), which is that of reflected abstractions (conscious products of the reflexive abstractions), the situation is modified in that cognizance begins to be extended in a reflexion of the thought on itself. In the logicomathematical field, that is, with regard to the movement of interiorization, this means that the subject has become capable of theorizing (a capability on which those responsible for devising educational programs make too many demands) and no longer only of "concrete," although logically structured, reasoning. The reason for this is the child's new power of elaborating operations on operations (set of parts and combinatory set, INRC group, and the like). With respect to the externalization, he thereby becomes capable of varying the factors in his experiments, of envisaging the various models that might explain a phenomenon, and of checking the latter through actual experiment. Briefly, the links between the logicomathematical movement of interiorization and the physical and causal movement of externalization become even closer than at preceding levels, both as a result of the progress of the abstraction, and by virtue of the well-known paradox that adaptation to the concrete experimental facts is dependent upon the abstract character of the theoretical framework, which allows analysis and apprehension of these facts.

To sum up, the study of cognizance has led us to place it in the general perspective of the circular relationship between subject and object. The subject only learns to know himself when acting on the object, and the latter can become known only as a result of progress of the actions carried out on it. This explains the circle of the sciences, of which the solidarity that unites them is contrary to all linear hierarchy. Further more, and most importantly, this explains the harmony between thought and reality, since action springs from the laws of an organism that is simultaneously one physical object among many and the source of the acting, then thinking, subject.

Index